Philip L. Hosford,
Chairperson and Editor

**Association for Supervision
and Curriculum Development**
225 North Washington Street
Alexandria, Virginia 22314

Using What We Know About

Teaching

ASCD publications present a variety of viewpoints. The views expressed or implied in this publication should not be interpreted as official positions of the Association.

Stock number: 610-84322
Library of Congress Catalog Card Number: 83-073411
ISBN 0-87120-122-4

Price: $12.00

Contents

SECTION II. GETTING KNOWLEDGE

SECTION III. USING KNOWLEDGE

Foreword

Several recent reports by prestigious national groups have confirmed the American public's disenchantment with their schools. Everywhere, people are demanding higher standards and better results.

If this were the situation in other professions, we would probably see increased emphasis on research and development. When Americans were concerned about the spread of polio, we did not blame general practitioners; we supported medical research. When we were shocked by the launching of Sputnik, we recognized that the way to put a man on the moon was through scientific experimentation.

For many reasons, education is different. Not only the general public, but educators themselves, have little faith in educational research. We sometimes look for research findings to justify what we are doing or believe we should be doing, but we are seldom persuaded to act on the basis of research alone. What is more, researchers and practitioners live in separate worlds, with limited interplanetary communication. And when some researchers begin to build the body of "knowledge," as the "effective teaching" researchers have been doing, other authorities condemn this "scientific" approach as shortsighted and a threat to the *art* of teaching.

How do educators develop the special knowledge that marks a profession? How much can "quantitative" research, with its precise operational definitions, replicable treatment of data, and choice of manageable problems, contribute to our knowledge of what to do? Can the findings from this process be reconciled with the intuitive good sense traditionally shown by untrained teachers—including many parents—and with the insights of occasional great teachers who have inspired our commitment to human values? How can the best of all this be synthesized and applied by millions of teachers all over the world? More important, can the education system be redesigned so that childrens' success or failure are not so dependent on the experiences and preferences of individual teachers?

These issues are addressed by the distinguished educators who planned and wrote this yearbook. Warning: they did not reach agreement so you will have to decide for yourself who is right. In fact, you may decide that each of them is at least partially right. But we will have to keep trying to bridge the chasm between developers and users of knowledge about teaching. Only by orchestrating our efforts more skillfully will educators be able to fulfill public demands for more effective schooling.

—Lawrence S. Finkel
ASCD President, 1983-84

Section I.
Stage Setting

1 Introduction: The Problem, Its Difficulties, and Our Approaches

PHILIP L. HOSFORD

*T*he skillful use of knowledge is often an enormous step beyond knowing. Having knowledge about the stock market is one thing—using that knowledge to make money is quite another. Knowing how to hit a golf ball does not mean we will hit it well, but the knowledge does give us a better chance.

And so it is with teaching, supervision, and curriculum development—the more we know, the better our probable performance. We gain the needed knowledge through experience, formal education, research, coaching, and intuition. We test theories generated from our knowledge in our attempts to solve problems, gain new knowledge, or improve our skills and artistry.

This orderly, straightforward process of gaining knowledge and translating it into artistic practice is often slowed by controversies generated through the process itself. For example, advocates of the scientific approach and the artistic approach to education sometimes seem to spend as much energy discrediting each other as they do in offering support for their own views. Other such conflicts have at one time or another been created between behaviorism and humanism, between quantitative and qualitative research procedures, and between the developers of knowledge and those who fear the possible misapplication of that knowledge.

As the committee worked toward an organization for this book, we found most of our discussions and writings centered on one of the following questions:

Philip L. Hosford is Professor, Department of Curriculum and Instruction, College of Education, and Department of Mathematical Sciences, College of Arts and Sciences, New Mexico State University, Las Cruces.

3

1. How do we get what we know?
2. Once known, how do we get it into common practice?
3. Once in practice, how do we develop skill and artistry in that practice?

Three very difficult questions—but they are, after all, what this book is all about. The comments on these questions by our major authors, which are provided in this Introduction, were not taken from any of the chapters that follow, but rather were obtained from our discussions and other writings during our organizational efforts.

How Do We Get What We Know?

How do we gain the knowledge we need? How do we verify that knowledge? If it is true, how do we judge its value? In the chapters that follow, much more will be said regarding this problem. But for now, two of our committee members comment:

Madeline Hunter:

There are many ways of knowing. Realization of this may eliminate the either-or dichotomy between theoretician and practitioner that, in the past, has interfered with each contributing productively to the questions asked and the answers sought by the other. Lack of communication has resulted in arguments at the level of, "Which is more important in running, your right leg or your left?" If you don't use both, you won't run. If educators don't base practice on theory derived from validated research and if the results of that practice do not infuse research with correction and with new questions that need to be answered, then education won't "run" successfully.

Educators use three ways of knowing, each way contributing to certain facets of effective professional practice. No one way yields omniscience in all facets.

In every profession the first way of knowing emerges from the perceptions yielded by experience. Practice often reveals certain actions or sets of circumstances that can be used for prediction. The "look" of the sky eventually enables certain "experienced" individuals to predict weather conditions. In the same way, the "look" ("sound," "feel") of students or class situations enables a sensitive teacher to predict future events. "The way John looks, I know we're going to have a rough day."

Science, a second way of knowing, was born out of human attempts to identify significant perceptions so people could explain, extend the accuracy of, and generalize their predictions. Understanding which were the significant clues often enabled humans to identify cause-effect relationships that made control a possibility. When meteorology emerged as a science, it enabled humans to "see" more accurately, farther away and farther ahead; therefore, prediction achieved higher accuracy but seldom certainty. Even with this greater accuracy made possible by science, the aviator, sailor, teacher, and a woman hanging out her wash do not discard the knowledge generated from experience. In dry southern California, teachers know from the restless behavior of their students when it is going to rain without consulting the weather report.

An advantage of knowing from science is that systematized and disciplined inquiry increases the accuracy and generalizability of findings. When the weatherman predicts rain, the teacher can change teaching plans, if that is indicated. The advantage of knowing from experience is that the knowledge is forged in the real world and often tempered by immediate and consequential validation or impeachment. Should a teacher attempt to introduce a new and difficult learning task when the barometer is changing and students are inattentive, the vividness of the disappointing, if not disastrous, results has a lasting effect on that teacher's future decisions.

An additional advantage of knowing from experience is that the human mind processes perceptions that the person may not have identified as significant or in some cases, even admitted to consciousness. Yet those perceptions may be a critical variable in explanation or prediction. This highly functional but inarticulate knowledge is usually classified as intuition, which is a third way of knowing. Many "hunches" or insights are simply knowledge that results from non-deliberate and subconscious (not unconscious) processing of articulate or inarticulate past experience and present perceptions.

Computers now enable us to factor out these perceptions, which made intuitive knowledge possible as the computers systematically process the multitude of data available. For example, in one medical school, certain physicians could identify some brain damage at birth but didn't know what clues they were using so could not transmit their "intuition" to other doctors. Computer analysis of every facet of those births finally narrowed the clues down to the cry and eventually to the timbre of the cry. Once the significant perception was identified and articulated it could be taught to others.

Vincent Rogers:

Finding out what is really going on in children's minds as they go through the process of schooling is unquestionably one of our most difficult and neglected tasks. We have an enormous amount of test data dealing with outcomes, but very little information at the level that probes beneath the surface of a child's written response.

This, of course, is what John Holt did so effectively in his classic, *How Children Fail*; it is what Piaget did as he studied the cognitive growth of children; it is what Erlwanger is doing now in mathematics education, Janet Emig in writing, and Ann Bussis in reading. All of them and many others as well are using one-on-one interviews as well as a number of other devices to probe into the mind of the child and study what Goodlad calls the "experienced curriculum." This movement seems to me to be long overdue.

How Do We Get What We Know into Common Practice?

When and how do we discern the value of what we know? How do we determine its applicability in another context? How much do we know that is not widely used? What might quicken the pace from knowledge to practice? Three committee members comment:

Ralph Tyler:

Does the educational practitioner—teacher, supervisor, administrator—use the results of educational research? In 1970, Stephen Bailey sent questionnaires to a sample of school administrators, asking about their uses of the products of educational research and development. Their replies cited very few research findings that they were employing in their schools. Teachers and supervisors often complain about the lack of usefulness of research studies.

One obvious explanation for the fact that most teachers and administrators do not report that they use the results of educational research in their work is the cumulative nature of systematic knowledge, and, therefore, much of it that we use was formulated in the past. For example, we now take for granted that interest in a learning activity is an important positive factor in a pupil's learning. However, when John Dewey discovered this in his work with his laboratory school in Chicago, it was a new finding contradicting the folklore of education— that learning tasks to be effective must be hard and unpleasant. His little book, *Interest and Effort in Education* (1918), created a debate among professionals for 10 years before the idea became an accepted pedagogical principle.

The Department of Defense conducted a study of the source of knowledge used in designing a modern weapons system and found that more than 80 percent of the research findings used in this project were published 25 or more years before. When new knowledge is incorporated into the common practices of a profession, practitioners rarely know the source of the knowledge and are not likely to appreciate the contribution that earlier research has made to their work.

Madeline Hunter:

Ways of knowing lead to ways of doing. The more accurate the knowledge, the more powerful can be its potential for action. Teaching and supervising are performance behaviors; so that performance needs to take advantage of all three ways of knowing yet be responsive to the assets and limitations of each.

Research, in its effort to maintain purity can become sterile so the knowledge yielded is not valid in the "impure" environment of the classroom. For example, when behavior in the laboratory is not reinforced it will be extinguished. In a classroom, however, a teacher may ignore a smart remark but the responses of other students may constitute a positive reinforcer.

Still the teacher finds the concept of extinction a useful one. Knowing that the inappropriate remark is a bid for attention, the effective teacher ignores the remark rather than making a federal case of it. If ignoring is not possible or appropriate, the teacher can respond with a quiet and unemotional, "We won't take class time for that, I'll see you at break."

This research-supported action accomplishes three things: (a) it eliminates the possibility of positively reinforcing the student for interrupting the class; (b) it gives the culprit time to repent in anticipation of what the teacher will do; and (c) it gives the teacher time to think of something intelligent to do.

Experience, however, tells the teacher that this strategy won't always work. Sometimes the responses of the other students constitute such a powerful positive reinforcer that ignoring by the teacher is ineffective.

Intuition, which results from processing past knowledge with perceptions of the moment, may tell the teacher to pretend to be amused and laugh heartily with the other students *or* to "land on the student like a ton of bricks" *or* to eject the student from the class *or* let the culprit go and punish the other students for encouraging such behavior by their laughter.

These examples suggest that nothing is more powerful than research-based theory, tempered and augmented by knowledge that is derived from informed practice, whether it be articulated or intuitive.

Vincent Rogers:

Perhaps more effective use of research in education has at least something to do with the notion of reciprocity; that is, that research ought to be as much for the subjects being studied as it is for the researcher. More involvement on the part of teachers and others in the design of the research itself, more involvement as the research progresses, sharing of preliminary results, and most important, dialogue about and follow-up of the results of research in participating schools might make a difference. As things stand now, many teachers are suspicious of educational researchers because they feel they are serving their own purposes and not necessarily the schools.

I believe that teachers get less respect than they want, and that we demonstrate this inadequate respect by our approach to their professional growth. The Teachers Center movement began in this country as a response to this problem. In some of the best centers, teachers designed the workshops and seminars to be offered, selected speakers and workshop leaders, and sometimes participated in locally designed research projects.

Perhaps if university teachers, school administrators, and others higher up in the educational hierarchy tried a bit harder to treat teachers like genuine professionals in all aspects of their work, including educational research, the results of research would be applied more effectively.

How Do We Develop Skill and Artistry in Our Practice?

Once knowledge is in common practice, how do we increase the artistry of that practice? How do we overcome resistance to skillful and aesthetic application of knowledge—resistance that may arise from stubbornness, independence, lack of confidence, or fear of the unknown? How do we cause real impact on the desire of practitioners to apply knowledge in their teaching, supervisory, and administrative activities in the most rewarding, artistic ways possible? Once again, two authors comment:

Asa Hilliard:

Questions arise frequently regarding the gap between the development of knowledge in education through science and the application of that knowledge in practice. Questions also arise regarding whether the practice of education is an art or a science or some combination of the two. Both of these questions reflect a continuing infection of our belief system with the type of dualisms against which John Dewey warned us years ago. In the two questions above we note a dualistic concept, first, between theory on the one hand and practice on the other. Second, we note another dualism between art on the one hand and science on the other. The easy, almost natural emergence of dualistic thinking among educators when analyzing educational phenomena may well be rooted in a more deeply pervasive implicit philosophical orientation within the society at large. That orientation is toward either-or thinking, of which theory and practice, art and science, are but two manifestations.

Unstated but present in such dualistic thinking is the notion of hierarchy. For example, not only are theory and practice seen as separate, and art and science seen as separate, but they are ranked with respect to each other. Therefore theory is seen as higher than practice, and science is seen as higher than art. This also suggests a desired direction for evolution in professional thought. Presumably, education will get better to the extent that it deals more with theory than with practice, and to the extent that it is more scientific than artistic. Thus along with the cognitive separation of educational phenomena into poles of a dualism, we tend to be compelled to regard existing positions with respect to the dualism as better or worse, advanced or retarded, and even amateur or professional.

Theory, practice, art, and science may be regarded simply as points of view from which a common reality can be analyzed. Theory need not be regarded as the opposite of practice, nor as separate from practice, any more than art need be regarded as the opposite of science or separate from science. The moment either of these dualisms is seen as being differences in the real world, a whole host of undesirable consequences must follow inevitably. Not only will theory and practice be separated and art and science be separated, but theoreticians and practitioners, artists and scientists, will also be separated, with individual educators becoming specialists in one or more aspects of the educational operation, as if such aspects represent a real-life separate category.

It is useless to protest that as educators we do not think this way in general. Evidence that we do is found in the organization of our colleges of education and in the roles that are played by educators. Quite simply, most of our theoreticians do not practice, and most of our practitioners do not theorize. Similarly, most of our artists do not see themselves as scientists, nor do most of our scientists see themselves as artists. The major outcome of such an arrangement is that the real problems that exist in American education remain unsolved.

Ralph Tyler:

The nature of research and the difference between research and development are not well understood. Research is an activity seeking to gain greater understanding of a phenomenon, while development is an effort to design a system that will achieve desired ends under specific constraints. There is also evaluative research that compares the realities of the system with the intentions and conditions, specific or implied, in the plans. Often, practitioners do not understand these distinctions and will ask of research such questions as: How can I eliminate disruptive behavior in the classroom? How can we get the school tax levy raised? How can I give instructional leadership in my school? How can I teach disadvantaged children to read?

Research may provide greater understanding of such a problem as disruptive behavior in classrooms by studying instances of it that may lead to the building of a taxonomy of types, identifying kinds of students involved, describing the contexts in which they occur, the antecedent events, and the consequences. But systematic efforts to eliminate or reduce this behavior requires the design of a procedure (development) and the testing of the procedure in practice (evaluative research). Practitioners in most fields have not had much experience in calling upon research, development, and evaluative research in connection with their own work; thus, they have not learned to make distinctions, nor discovered their usefulness.

Researchers and many academics also misunderstood educational practices. The practice of every profession evolves informally, and professional procedures are not generally derived from a systematic design based on research findings. Professional practice has largely developed through trial and error and intuitive efforts. Practitioners, over the years, discover procedures that appear to work and others that fail. The professional practice of teaching, as well as that of law, medicine, and theology, is largely a product of the experience of practitioners, particularly those who are more creative, inventive, and observant than the average.

Research and development activities furnish a more systematic basis for building a body of practices and an intellectual doctrine to explain them, and they can also provide a basis for dealing with new problems and improving practice. But science explains phenomena, it does not produce practices. Hence both researcher and developer must turn to the phenomena of learning and teaching, of schools and other institutions where learning takes place in order to derive relevant data for their work. This seems, sometimes, to be forgotten. Part of the lack of utilization of research by the practitioner is the failure of some researchers to investigate actual educational phenomena.

On Becoming Bridge Builders

We on the committee are grateful to those in the field who wrote the thoughtful responses to the major sections of this book. Those who responded represent teachers, supervisors, administrators, teacher trainers and others from public and private sectors concerned with education. These responses challenge, clarify, or support by example the concepts presented by the major authors. I need make only one further point appropriate to an introduction to this book.

Between the discovery of knowledge and its successful application lies a swampland of fears. Historically, these fears are rooted in religion, self-defense, ignorance, and assorted emotional needs. Fearful resistance to translating new knowledge into practice is not unique to the field of education. Socrates, Ptolemy, and Gallileo all suffered at the hands of those who feared the meaning and possible consequences of the new knowledge they proclaimed. The history of the discovery, development, and use of anesthetics in medicine illustrates the serious difficulties that confront the bridge-builder toiling to connect knowledge with usage. The relationship between cancer and smoking has been well established and publicized, but the most obvious application of this knowledge today seems to be only the Attorney General's warning printed on each package. These examples from other fields illustrate the continuing difficulties encountered in linking knowledge to its logical application.

Bridge-builders in education, whether they be teachers, supervisors, administrators, or theorists, must be prepared to encounter resistance to their efforts to bring new knowledge into common practice. In our field much resistance arises from those who (1) doubt that something needs to be done, (2) doubt that the proposed solution will do any good, (3) fear offending their colleagues by openly departing from traditional practice, or (4) are reticent to depart from the comfort of the status quo or anticipate failure in adopting the new practice.

Knowledge gained through sound research in the area of teacher effectiveness serves as a current example. The time-on-task knowledge reported during the 1970s provides all of the historical challenges to bridge-builders attempting to span the swampland. The bridge-builders, in their efforts to develop the time-on-task knowledge to an acceptable state of application may be attacked by a mixed group of people I will call the Fearful Ones. Their concerns arise from the fear that the bridge-builders are:

1. Being dynamically ignorant of the many integrally related aspects of teacher effectiveness now supported by research
2. Being cold-hearted measurement people determined to evaluate teachers on the basis of time-on-task data alone
3. Not evaluating the quality of time-on task
4. Not questioning the value of the task
5. Failing to note the efficiency of performance of the task
6. Using invalid, unreliable instruments for measuring time-on-task.

In spite of support for the bridge-builder's attempts to develop acceptable foundations for time-on-task knowledge, an increasing number of people beleaguer the work with one or more of the above charges. As the attacks from the Fearful Ones increase and possibly border on the vitriolic, we witness a sociological phenomenon—namely the rise of still a third group, which I will call the Anti-Fearfuls.

Beyond any specific example such as the preceding time-on-task illustration, the Anti-Fearfuls are not so much in favor of the bridge-builders, in general, as they are antagonistic toward the Fearful Ones. They rise to oppose the Fearful Ones like an essential counter-force of Newton's Third Law. So now the bridge-builders are caught in a distracting if not disabling cross fire of charges and counter charges. Both the Fearful Ones and their anti-group proclaim, "If you're not with us, you're against us." Their distracting quarrel becomes politically based rather than issue oriented and again we see their energy being expended in discrediting each other instead of supporting their respective views.

Under these circumstances, the bridge-builder's lot is not exactly a happy one. Even though bridge-builders play the role of the "good guys" in this scenario, we can wonder that any bridges are ever completed, much less stand the test of time. The observation that practice commonly lags 20 years or more behind knowledge becomes more believable in this context.

One more current example of linkage difficulty may further illustrate the point. For over ten years now, mostly on the research side of the swamp, some of us have been intrigued by patterns and unique correlations found in teacher evaluation research using videotape. One such pattern is the surprisingly clear consensus achieved by professionals when they are asked to respond to the question, "Would you want this teacher for your child, or little brother or sister, next year?" The consensus occurs regardless of the subject matter, grade level, or sex of the teacher being viewed.

As such bits of knowledge emerge, some Fearful Ones announce their concern that the knowledge might be hurried into inappropriate application. A few students of the research then join the Anti-Fearfuls and attempt early application without first developing the necessary bridge between knowledge and practice. As a result, most of their work disappears into the swamp. A few students attempting a more cautious development report their surprise at the attacks on their efforts. Many of these young professionals begin to hesitate—to question the rewards of the bridge-building effort. A forceful affirmation by their mentors that they are, indeed, serving their profession well, may be critical to their continued efforts to develop acceptable applications of new knowledge.

Many bridge-builders are at work today. The experiences, skills, and insights of some who have successfully linked knowledge to application are presented in this volume. All readers will identify with either the researcher, developer, research evaluator, or practitioner so clearly defined by Tyler. Similarly, readers will appreciate Hunter's ways of knowing, Hilliard's historical/contextual view, Roger's qualitative analysis imperative, and Berliner's context for quantitative research.

Tyler asserts that practitioners do use research, but their use is limited by lack of information about recent research, by lack of understanding of the kind of practical values research can provide, and by the confusion created by reports of research not based on the realities with which practitioners deal.

The purpose of this yearbook is to provide a thoughtful examination of such problems, looking at how we get our knowledge, how we translate that knowledge into practice, and how that practice becomes artistic. We hope that large numbers of educators as well as others interested in education become compulsive readers of this volume. The chapters may be read as separate entities, but they are so ordered that a sequential reading should bring an integrity of content to the reader that otherwise might be missed.

Much is yet to be learned regarding the knowledge, skills, and values of the bridge-builder in education. If you are not already an industrious bridge-builder, this book may hasten your stride toward that goal.

2 Comparing the Use of Research in Other Professions With Research in Education

CHRISTINE H. McGUIRE AND RALPH W. TYLER

PART I. DIFFUSION AND APPLICATION OF NEW KNOWLEDGE IN MEDICINE

Christine H. McGuire

On December 3, 1967, the first successful human heart transplant was performed half a world away in South Africa. Within hours newspapers, radio, and television carried headline stories of this event to every town and city in the United States; within days terminally ill patients and their families across the land were beseeching their physicians to tell them how they could obtain this lifesaving measure; within months the first team was organized to perform this procedure in a U.S. hospital, and similar teams at other institutions soon followed.

While this is a particularly dramatic case of the diffusion of innovation in medicine, it provides a striking illustration of five important characteristics of the health professions that *generally* act in concert to encourage rapid application of new knowledge by the practitioner.

Christine H. McGuire is Professor of Medical Education, University of Illinois at Chicago. Ralph W. Tyler is Director Emeritus, Center for Advanced Study in the Behavioral Sciences, Palo Alto, California.

13

First, lifesaving developments and even less dramatic breakthroughs in medicine are treated as front-page news by the press; in many cases the public becomes aware of the development almost as quickly as professionals. This phenomenon is not new; when Louis Pasteur apparently conquered hydrophobia (a rare but terrifying disease) in the 19th century "the news flashed round the world, and frantic individuals from many nations rushed to Paris as to a savior."[1]

Second, the public recognizes immediately the possible import of such developments for extending the length and/or improving the quality of their lives; thus, they have a strong interest in seeing that practitioners employ the latest and best methods. Third, potential beneficiaries of the new knowledge bring direct and immediate pressure on individual practitioners to utilize it. True, the public, desperate for a "cure" for serious diseases, may press for dubious but highly publicized remedies, such as krebiozen or laetrile. Even 100 years ago the public was alert to new discoveries that promised relief from suffering and demanded their application. For example, in 1881 at the request of an agricultural society, Pasteur conducted his famous experiment with anthrax, and demonstrated before awed onlookers at Melun, France, that while all unvaccinated sheep succumbed to a deadly injection of anthrax bacilli, not one of his vaccinated animals was harmed. "The world received this news and waited, confused, believing that Pasteur was a kind of messiah who was going to lift men from the burden of all suffering. France went wild and called him her greatest son and conferred on him the Grand Cordon of the Legion of Honor."[2]

Fourth, as suggested by this anecdote, the practitioner's reputation and, to a certain extent, income depend on his or her willingness and ability to respond positively to public pressures for treatment and cures.

Fifth, because of the extreme specialization now characteristic of many health fields, the relevant community of practitioners is a small, tightly knit group. Most of them are in direct contact with one another, creating a highly functional communication network that continues a long tradition which places high value on "keeping up" with the latest developments.

As evidence of this last point, most medical specialists belong to societies that sponsor national meetings and produce specialized journals, both of which are dedicated to publication of the latest research. In addition, most of these societies require continuing education credit as a condition for specialty certification. Further, the staff of each hospital, as well as the local medical society, conduct various continuing education

---

[1]Richard Harrison Shyrock, *The Development of Modern Medicine* (Madison: University of Wisconsin Press, 1979), p. 336.

[2]Paul de Kruif, *Microbe Hunters* (New York: Harcourt Brace and Co., 1966), p. 164.

programs; participation in these, or comparable groups, has become a requirement for maintaining licensure in a number of states. Finally, the work setting for practice of the medical profession encompasses not only the traditional independent private office, but more and more frequently an office that is in a group practice as well as a hospital. In both settings there is not only opportunity to learn from one's peers, but also a dependence on their esteem, which directly affects personal income from practice.

The pharmaceutical industry also plays a role in the rapid diffusion and application of some kinds of new knowledge. That industry spends tens of millions of dollars annually investigating new drugs. For those drugs that survive animal and human trials (and there are hundreds such each year[3]), there is a marketing race that involves armies of "detail men" who call on physicians to explain and urge the use of these products.

Lest the process of the diffusion and application of knowledge about organ transplants be thought to be unique, numerous other less dramatic but more significant examples of prompt application of new knowledge in the U.S. can be cited. Among them are the closing of tuberculosis sanitoria following the rapid spread of antibiotic therapy during and following World War II, the virtual elimination of poliomyelitis following the introduction of the Salk vaccine, the reduction of mortality from pneumonia, and significant reductions in the disabling consequences of venereal disease.

However, these and many other possible examples share two characteristics that may suggest limitations on the kinds of knowledge likely to be rapidly applied by the majority of practitioners: first, all are the products of applied research; second, each represents a very specific intervention (a pill or procedure) undertaken by the physician. When the application of new knowledge entails a fundamental change in the life style or habits of either the patient or the health professional, it finds less ready acceptance by both.

In the field of preventive medicine these attitudes have impeded progress in virtually all areas except sanitation, vaccination, and immunization. Even in these areas application of knowledge has often been excruciatingly slow. For example, the basic discovery on which smallpox vaccination is based was made prior to 1800; but it was not applied on a wide scale until after the Franco-Prussian War (1870-71) when a controlled experiment was inadvertently conducted. In that war the German army, which had been systematically vaccinated, lost only 300 men to smallpox while the unvaccinated French army lost over 20,000 men to the

---

[3]For example, it has been reliably estimated that 90 percent of the drugs now used by physicians were not known 25 years ago.

disease. More than another 100 years passed before the World Health Organization could announce that the last case of smallpox had been found, and the disease eradicated. Thus, it required almost 200 years to conquer the "most feared of all eighteenth century plagues," the elimination of which entailed only a simple procedure and the use of a cheap and plentiful supply of vaccine.

It should, therefore, not be surprising that when prevention of disease involves changing cherished habits or making other perceived sacrifices, the public will be more resistant to new advancements in knowledge. For example, though the doctor's role in spreading puerperal ("childbed") fever had been amply demonstrated by the mid-19th century, thousands of women continued to die from the disease because physicians could not be persuaded to take the simple precaution of washing their hands before examining each patient. More recently, 20 years after the Surgeon General's widely publicized report demonstrating the relationship between smoking and both lung cancer and heart disease, thousands of avoidable deaths continue to occur each year. Similarly, while our workplaces have become safer and more pleasant in some respects, new toxins have been introduced, and progress toward removing them has been frustrated by powerful lobbies that resist the expense of applying fully the knowledge we do have.

Finally, issues regarding the utilization of findings from basic research are complicated, and the lag time between discovery and application varies greatly. For example, knowledge of the effects of particular molds on skin infections is part of our folk wisdom. For countless years, individuals worldwide have used moldy bread as a poultice. Yet, Fleming's accidental discovery of penicillin and his report in 1928 of its remarkable effect on bacteria were greeted by a total lack of interest from his medical colleagues. It was only after a report of the results of the first clinical trial on February 12, 1941, with one dying patient, that the medical community evidenced any real enthusiasm for this important discovery. Then progress and recognition came rapidly, and in December 1945 Fleming and two colleagues were jointly awarded the Nobel prize.

In contrast, the earliest publication of a piece of obscure, esoteric basic research on the action of certain enzymes in splitting genes was followed by a flurry of activity. Within ten years, and despite a self-imposed and partially voluntary moratorium on recombinant DNA research, the field of genetic engineering was flooded by the formation of some 150 commercial manufacturing firms. These companies were prepared to utilize the newly discovered gene splicing techniques to produce on consignment new forms of life capable of "eating" oil spills, manufacturing natural insulin, or producing other organic materials.

These two examples suggest that, overall, the time between medical discoveries and general application of this knowledge may be diminishing. To the extent that this has occurred, it has been due to three factors.

First, the more extensive the initial information base, the more likely that new knowledge will provide a missing element to unlock numerous areas. Second, technological advances in instrumentation (for example, the electron microscope, the CAT scanner, and so on) and in data processing (the main frame, mini, and microcomputers) have facilitated more rapid follow-up of each new discovery. Third, the federal government has until recently put high priority on biophysical and biomedical research, supporting such research with billions of dollars distributed through the National Institutes of Health and the National Science Foundation. Though many seem disappointed that some ten years after President Nixon declared "a war on cancer" we have not yet eliminated that disease, the fact is that large amounts of federal dollars have permitted us to mount a concerted attack on the problem at every level—from basic research, through applied research, to demonstration projects in cancer control centers. The availability of resources and the coordination of effort have advanced our understanding and have reduced cancer mortality and morbidity more rapidly than would otherwise have been possible.

There are, however, signs of a disturbing countertrend that may have adverse consequences for research and development in the health sciences. In many areas, basic research that results in patentable discoveries can produce significant profits for the owners of the patents. Given these circumstances, the tradition of free and open discussion and collaboration among scientists may be seriously compromised, and the rate of future progress jeopardized.

Summary

Because they supply a service to people with clearly perceived problems, practitioners of medicine are under pressure from those they serve to utilize the latest advances in the field. These pressures are reinforced by the organization and structure of the profession, the values it espouses, the settings in which its members work, the rules and regulations to which they are subject, the reward system in which they participate, and the economic motivations of industries which support them. All of these conditions act to encourage and assist medical practitioners to "keep abreast" of new knowledge and to apply it in their practices. The willingness of the public to commit substantial resources to biomedical research and development over the past two decades has further accelerated both the advance of knowledge and its rate of diffusion and utilization. However, the prospects of sharply reduced federal funding for both research and training, together with the limitations on and competition for private funding, strongly suggest that the stimulus to progress from that source will be sharply curtailed. Finally, rapid utilization of new knowledge will be further inhibited to the extent that its application requires economic and/or other sacrifices.

PART II. THE USE OF RESEARCH BY ENGINEERS

Ralph W. Tyler

Engineers design systems to accomplish certain functions within given constraints. Thus engineers are called upon to design solar heating systems, fuel-efficient automobiles, space vehicles, and so on. Like physicians they are responsible for getting something done. This function is in contrast with that of scientists, which is to gain increased understanding of phenomena.

However, both professions, medical and engineering, benefit greatly from the research of scientists. Biologists, seeking to understand the structures and functions of living things, produce knowledge, much of which is helpful to physicians. Physicists and chemists produce knowledge about physical phenomena, much of which is helpful to engineers. For example, the research of organic chemists in the early 1900s identified the benzine ring group of organic compounds. This was picked up quickly by German chemical engineers who designed equipment to produce synthetic dyes and smokeless powder. French, British, and American engineers realized the significance of this research during World War I when the Germans, using smokeless artillery powder, easily concealed their positions and inflicted heavy losses on the Allies.

Not only do chemical engineers utilize research but also mechanical, electrical, radio, and civil engineers have benefited from research in new metals, crystalline structures, semi-conductors, soil analysis, and the like. The incentives for engineers to apply research are similar to those of physicians; their work will be more effective, their efforts will be applauded by their peers, and their incomes will be higher. However, the public is not as concerned with systems designed by engineers as they are with saving lives or improving health—the work of physicians. Hence, the mass media pay little attention to new developments in engineering. The diffusion of research to the engineering profession is largely done through professional publications, meetings, and other communications networks of engineering specialists.

Furthermore, faculties in schools of engineering, particularly graduate schools, keep in close touch with research programs that have produced useful findings for the engineering profession. The continuing education programs of engineers place great emphasis on these new developments. It is estimated that physical and chemical research results that appear to have significant implications for engineering are widely known and utilized by leaders of the profession within 10-15 years after the reports are published.

The rapid diffusion and adoption of research in medicine and engineering are in sharp contrast to the time required for relevant social science research to be widely utilized by educational practitioners. Paul Mort and his students at Teachers College, Columbia University, studied the diffusion of innovations in the practice of education in the United States. They reported that at least 30 years were required for any innovation that was found to be effective in school practice to be adopted by half the schools in the U.S. What accounts for this difference between the diffusion rate in education and that found in other professions such as medicine and engineering?

PART III. DIFFUSION AND ADOPTION IN EDUCATIONAL PRACTICE

Ralph W. Tyler

Professor McGuire, in the first section of this chapter, lists important characteristics of the health professions that generally act in concert to encourage rapid application of new knowledge. Several relate to the influence the mass media exerts to stimulate members of the health profession to utilize research in their professional practice. McGuire points out that breakthroughs in medicine are treated as front page news by the lay press. Thus, the public recognizes immediately the import of such developments for extending the length of and for improving the quality of their lives; and so has a strong vested interest in seeing that the latest and best means are regularly employed by medical practitioners.

New research in engineering and education is not generally regarded by the mass media to be of front page significance. Mass media program directors believe that most adults are concerned about their health and want to know anything that would appear to have implications for longer or healthier life. But they do not believe that most people are generally interested in the products of engineering such as machines, buildings, and roads. The program directors similarly do not believe that most people are concerned with improving the effectiveness of education. Research results that have implications for improving educational practice are not commonly presented by the mass media. Programmers think that only startling or "bad" news about education will have an audience. Thus, on those occasions when positive research is publicized, its implications for education are often misunderstood and misinterpreted by the press.

As an example, the mass media publicized the discovery of the effects of certain dietary compounds on hyperactive children as a panacea for education. The reporters did not know how rare physical hyperactivity is, nor the role of children's energy and motivation in learning. Similarly, programmed instruction was widely publicized as a guaranteed procedure for individualized learning. No publicity was given to Sidney Pressey's experiment that showed that programmed materials generally increased learning only for a fraction of the so-called "slow learners" and decreased the efficiency of learning for the majority.[1]

Cases exist where parents believed that a profound research finding was presented in a popular book or article. In actual fact, someone unfamiliar with relevant research was merely expressing, with moving passion, totally unsupported beliefs. Such publications often have aroused parents to press for costly but nonproductive changes in school practices. For example, Rudolph Flesch published *Why Johnny Can't Read,* which caused parents in many middle-class communities to pressure for change in the teaching of beginning reading. They were aroused because of Flesch's assertions concerning the low level reading ability of most children. Parents did not ask their local schools about the reading achievements of their own children. Had they done so, most parents would have found that a large majority of American children had learned and were learning to read. The children having serious difficulty in learning were generally less than 20 percent of those enrolled.

Parents might also have been informed of the research of Jean Chall who found that all of the widely used methods of teaching beginning reading are about equally effective when employed by a competent teacher. But, failing to investigate the matter, many school districts changed their programs without obtaining any observable benefits. This illustration suggests the importance of evaluative research that seeks to distinguish constructive innovations from those that produce little or no improvement in school learning.

If the present pattern of news selection continues, neither engineering nor education can depend upon the mass media to correctly inform the public about research that may have significant implications for improving the practice of these professions. The public, therefore, will be unable to influence these professions to develop and adopt research-based practices.

McGuire states that the medical "practitioner's reputation and, to a certain extent, income depend on his or her willingness and ability to

---

[1]Sidney Pressey, "A Puncture of the Huge Programming Boom?" *Teachers College Record* 64 (1963): 413-18.

respond positively." This incentive to use research is also common in the engineering profession. Individual engineers and engineering firms become known for their designs and products—qualities that depend to a considerable degree upon the use of research methods and findings. The competitive bidding system of engineering firms affects income and enhances reputations. Their designs and products are often cost-effective because of the utilization of research on materials, manufacturing processes, and end products.

There is no such simple relationship between the application of research and the reputation and income of educational practitioners. It is true that teachers who remain in the same school for several years develop a reputation. Parents will often compare notes on "good" teachers and sometimes try to place their children in the classes of teachers with fine reputations. A good reputation can be a good incentive for a teacher to become better, keep abreast of promising ideas, and try new methods. In the past, reputations have been an important factor in the diffusion and utilization of innovations. However, the number of persons who are confident of their teaching effectiveness and seek to improve by making use of new knowledge is too small to furnish the major channel for stimulating the use of research by the practitioner. School principals and parents could and should do what they can to increase the reputation of good teachers and encourage them to try out promising ideas.

McGuire also points out that hospitals and local medical societies conduct continuing education programs. So do large corporations employing engineers, and engineering colleges also conduct programs of continuing education. A considerable number of these programs report on research that has implications for engineering, and some require the student to carry on a project employing recent research in the design of a procedure, process, or product.

In contrast, education practitioners involved in continuing education programs find that very few courses review research that is relevant to improving practice. Educators generally are not taught how to implement new practices. But there are some notable exceptions. For example, Roland J. Long, principal of Hubbard High School in Chicago, reports that his school is establishing inservice programs that explore and resolve problems on research methods and techniques. This program is based on the view that "theory and practice is a continuum which links elements of the educational process, rather than a dichotomy which imposes an artificial compartmentalization upon mutually dependent activities."[2]

---

[2]Roland J. Long, "A View of Educational Research from the Local School Level," *Phi Delta Kappa, CEDR Quarterly* 14, 3 (Fall 1981): 11.

This exception to the general focus of inservice programs demonstrates the possibility of more closely relating research and practice through continuing inservice education.

McGuire also states that in medicine the pharmaceutical industry plays a role in the rapid diffusion and application of some kinds of new knowledge. This industry depends heavily on its profits from the development of drugs and medicines and their use by members of the health professions. These products result from biological and medical research. Hence, the industry is highly motivated not only to inform health professionals about research and products but, if necessary, to facilitate the use of such products. This is a powerful dynamic factor in diffusion of medical knowledge.

The purveyors of materials, machines, and measuring instruments perform the same function for engineers as the pharmaceutical industry does for the health and medical professions. The nearest equivalent to these industries in the education field is that of educational publishing. Educational publishers played a major role in informing practitioners about the results of early studies of the psychology of reading and arithmetic. Even today, publishers are significant elements in the diffusion of new information. Unlike medical and pharmaceutical products, which are the major elements in the physician's world, textbooks and other instructional aids are merely auxiliary materials for the teacher. Pharmaceutical companies can sell a product that heals a physician's patient. Publishers do not distribute materials that cause or create the learning process. Thus, new educational practices are not necessarily diffused through printed matter.

Another of McGuire's characteristics refers to a "highly functional communication network that continues a long tradition of 'keeping up' with the latest developments." The education profession has a variety of communication networks, but the participants are more likely to talk about novel ideas and fashions rather than about the implications of sound research. I think that this may be partly due to the complexity of the teaching-learning situation.

Most physicians have a similar conception of the structure and functioning of the human body. In most respects, the conception is that of the research biologist. For example, when the research biologist speaks of the malfunctioning of the thyroid gland, medical practitioners have an accurate notion of what the gland is and how it functions. Unfortunately, the complexity of school learning is such that each teacher is likely to have a different map in his or her mind about the teaching phenomenon. Until we share a common map, we will not have an adequate basis for the practitioner to judge both the positive and negative effects of a proposed innovation as well as the costs of implementation.

To construct a common map, educational and social science researchers must first build an interpretable common body of knowledge. They must play down conflicting schools of thought and emphasize common elements. As the education profession (through artful teaching) begins to use science constructively, we will be encouraging the building of a cumulative body of knowledge. This will be a more positive approach than rewarding those persons who completely reconstruct the school learning experience to magnify the contributions of their own work.

Finally, we must be realistic in our expectations; we cannot expect the rapid implementation of research observed in the medical field. Medicine has been most successful when the procedure was performed on, not by, the patient.

But total health also depends upon the habits, attitudes, interests, and practices of human beings in regard to such matters as nutrition, exercise, sanitation, stress, rest, and recreation. In these matters, physicians have faced the same problems as teachers. Doctors and teachers cannot learn for the patient or the student. Telling patients they should not smoke is no more effective than telling students they should read better. Increased physician-patient interaction and dialogue has forced medical practitioners to recognize the age-old teaching problems of arousing interest, encouraging and guiding the learning experience, and rewarding desired behavior. There is no simple panacea. But, we can reasonably expect research to help us gain a greater understanding of the complex human learning experience in contemporary situations.

A Response to the McGuire-Tyler Statements

FRANK TOUT

The McGuire-Tyler statements need some additional comment. For example, in education we much admire what "works." Past practices are considered sound and even acquire undeserved virtues. A timid departure from tradition can be met with skepticism and, sometimes, hostility. New practices, even those based on substantial research, are criticized as being "untested." The public expects "new and improved" products from industry and "breakthroughs" from medicine but does not "buy" school programs that are unlike those of yesteryear. In education, to stick with a "proven" practice is often thought to be the wise and safe choice. Such an attitude reminds us that education may be neither art nor science but politics.

Educational practices are often responses to perceived public concerns. More curriculum changes have likely been mandated by legislatures, state education offices, or school boards because of public interest in eroding standards than have been stimulated by any body of recent research. Research findings that conflict with existing practices are given limited consideration and often are dismissed as being "impractical."

Critics of educational research argue from the standpoint of practicality and hold that most teachers cannot duplicate the rigid controls found in the scientific laboratory or the engineering workshop. They state that the human variables in education prevent a wholesale "vaccination" and immunization against poor learning. What works effectively in experimental classrooms can work in others only if all the variables are duplicated; that in itself spells a likely failure for the universal application of learning theories. More likely is the probability that the new products or methods created by research and development will not be available to the educational practitioner. And, in most cases, practitioners find that they lack the decision-making authority to implement new procedures.

Research and development are not significant budget items for school systems, and there is no ready practice for passing on costs to the educational consumer. Exemplary programs, usually funded by government and foundation grants, face an uncertain future even if the value has been well documented.

The experience of John T. Molloy, author of *Dress for Success*, illustrates the problem of disseminating research. As a teacher supported by a government grant, Molloy studied the dress of teachers in the classroom

Frank Tout is Principal, Thomas Carr Howe High School, Indianapolis, Indiana.

and concluded that dress had a significant effect on discipline, work habits, and student attitudes. However, at the conclusion of the study, Molloy's superiors informed him that the experiment was over, further funding was not available, and even if his results were valid, his superiors would not know how to apply them (Molloy, 1975).

Education, unlike business and medicine, has limited avenues by which research findings can be disseminated. There is no well-developed implementation model. Even with a model, its effect on the decision-making process is questionable.

Reference

Molloy, John T. *Dress for Success.* New York: Warner Books, 1976.

On Contrasting Rates of Diffusion of Professional Knowledge: A Response to McGuire and Tyler

STANLEY J. GROSS

McGuire and Tyler compare the factors involved in the diffusion of knowledge in the fields of medicine, engineering, and education. A rough parallel may be suggested by their examples from clinical and preventive medicine on one hand, and from engineering and education on the other. There are differences in the nature of the knowledge involved and in its social relevance, which may explain the differences in the rates of diffusion of new knowledge.

Interventions in the fields of clinical medicine and engineering appear to have consequences that are relatively clear and immediate. An artificial heart or liver transplant works or fails. A bridge stands or collapses. In effect, the public often connects the intervention and its consequences.

Education, however, at all levels is swept by fad after fad and powered by a public so eager for improvement that it is unwilling to await the evidence of impact. In education, just as in preventive medicine, connections between intervention and consequence are often unclear, if they are made at all. It takes no great intuitive leap to suggest that knowledge that can be connected to consequence will be valued more greatly and be diffused more quickly.

An intriguing aspect of the knowledge of clinical medicine, sets it apart from other areas of knowledge and pertains to its social relevance. McGuire notes the life-giving and life-enhancing quality of medical knowledge that gives it an image of power and progress that is, in fact, unrelated to its actual effect. We are made aware periodically of highly dramatic breakthroughs in clinical medicine that are small in proportion to the total knowledge base for the physician.

This dramatic knowledge is the basis for an image that is out of proportion to the real difference a physician can make in his or her daily practice. Two consequences tend to be ignored. First, there is a price to be paid. Iatrogenic (physician-caused) diseases result, as Hamilton (1982) indicates:

> . . . few technologies are completely innocuous in their effect. The occurrence of iatrogenic disease increases with each new procedure or product. Diagnostic roentgenography; birth control drugs, products, and devices; and pharmaceuticals for the treatment of diabetes and hypertension were all lauded as fantastic breakthroughs, but they have since been implicated as serious threats to health. (p. 140).

Stanley J. Gross is Professor of Counseling Psychology, Department of Counseling, Indiana State University, Terre Haute.

Second, the actual power of clinical medicine is more limited than the image suggests. A recent review of research indicates that only 10 to 20 percent of medical procedures are validated by scientific studies (U.S. Congress, 1978). While clinical medicine may be effective in the treatment of bone fractures, infectious diseases, and surgery for removing pathogenic organs, it has little effect on the major diseases of modern society. These, the degenerative diseases—cancer, heart ailments, arthritis, stroke—require what clinical medicine ignores—large scale social prevention and the role of the individual in achieving health. As Carlson (1975) has said, "Medical care as provided by physicians and hospitals is having less and less impact on health" (p. 1).

The image of medicine as life-giving and life-enhancing permits the denial of these major shortcomings. A sleight-of-hand is at work by which physicians reap great rewards and acclaim while the public is encouraged to believe it is getting something it is not. The means by which this situation is maintained is an example of superstitious behavior recognizable to psychologists as a variable ratio reinforcement schedule. The dramatic breakthroughs periodically reinforce a desperate and grateful public. The hope for success permits the public to dismiss the more predominant failures. The image also creates an expectancy of influence which of itself aids in treatment (placebo effect) and which may be further reinforced by a prescription or by surgery. There is no implication here that physicians are consciously malevolent in using this situation to exploit the public. Rather, sad to say, many physicians themselves are taken in by the sleight-of-hand that also acts to reinforce the image. Bucher and Stelling (1977) report that physicians learn early about the faulty nature of the knowledge base on which professional claims are based. Thus they

> come to give greater emphasis to the actual process of doing their work than to the results of that process. If one is not sure whether one will be able to control, influence, or even predict an outcome, one is understandably loath to take responsibility for it or to base one's self-evaluation on it (p. 283).

Interventions that are implemented in the education and prevention arenas tend to express the current value position of the society rather than change society for the better. Tyler notes the flap following the publication of *Why Johnny Can't Read.* He faults the schools and the parents for not being more aware of sound evaluation research indicating that in the hands of a competent teacher there was no difference in the effectiveness of the commonly used methods of teaching reading. One explanation for this is that a social value was being debated here. The Flesch book received much of its support, as Chall (1967) indicated, because this " 'return to phonics' can be associated with the general reaction against progressive education" (p. 290). Convinced that high standards were not being upheld by the schools, mostly well-educated parents were concerned that their children were not getting a sufficient foundation in the early grades to enable entrance into the college of their choice. Privileged people acted to secure their advantage rather than examine the system that makes choice colleges rare.

Exceptions occur, of course, in education and prevention—exceptions probe the rule. Witness the current rapid introduction of the minicomputer into education at all levels. This innovation, however, has obvious economic consequences and disturbs no significant vested interest. The parallels and examples noted in these comments support the suggested rule that knowledge will be diffused in the professions according to its economic impact and its service in maintaining entrenched social interests.

References

Bucher, Rue and Stelling, Joan G. *Becoming Professional.* Beverly Hills: Sage Publications, 1977.
Carlson, Rick J. *The End of Medicine.* New York: Wiley, 1975.
Chall, Jeanne. *Learning to Read: The Great Debate.* New York: McGraw-Hill, 1967.
Hamilton, Patricia A. *Health Care Consumerism.* St. Louis: C.V. Mosby, 1982.
U.S. Congress, Office of Technology Assessment. *Assessing the Efficacy and Safety of Medical Technologies.* Washington, D.C.: U.S. Government Printing Office, 1978.

3 Curriculum Development and Research

RALPH W. TYLER

What Students Are to Learn

What we call today the field of curriculum development arose from the recognition by educators of the implications of the research findings of the 1890s and the 1900s. The American school curriculum at that time was a list of subjects and topics to be taught and a plan for their organization into a course of study. This course of study had its origins in the old English and European folk schools and secondary schools. The selection and placement of subjects were largely based on earlier tradition, somewhat modified by the experience of teachers and the judgments of intellectual leaders. The report in 1893 of the Committee of Ten of the National Education Association was the dominant influence in defining the academic curriculum of the American high school for at least 40 years. Subjects were justified for inclusion by the claim that they trained the mental faculties of students or that they disciplined the mind, or both. Thus, geometry was believed to train the student's logical faculties, Latin was thought to train the faculty of imagination. The study of classical languages was believed to produce general mental discipline. These beliefs and assumptions were seriously questioned by the research investigations of E. L. Thorndike on transfer of training.

In his experiments, Thorndike found that students who had studied geometry were no more logical in their efforts to deal with non-geometric material than were students who had not studied geometry. Latin students did not remember English words any better than those who had not studied Latin. In brief, the notion that the study of certain subjects would in itself produce a trained mind had to be discarded as the basis for

Ralph W. Tyler is Director Emeritus, Center for Advanced Study of the Behavioral Sciences, Palo Alto, California.

curriculum development. This led curriculum makers to stimulate re-search and to examine and use the results to provide a more acceptable basis for selecting what should be taught, for designing learning experiences and teaching procedures, and for organizing them into a coherent course of study.

In arithmetic, for example, investigations were conducted in several different localities in the 1920s to find out the transactions in which arithmetic was used by adults. Studies were also made of the ways in which students were learning arithmetic concepts and skills, and the kinds of difficulties they were encountering. As a result, some of the courses of study in this subject were discarded. They had included such topics as *square root* and *ciphering,* processes not currently used outside of school. The new courses of study listed topics that were more relevant to the current activities of American adults. The topical order and the plan of instruction of the new courses were derived from the research on arithmetic learning.

Similarly, in the field of reading during the same period, research efforts increased rapidly as studies were made of the kinds of reading done by adults—news, fiction, directions to follow in assembling appliances and in constructing objects. Word counts were made of the vocabularies of these common reading materials, and children's interests in various kinds of reading were investigated. The psychology of the reading process was studied and the effects of different ways of guiding children in learning to read were examined. Older courses of study for reading that began by teaching children the letters of the alphabet, then the recognition of syllables, then words and later the reading of sentences were replaced by courses in which word recognition and sentence comprehension preceded analyses. The content of the new reading courses of study was expressed in a carefully restricted vocabulary.

These illustrations from the subjects of arithmetic and reading were paralleled by investigations in sciences, the social studies, and foreign languages. By 1927, the field of curriculum development with its use of research was well enough established for some of its workers to provide the substance of the two parts of the 26th Yearbook of the National Society for the Study of Education (1927).

The early history of curriculum development shows the use made of three kinds of research. E. L. Thorndike's study of transfer of training was an instance of basic research; that is, it furnished research findings that are widely generalizable. It indicated that what a student learned in school was not applied by him or her to situations outside the classroom unless the student saw the similarity of the out-of-school situations to the context in which the learning took place and had learned how to make the application. This altered some curriculum makers to the problem of transfer of learning but it did not give them a particular solution to the problem.

However, it led to a second kind of research that could furnish some guidance to the effort to identify educational objectives; that is, to define what students are to be helped to learn. This applied research investigated the question: What are the contemporary out-of-school situations in which school learning could be constructively used? The studies of adult uses of arithmetic and the uses of reading by children and adults illustrate this kind of applied research. From the results of these investigations, curriculum makers selected topics that involved arithmetic processes widely used outside of school and they developed learning exercises in which students could practice the use of these processes in common out-of-school situations.

In the field of beginning reading, they selected teaching materials, whose content, vocabulary, and sentence structure represented the kinds of reading done by a considerable number of children and adults and they developed learning exercises in which students could practice these kinds of reading in common out-of-school situations.

John Dewey's studies of interest and effort in education furnish another example of the influence of basic research on curriculum development. Contrary to the folklore of that time, he reported from his experiments that student interest was not antithetical to the efforts students put forth in learning but rather the deeper his or her interest in the learning activities the greater was his or her effort. The results of Dewey's studies impressed curriculum makers with the importance of the student's motivation but it did not solve the problem of how teachers could help students develop interest in their school work. However, it did stimulate applied research on the question: What are the interests and motives of contemporary children and youth? From the results of such investigations, curriculum makers gained an additional basis of selecting topics and processes to include in the curriculum and kinds of learning to assign that would appeal to the interests and motives of the students.

Action Research

In order to utilize intelligently the results of basic research, applied research is generally necessary to translate general concepts and principles into more particular contents or processes. But the implications for the curriculum of much of the basic research findings require investigations carried on at the particular school and classroom level. For example, Dewey's basic research indicated the importance of the student's interests in stimulating and maintaining learning. Applied research sought to find out what the reading interests were of samples of children, youth, and adults. However, a particular group of students is enrolled in a particular school and the teachers in this school should find out what the interests of their students are. This level of specific investigations is often called action research. It does not seek generalizable knowledge but rather to obtain helpful information about the persons and situations which the particular school or teacher encounters.

Research useful in identifying what students are to be helped to learn is not limited to studies of contemporary society and of the interests of students. For example, research of the Herbartians and many more recent investigations have indicated the significance of basing learning tasks on the previously acquired knowledge, skills, attitudes, and habits. Responsive to this generalization, curriculum makers have conducted applied research to ascertain what different groups of students have learned that can serve as the basis for new learning. This concern has been intensified with the efforts to develop bilingual, bicultural, and multicultural programs of instruction. Applied research has been conducted on the concepts, attitudes, and skills of children in several large ethnic populations, and teachers in particular schools are encouraged to conduct studies of their own students in planning instructional programs.

In the Eight-Year Study of the 1930s, another focus of research was found useful in selecting what students would be helped to learn. A subject like English, science, or art is not a single body of knowledge. A subject is often called a discipline because it is a continuing enterprise of scholars seeking to gain further understanding of phenomena that fall within the area they have selected for study. Their investigations are not casual. They have disciplined themselves to follow the procedures that have been worked out by their profession to ensure common understanding of the questions being studied, the kind of data that are relevant to these questions, and the meaning of the results obtained. As the years have passed, each subject has amassed a great deal of information, of concepts, of principles, of techniques of data collection and interpretation, and of the scope and limitations of the area encompassed by the subject. This mass of material is far more than any one scholar can comprehend, and, of course, it is far more than could possibly be included in any course or educational program. Most of the courses that have been offered in high school and college represent selections from the subject that scholars in the subject believe are appropriate for the initial training of persons who are to become scholars or specialists in the field. The courses have not usually been based on research that identifies the particular material from that subject that can be helpful to the non-specialist in understanding language, science, the social system, or other phenomena, and the skills that the non-specialist will find helpful in dealing with the problems and opportunities arising in his or her life.

Here is an area of research that can greatly influence what the school can help students learn.

Little Bits of Behavior

When curriculum makers are formulating educational objectives, that is, when they are defining what the school will help students to learn, the question of the desired specificity of the objectives arises. The early research of E. L. Thorndike, which discredited the notion of general mental faculties and general mental discipline, was frequently interpreted to mean that children could not generalize from their learning experiences and everything to be learned must be specific—little bits of behavior. Hence, Thorndike's psychology of arithmetic listed about 3,000 specific objectives for elementary mathematics. Pendleton's work on high school English produced a list of 2,800 specific objectives. Then Charles H. Judd and his students conducted investigations of the extent to which pupils could generalize. As an example, I was in an advanced psychology course taught by Judd where each of us studied generalizations by primary school children. I found that by having children practice addition of two one-digit numbers and accompany this with an explanation of what the process of addition was, that these children were able to add correctly all the 100 combinations of two one-digit numbers after practicing only 21 of them.

Judd's investigations indicated that children could generalize, and that the level of their generalization increased with experience. The implication of these findings for the curriculum makers is that the objectives for an educational program should be at as high a level as the students could attain. This basic research led to applied research seeking to find out what level of generalization different age groups could attain. Then, in the local school, action research was helpful in identifying the level of generalization particular students could attain. Unfortunately, we have just been through a period in which this earlier research has been overlooked and many schools have formulated very specific objectives. These are stated as little bits of behavior as though the school were training rats to run mazes rather than children to use general concepts and principles to aid their understanding and to develop generalized habits and skills to help them attain their goals in life. More recently, however, research reports on transferable skills have revived interest in generalization in learning. Curriculum makers are finding these studies useful in furnishing guides to the formulation of educational objectives.

One of the important problems in selecting objectives for a school curriculum is to distinguish the learning for which the school will take major responsibility from the learning which is the major responsibility of the home, the employer, or other non-school educative institutions, and the learning that will be a shared responsibility. Earlier research indicated the significant influence on children's school learning that came from the consistency of emphasis in school and home and the negative effect of conflict between home and school. Studies of the community environment also indicated the importance of workplace, peer groups, and other non-school experiences on children's learning.

Recent applied research investigations have documented the changes that have recently taken place in the home, in the work-place, in religious institutions, and other local institutions as they affect the education of children. For example, in 1960 only 26 percent of the mothers of school-age children were in the labor force. By 1980, this figure had increased to 59 percent. Many of these working mothers had made no provision for the supervision of their children from the end of the school day until a parent got home from work. Action research is needed to establish the facts for the local school. If the non-school environment has changed markedly for the children of the local school, it will require new discussions with parents and other interested members of the community to work out a mutually acceptable division of responsibility for particular educational objectives.

Planning Learning Experiences

Until the latter part of the 19th century, the guide for teachers was provided by the proverb, "Practice makes perfect." Material was presented to students either orally or in writing and the learners were required to repeat what was presented. Often there were a dozen or more repetitions in an effort to memorize the content. For a skill like handwriting, the teacher demonstrated the way in which the letters were to be formed and the students practiced the writing many, many times.

E. L. Thorndike interpreted his early research on learning in terms of the *Law of Exercise,* a somewhat more precise formulation of the maxim, "Practice makes perfect." His later investigations added a second generalization: The Law of Effect, which emphasized the influence of rewarding successful practice in bringing about learning. Thorndike viewed learning as building connections in the mind between stimuli and appropriate responses to these stimuli. The research of Pavlov and his formulation of learning as conditioned response enhanced the acceptance of this view of learning and it became a guide to many curriculum makers in the planning of learning experiences. This meant that courses of study and teaching units were designed to emphasize: (1) That learning involved the activity of the learner since the responses of the learner to the teacher's stimuli were the behaviors the student learned. (2) These activities should be designed to elicit the behaviors implied by the educational objectives. (3) The teacher should make sure that the student gained satisfaction; that is, was rewarded as he carried on the learning activities successfully.

The stimulus-response theory of learning developed by Thorndike and the theory of learning as conditioning initiated by Pavlov served teachers well when they were planning experiences to help students learn to respond appropriately to situations in which the reaction of a person is initiated by a clear stimulus and consists of an automatic, fixed response. It is a necessary and important type of learning, but it fails when the learner acquires a fixed automatic response where such a reaction is inappropriate.

The inadequacy of conditioned responses arises from the fact that the modern human environment is continually changing and requires new human behavior patterns for coping with these changes. Hence, for the past fifty years, students of learning have sought to develop generalized models that can guide the design of educational programs that are likely to help students gain these more dynamic goals.

Among the most recent of these efforts are those conducted by researchers who call themselves cognitive scientists. Currently their studies indicate that much learning is a highly personalized mental activity involving an active struggle on the part of the learner. It takes time and mental activity for the student to bring existing knowledge, skills, activities, and interests to aid in interpreting and internalizing new knowledge and developing new skills. Furthermore, the studies suggest that applying the knowledge in new situations involves active reconstruction and not simple recall and use of the knowledge (Spiro, 1977).

John Dewey, in 1918, characterized learning as the "reconstruction of experience" and emphasized the importance in teaching to provide ample opportunity for reflection and interpretation of experience rather than using most teaching to present new information. The verification of Dewey's views by recent research should have a strong influence on practice, which has not generally heeded Dewey's emphasis. For example, M. B. Rowe (1974) analyzed hundreds of audio recordings of elementary science classrooms and found that the average time teachers waited for a child to respond to a question was only about one second. When teachers were trained to wait for about three seconds before expecting a meaningful reply, the number of students participating and the appropriateness of their responses improved significantly. She found from her analysis of nearly 1000 audio recordings that when students are given more time to respond the length of student responses increases, the failure to respond appropriately decreases, the number of unsolicited but appropriate responses and speculative responses increases, and students make more statements of inference based on evidence and compare data with other students. Students also ask more questions so that the classroom dialogue changes from an inquisition to a conversation. Further-more, the incidence of responses from "slow" students increases and teachers expect more of such students as well.

From these studies of conscious, complex human learning, curriculum makers are developing new conceptions of the learning of problem-solving skills, and of other kinds of dynamic coping behavior. For exam-ple, some conceive the learning situation as one in which the learner actively seeks to acquire new behavior and the rewards of learning are largely intrinsic rather than extrinsic; that is, the learner derives great satisfaction in using the new behavior successfully as he copes with the problems he encounters or tries to enjoy the experiences of his daily life. From this conception, curriculum makers outline learning situations which are designed to stimulate the student initiative in seeking new understanding, new skills, new attitudes and interest. Research on learn-ing and the development of theories of learning that are more appropriate to some of the important objectives of the curriculum are profoundly influencing practice in design of learning experiences.

Organizing Learning Experiences

During the 20th century, research that has been perceived as useful in guiding the task of organizing learning experiences has been limited both in amount and scope. Prior to this century, both Herbart and Dewey interpreted their experience in planning effective educational programs as requiring continuity and integration of experiences. Herbart empha-sized the importance of beginning with the development of the appercep-tive mass and building gradually and sequentially on that. Dewey's earlier work showed the significant effects on student performance when learning experiences furnished opportunities for continuity and a wealth of interrelations. His small volume, *Experience and Education,* elaborated more fully on these basic criteria for the organization of learning experi-ences—continuity and integration. More recent research has shown the increased effectiveness in learning when experiences are organized to enable the student to progress from unit to unit in which each subsequent unit builds on the preceding ones. Curriculum makers today can benefit by reviewing earlier work and more recent studies in developing their plans for organizing learning experiences based upon the results of re-search.

Appraising the Effects of Program of Instruction

It is not necessary here to elaborate on the ferment now found in the practice of educational evaluation. Much of this can be attributed to the demands for evaluation of programs receiving federal support. Evaluation research is producing new procedures, new instruments, and heated debates as well as increasing so rapidly that the field is often called "exploding." This research is influencing practice in diverse ways and is resulting in confusion among practitioners as well as researchers. Until there is greater clarity about the purpose of evaluation and the methods and instruments are sorted out in terms of purpose, the practice of evaluation in the service of curriculum development appears unlikely to benefit greatly.

From the research of the 1930s and 1940s, however, the practice of program evaluation has developed certain concepts. One has been the identification of four phases of evaluation corresponding to the stages of program development. At the stage when a new program is being planned it is helpful to appraise the objectives, the basic assumptions and the learning procedures proposed, checking them against previous research and obtainable evidence of their soundness. At the stage when resource units and other groups of learning experiences are being selected, an appraisal of their effectiveness and practicability should be made through the use of tryouts. The results of this evaluation should be the basis for necessary revisions and improvements. During the stage when the program is being implemented, a detailed evaluation of the implementation should be conducted in every setting where the program is adopted. Research has shown that many teachers have difficulty in conducting a new program as intended. Most new programs require several years before being fully implemented. During the operation of the program, appraisals are needed of actual outcomes to find out what the students are really learning. Furthermore, from time to time, an evaluation of the permanence of the learning should be made involving students who completed the program a year or more earlier. Information from these appraisals of outcomes should serve as a basis for further improvement of the program. Finally, monitoring evaluations are necessary. Programs may be highly effective in the initial years and lose their effectiveness. In some cases this is due to the employment of new teachers who have not been given adequate training in conducting the program. In some cases the decline in effectiveness can be traced to the loss of interest of teachers and students and to their losing flexibility in making the continuing modifications necessary with changing conditions. Monitoring evaluations can furnish a basis for reinvigoration of the program.

Communication Between Practice and Research

The previous examples indicate that research can assist curriculum makers in developing and improving the school curriculum and show that it has been doing so for most of this century. But it is not generally known how research reaches the practitioner in the field of curriculum development. A review of recent history shows that there have been several channels through which research has influenced curriculum development. One is the graduate schools of education. For example, pioneer research on transfer of training was done by E. L. Thorndike, a professor at Teachers College, Columbia University. His studies were widely discussed in graduate classes there which were attended by many school administrators and supervisors. One of them, G. M. Wilson, an Indiana City School Superintendent, returned home from a summer session at Teachers College and decided to conduct an applied research study on the uses of arithmetic by the adults in that locality. The results were used in the local elementary school. He also published the results in a professional journal where it was read by an editor of a textbook publishing company. The editor saw this kind of study as a good basis for developing a new set of textbooks in arithmetic. As the texts were produced and marketed, their use stimulated changes in the arithmetic course of study in many school districts.

Another channel was the demonstration school. John Dewey started the Laboratory Schools at the University of Chicago. He did not produce textbooks but he directed and closely monitored the instructional program of his school. Administrators and teachers who visited the school were impressed by the constructive learning activities carried on by students in contrast to the passive silence of the classrooms that was characteristic of that time. The direct influence of demonstration schools was not as widespread as the influence of new textbooks but several schools and school systems rebuilt their instructional programs to provide for student motivation and student-initiated activities. Perhaps the greatest direct influence of the Chicago Dewey School was on the development of the curriculum of the Lincoln School, an experimental school endowed by the General Education Board of the Rockefeller Foundation and conducted under the auspices of Teachers College, Columbia University. The original director of the Lincoln School was Otis Caldwell, a former professor at the University of Chicago. He was very familiar with the Dewey School and sought to exemplify its principles in the Lincoln School. He brought another Chicago faculty member, Harold Rugg, to guide curriculum development. The influence of the Lincoln School upon school practice was greatly facilitated by the presence in the summer sessions of Teachers College of large numbers of school administrators from all parts of the country.

One of these administrators was Jesse Newlon from Denver. He was greatly impressed with the need for curriculum reform in the public school and instituted a districtwide program of curriculum construction in the elementary schools of Denver, where the staff was quickly involved in applied research to obtain information about the interests of Denver children and the uses of school subjects by adults in that city. Later Jesse

Newlon moved from the superintendency of Denver to be Director of the Lincoln School. Walter Cocking was another administrator who learned of the research of Thorndike, Dewey, Rugg, and others at Teachers College and was impressed with the need for developing a curriculum that was relevant to the activities of contemporary society and capable of arousing and maintaining the interest of school children. In 1928, he instituted a citywide curriculum project in St. Louis.

Hollis Caswell was another channel of research information to the work of curriculum. He had been superintendent of schools in a small Nebraska town when he came to Teachers College to do graduate study, receiving his doctorate there in 1929. He then joined the faculty of George Peabody College for Teachers in Nashville and in 1930 became consultant to the Virginia State Department of Education in a massive statewide curriculum development project. The Virginia project plan greatly underestimated the time required, the teacher training needed, and the applied and evaluative research costs in order to develop an effective new instructional program in the thousands of classrooms in Virginia. As a result the study was never completed but its influence was an important factor in curriculum changes in a number of Virginia schools for at least a decade.

The supporting staffs of the Eight-Year Study were a major channel for communicating relevant research to the many practitioners in the Thirty Schools and School Systems. These supporting staffs largely consisted of university faculty members but several of them were drawn from the secondary schools where they had already demonstrated interest in research related to curriculum development and were widely read in various fields of the social sciences. The staffs of the Michigan Secondary School Study, the Southern Association High School Study, and the Negro High School Study, all of which were conducted during the Great Depression of the 1930s were mostly drawn from the high schools and a smaller number from the universities.

Several state departments of education have served as channels for bringing research to the attention of curriculum practitioners. For example, J. Casey Morrison, Director of Research in the New York State Department influenced the development of the Activity School Curriculum in New York City, as well as several less-well-known projects. Robert Koopman, in the Michigan State Department of Education, Helen Hefferman of the California State Department of Education were very actively influencing curriculum development in this way in the 1930s and 1940s.

The Metropolitan Associations of school administrators and supervisors that were initiated by graduate schools of education have been channels of two-way communication. They have been in contact with graduate schools and sometimes with the researchers themselves. These contacts have served to inform practitioners about relevant research and have also been a means of suggesting critical problems to researchers that have in some cases led to the focusing of research efforts on problem areas identified by practitioners.

Finally, but not least, mention should be made of the professional organizations of practitioners which in some cases have brought about very effective two-way connections. ASCD, for example, has often identified significant research and 'brought it to the attention of its members both through publications and conferences. ASCD has also publicized problem areas and in several cases stimulated important research that has illuminated these areas.

In summary, research has been reaching practitioners in curriculum development through graduate schools of education, demonstration schools, purveyors of instructional material and equipment, consultants to curriculum development projects, state departments, organizations of school systems professional organizations, and less frequently but significantly through the reading of active practitioners. Communication can be doubly effective if it brings to the attention of researchers the significant problems of the practitioners. The attitude of practitioners toward research greatly influences its use. Where practitioners perceive no serious problems or difficulties in their work, research reports have little interest. But when they are experiencing and recognizing serious difficulties, findings that appear to help in overcoming these difficulties are likely to be seized and efforts made to apply them where they appear to be relevant.

Improving Research Utilization

There are many cases of research findings that appear to have significant implications that are not being utilized by curriculum makers. Furthermore, the time between the publication and validation of research findings that appear to have important implications for practice and their application by curriculum practitioners is often greater than necessary. This means that opportunities available to children for better educational programs are delayed for several, perhaps many years.

On the other hand, there are occasions in which curriculum makers have heard of new research and hastily sought to apply it without careful considerations of its implications in practice and the impact the proposed changes in the curriculum are likely to have on other important factors in school learning. The problem is to identify quickly and comprehensively research with likely implications for curriculum development, to explore its implications for practice, noting especially its relation to other important curriculum factors, particularly the changes its adoption would necessitate in present practices and the new knowledge, skills, and attitudes required of those who are to apply the research effectively. Finally by tryout or other means for making estimations, the cost in time, effort, and in training of personnel will need to be compared with the estimated degree of improvement in student learning before widespread adoption of research findings are undertaken.

Who in the educational community can be expected to participate in this search for studies whose findings have significant implications for curriculum makers and who will work out their meaning and practicable value for practitioners? The review of research is more likely to be done by those whose professional interests include continuing touch with research in a particular field, than is by curriculum makers. However, to recognize the relevance of research to practice requires close touch with practitioners. As described in the previous section, schools of education, some state departments of education, and certain professional associations have played such a role. But, in general, their activities in research utilization have been neither continuous nor comprehensive. Perhaps it is not possible to organize and maintain an association of persons knowledgeable about the main fields of research and other persons in close touch with practitioners' problems and opportunities who are willing to devote time and effort to effect a constructive union. It would represent a joining of interests that is unusual in the field of education, although well developed in medicine. But without this concerted and continuing effort the utilization of research by curriculum makers will be spotty and somewhat haphazard. The stimulation and encouragement of such an association could be an important activity for ASCD.

References

National Society for the Study of Education. Curriculum Making: Past and Present, Part I. The Foundations of Curriculum Making, Part II. Twenty-sixth yearbook. Chicago: NSSE, 1927.

Rowe, M. B. "Wait Time and Rewards as Instructional Variables, Part I, Wait Time." *Journal of Research in Science Teaching* 11(1974): 81–84.

Spiro, R. J. "Remembering Information from Text: The State of Schema Approach." In *School and the Acquisition of Knowledge*. Edited by R. C. Anderson, R. J. Spiro, and W. E. Montague. Hillsdale, N. J.: Lawrence Erlbaum Associates, 1977.

A Response to Tyler

BARRY M. FRANKLIN

Professor Tyler is certainly on the mark in raising the question of the relationship between curriculum research and the work of curriculum development within the schools. It is, I believe, an important topic that has not been given the attention it deserves (Kliebard and Franklin, 1983). Unfortunately, however, the picture he gives us of that relationship is less, so to speak, on the mark.

Since my own research interests fall within the area of curriculum history, I will focus my attention on the historical adequacy of Tyler's view of the relationship between curriculum research and curriculum practice. My response is based on three of the very few existing studies that have looked at the history of curriculum practice: my own examination of the social efficiency movement in the Minneapolis Public Schools during the first half of this century (Franklin, 1982); Carol O'Conner's investigation of curriculum change in the Scarsdale, New York Public Schools during the decade of the 1920s (O'Connor, 1980); and Wayne Urban's account of curriculum reform in the Atlanta Public Schools from 1890 to 1925 (Urban, 1981).

Tyler offers us a view of the relationship between curriculum research and curriculum practice that does not square with the empirical evidence available about the history of curriculum development within the schools. First, he seems to suggest that the ideas of such diverse individuals as Thorndike, Dewey, Judd, and the Herbartians have had an equal impact on the work of those individuals who were responsible during the first half of this century for curriculum development within the schools. In Minneapolis, Scarsdale, and Atlanta, educators seemed to be more interested in those ideas that we would associate with the social efficiency movement and with the notion of scientific curriculum making than they were with any competing ideas, particularly those ideas identified with Dewey or with the child-centered education movement. Similarly, Tyler seems to assume that the curriculum research that he describes affected all schools in the same way. That is, he talks about the relationship between curriculum research and practice as if regional differences among schools and the populations they serve are of no matter. Actually, when we consider the influence that efficiency minded curriculum reform has had in Minneapolis, Scarsdale, and Atlanta, a different picture emerges.

Barry M. Franklin is Chairperson, Department of Education, Augsburg College, Minneapolis, Minnesota.

Between 1920 and 1944, Minneapolis school administrators sought to restructure the curriculum along efficiency lines by introducing two reforms, curriculum differentiation during the 1920s and an integrated, functionally oriented social studies course known as Modern Problems during the late 1930s and early 1940s. Despite the commitment of the administration to the efficiency movement, both attempts encountered opposition that muted their effect. Throughout the 1920s, Minneapolis had a differentiated high school curriculum. The opposition of teachers to ability grouping on the grounds that it was "anti-democratic," however, prevented the institution of the kind of distinction between college preparation and vocational training that typified the idea of differentiation as it was proposed by such efficiency minded curriculum theorists as Franklin Bobbitt and David Snedden. In fact, throughout the 1920s Minneapolis high school students could meet college entrance requirements whether they were enrolled in what we might think of as an academic course of study or a vocational program.

Modern Problems

During the 1930s, the Minneapolis school administration attempted to replace the existing 12th grade social studies offerings, which included a required one semester course in American Government and one semester electives in sociology, economics, and commerical law, with an integrated, functionally oriented course entitled Modern Problems. The insistence of the State Department of Education that 12th grade social studies include the study of American government, however, prevented the institution of this change in anything but name. In 1944, a one year course in Modern Problems was substituted for the courses in American Government, sociology, economics, and commericial law as the 12th grade social studies requirement. In response to the demand of the State Department of Education, the first semester was devoted to the study of American Government. The second semester was devoted to the study of a number of functionally oriented problems, such as housing, consumer needs, labor, and population—issues that had actually been included in the content of the sociology and commercial law courses. The result was a supposedly new and different course, Modern Problems, whose content was virtually the same as the courses it replaced.

In Scardsdale, New York, during the decade of the 1920s, the social efficiency movement also played a role. Here, however, the intent was not as it was in Minneapolis to make the curriculum more functionally oriented. Scarsdale educators in response to the demands of the city's upper middle-class population for the kind of the preparatory education typically provided by Eastern, private boarding schools abandoned large group instruction in favor of an efficiency oriented system of individualized instruction utilizing student contracts known as the Dalton Plan.

These educators believed that a system of individualization would enable them to provide an elite education that would prepare the children of the upper-middle class for entrance into the nation's most prestigious colleges while allowing them at the same time to serve the more conventional needs of those children of humbler origin. For Scarsdale, then, efficiency minded curriculum reform meant something entirely different in practice than it did for those curriculum researchers who articulated its theoretical principles.

Atlanta offers a third and still different picture of the influence of efficiency ideas on curriculum practice. Throughout the last decade of the 19th century and the first two decades of this century, the Atlanta Board of Education called for the inclusion of vocational education within the curriculum. The Board, however, never quite seemed able to overcome the opposition of those on the City Council, in the school administration, and in the community at large who opposed this reform on the grounds that it would thwart the long standing commitment of the Atlanta Public Schools to preparing the city's youth, at least its white youth, for college.

As it turned out, the members of the Board who were most outspoken in their advocacy of vocational education were not really committed to this change. They advocated vocational education not really to transform the school curriculum but to appear as reformers in their struggle for higher political office and for control of the Georgia Democratic Party against those whom they wanted to depict as being more conservative. By the 1920s Atlanta had two vocational high schools, Commerical High School for girls and Technological High School for boys. The curriculum for these two schools was never, however, completely vocationalized. What was offered under the rubric of vocational education was a college preparatory curriculum with the addition of some functionally oriented courses.

In short, Professor Tyler presents us with a far too simplistic picture of the relationship between curriculum research and practice. Perhaps it was the case in the experimental setting of the Eight-Year Study, where he gained so much of his own experience in curriculum work, that innovative curriculum research was simply embraced in toto by practicing educators. That was, however, not the case in Minneapolis, Scarsdale, Atlanta, or, I would dare say, in any of a number of the nation's other school systems. Curriculum research obviously has had some effect on curriculum practice in the schools. What research does find its way into schools, what form it takes, and ultimately how successful it is, hinges, I believe, on the influence of what we might think of as local or regional mediating factors. These factors, which include such things as community pressure, legal restraints, ideology, and demography to name but a few, usually come between the research findings of scholars and the practices of school personnel. From what we have seen in our brief consideration of curriculum development in Minneapolis, Scarsdale, and Atlanta, these mediating factors have muted the influence of curriculum research on school practice. The question of the relationship between curriculum research and practice is, as Tyler suggests, an important issue that merits study. It is, however, a more complex and ambiguous relationship than Tyler's description seems to portray.

References

Kliebard, Herbert M., and Franklin, Barry M. "The Course of the Course of Study: History of Curriculum." In *Historical Inquiry in Education: A Research Agenda,* pp. 148–49. Edited by John Hardin Best. Washington, D.C.: American Educational Research Association, 1983.

Franklin, Barry M. "The Social Efficiency Movement Reconsidered: Curriculum Change in Minneapolis, 1917–1950." *Curriculum Inquiry* 12 (Spring 1982): pp. 6–33.

O'Connor, Carol A. "Setting a Standard for Suburbia, Innovation in the Scarsdale Schools, 1920–1930." *History of Education Quarterly* (Fall 1980): pp. 295–311.

Urban, Wayne. "Educational Reform in a New South City: Atlanta, 1890–1925." In *Education and the Rise of the New South,* chapter 6. Edited by Ronald Goodenow and Arthur O. White. Boston: G. K. Hall and Company, 1981.

A Response to Tyler

ROBERT S. GILCHRIST

All 40,000 of us ASCD members should be grateful to Dr. Tyler for this statement. I marvel at his ability to review so succinctly nearly a century of American education and its use of research. Dr. Tyler's classifying research as basic, applied, and action, and his pointing out that all three are necessary, emphasizes how each of us as curriculum workers might do appropriate research as well as using the findings of others. I was especially interested in his identifying areas of weakness such as

• Curriculum makers today are not generally basing their plans for organizing learning experiences upon the results of research.

• Until there is greater clarity about the purposes of evaluation and the methods and instruments are sorted out in terms of purpose, the practices of evaluation in the service of curriculum development appear unlikely to benefit greatly.

• There are many cases of research findings that appear to have significant implications that are not being utilized by curriculum makers.

The big question obviously is: What can each teacher, each school, each school system, and each teacher educator institution do to improve practice in

1. Identifying what students are to be helped to learn?
2. Planning these experiences?
3. Organizing these experiences?
4. Appraising the effects?

I wish I were 50 years younger and still could capitalize on the rich experiences it has been my good fortune to have since 1922 when I started teaching. This being impossible, perhaps I can make a contribution by telling a few of my experiences that relate to research and curriculum development. They may be a consistent extension of Dr. Tyler's remarks, and present ideas that the reader will find helpful.

Teacher-pupil planning at University School, Ohio State University. (I was Director of University School, 1941–46.)

In planning units of work, teachers did much research. They made serious efforts to find and use existing research. In addition, the teachers carried on research first hand. *How Children Develop* (1946) was published by the faculty as the culmination of an analysis of research in the whole development field. This booklet, based on four years of study, has been

Robert S. Gilchrist is Professor Emeritus, Curriculum and School Administration, United States International University, San Diego, California.

translated into many languages and sold in thousands of copies. It is clear evidence that the University School staff believed that curriculum development should be based on pertinent research, not tradition or whim.

I am convinced that today's schools, with very few exceptions, have not seriously considered how to organize for learning. Isn't it sad that students are left almost entirely on their own to put together what they have learned in various subjects and then to apply those learnings to their problems of personal and social living?

University School was one of the 30 schools in The Eight-Year Study (Aiken, 1942). Today's curriculum developers can profit greatly by reviewing the research produced in this project.

Curriculum and Staff Development in the University City (Missouri) Schools. (I was Superintendent, 1955–1964.)

When I arrived in the summer of 1955 the Board of Education and several staff members told me that they thought the time was ripe for both staff and citizens to review and evaluate the educational program of the University City schools. Also, they seemed to be saying that even though the program had served the community well over the years, the time was ripe to study ways for making the school system even better. They sensed that much was happening both in education and in life itself that that might have implications for their schools.

An appraisal program had been adopted in the University City School in the early 50s that was used primarily by the administration for the evaluation of teachers. Several principals, Central Office staff members, and I agreed that the appraisal program might well provide a base for curriculum and staff development. The emphasis would need to shift from an evaluation of teachers to an appraisal of the learning program for pupils.

Staff in leadership positions concentrated on ways to help teachers as they used preschool days in the fall to examine data about incoming pupils, and during September when each teacher wrote his or her plan for the year. These plans included goals, creating a good environment for learning, utilizing needed resources, and continuing evaluation throughout the year.

Principals were expected to work closely with teachers, not only in helping them in their offering the very best possible program for the children, but also in identifying curriculum and staff development needs both at the building level and systemwide.

Systemwide leadership meetings provided for cross fertilization of ideas on how to help teachers both individually and as building faculties. These meetings also provided a forum in which systemwide plans were examined, agreed upon, and, when appropriate, taken to the Board of Education for approval.

Summary

My experiences over the past half century tell me that:

1. Curriculum workers must work hard to include all four phases of curriculum development as described by Dr. Taylor. In spite of research findings the American school curriculum is still too much "a list of subjects and topics to be taught and a plan for their organization into a course of study." The pupils in each classroom and in each school deserve to have a live, meaningful curriculum that results from the staff of their school: (a) identifying what students are to be helped to learn; (b) plannng these experiences; (c) organizing these experiences; and (d) appraising the effects.
2. Curriculum development should be undergirded with an understanding of the needs of human beings; how they learn and develop and the opportunities and problems of contemporary living. This means that pertinent research—basic, applied, and action—must be utilized.
3. Those affected by the curriculum should be involved in its development. Research clearly indicates that children learn more when they understand and are motivated. Teachers teach best when they are participants in decision making. Citizens will support and approve public education more when they are involved and, therefore, better understand.

References

Faculty of University School. *How Children Develop*. Columbus: Ohio State University, 1946.

Aiken, Wilfred M. *The Story of the Eight-Year Study, Vol. I*. New York: Harper & Brothers, 1942.

Section II.
Getting Knowledge

4 The Half-Full Glass: A Review of Research on Teaching

DAVID C. BERLINER

*T*here is a well-known adage about what is seen when the liquid in a glass is at the midpoint. A pessimist describes the glass as half empty, while an optimist describes the glass as half full. Both statements are absolutely accurate. Nevertheless, the choice of the terms used by optimists and pessimists to describe what they see can lead to vastly different beliefs and actions. We see in this volume, especially in the papers by Hosford and Hunter, the prevalence of the optimists when the implications of research on teaching are examined. These authors see the glass as half full. They are, however, like me, a minority in a profession where too many observers see the findings of research on teaching as, at most, constituting a half-empty glass.

The pessimism we suffer from in our profession is, perhaps, understandable. Until 1963 and the publication of the *Handbook of Research on Teaching* (Gage, 1963), there really was no field of research on teaching. Only a small number of scientists could be identified as having a primary interest in research on teaching. Coincidental with the publication of the *Handbook* came massive federal involvement in educational research and development. Centers at Stanford, the University of Texas, and the University of Wisconsin, among others, were funded to study teaching and instruction. The mid 1960s also saw federal monies used to start educational laboratories such as the Far West Laboratory for Educational Research and Development and Reserach for Better Schools. The laboratories were given the mission of improving the practice of schooling and of teacher education. The result of federally supported and independent research efforts over the last 20 years has been an enormous increase in our knowledge about sensible, effective, and efficient teaching practices.

David C. Berliner is Professor, Department of Educational Psychology, University of Arizona, Tucson.

The glass is, I believe, at least half full. So why are so few drinking? Three reasons immediately come to mind.

First, the past has seen research on teaching being oversold to educators. At the turn of the century the eminent educational psychologist E.L. Thorndike promised a revolution in education. He believed that empirical science and statistical inference would allow us to determine optimum ways to teach. Thorndike's promise of a scientific revolution based on psychological inquiry was misguided for a number of reasons, among which was his failure to adequately recognize the political and sociological forces that affect the schools and teacher education programs. A second reason is an outgrowth of the Great Depression. In society at large there grew a general mistrust of science and technology and a lack of faith in scientific inquiry in education as a means of improvement. Finally, as noted above, the field of research on teaching took its modern form only about 20 years ago. Reliable and replicable research has accumulated rapidly, but only recently. There has been only a short time in which to change deeply held beliefs about the utility of research on teaching.

Thus, because of promises unkept, societal and unique professional conditions resulting in a pervasive mistrust of research (and researchers) in education, and the recency of the development of the field of inquiry called research on teaching, we find the professional educator slow to respond to the remarkably bountiful yield of knowledge acquired over the last two decades. There exists in education a belief that the glass is half empty. In contrast, I believe the glass has at least reached the half-full point.

What is it we now know about teaching that is so useful? Let me start by recognizing that teaching is a highly cognitive activity that requires an extraordinary level of competence for making decisions in complex and dynamic environments. Perhaps every teacher has always said this was the case. But with recent research we have learned something about how such complex decision making takes place, and what factors must be considered in the decision process. This review of research is framed as a review of factors that can be controlled or influenced by teachers and that are known to affect student behavior, attitudes, and achievement. Two purposes are served by organizing the review in this way. The complexity of the decisions teachers must deal with is made explicit and we see also that there are well-documented ways for teachers to make sensible choices about how they should go about teaching. Both are important points to make in any program of preservice or inservice education of teachers.

Preinstructional Factors

Content decisions, time allocation decisions, pacing decisions, grouping decisions and decisions about activity structures are among the many preinstructional issues to be decided upon by teachers. Each such decision is known to affect the attitudes, behaviors, and achievement of students. Thus, they must be carefully considered by teachers.

Content Decisions

Until recently it has always been assumed that the district curriculum directors, superintendents, school boards, and state departments of education determined the content that is taught. This is only partly true. The final arbiter of what it is that gets taught is the classroom teacher. The teacher makes the final content choices. In a study of how such content decisions are made (Fisher and others, 1978), one elementary school teacher was observed for over 90 days. During that period of time she taught nothing about fractions, despite the fact that the topic was mandated by the State for instruction at that grade. When the teacher was asked why she did not teach any fractions, she said, "I don't like fractions!" That is a very human response, illustrating the power that teachers have in deciding the content of the curriculum.

We have recently learned from the Michigan State research team (Schwille and others, 1981) that the perceived *effort* required to teach a subject matter area, the perceived *difficulty* of the subject matter area for students, and the teachers' *personal feelings of enjoyment* while teaching a subject matter area influence the teachers' choice of content. One striking example in their data illustrates this point. An elementary school teacher who enjoyed teaching science taught 28 times more science than one who said she did not enjoy teaching science. And from Carew and Lightfoot's (1979) intensive study of four classes we see how the content concerns of a teacher can come to dominate all aspects of classroom life. One of their teachers, Ms. Allen, made reading the central part of classroom life. Eighty-five percent of all interactions with her first grade students were in academic contexts and 75 percent of those were in reading contexts. For the students in her class all feelings of personal competence and self-concept as a learner derived from evaluations of their competence as readers. In that class the teacher's decisions about the importance of reading as the preeminent content area dominated all other aspects of classroom life.

The empirical data relating content coverage or content emphasis to achievement is clear (see the review by Berliner and Rosenshine, 1977). Walker and Schaffarzick (1974) wrote an insightful article on this issue a number of years ago. Even the summary of the International Evaluation of Achievement (Husen, 1967) noted that content emphasis was among the determining factors accounting for difference in achievement between countries. And, more recently, the empirical work of Cooley and Leinhardt (1980) resulted in their comment that the opportunity to learn a given content area was perhaps the most potent variable in accounting for student achievement in that area. With the evidence about the powerful effects of the content variable so clear, it is interesting to note the casualness with which such content decisions get made. As Buchmann and Schmidt (1981) of the Institute for Research on Teaching say:

During the school day, elementary school teachers can be a law unto themselves, favoring certain subjects at their discretion. What is taught matters, hence arbitrariness in content decisions is clearly inappropriate. If personal feelings about teaching subject matters are not bounded by an impersonal conception of professional duties, children will suffer the consequences. Responsibility in content decision-making requires that teachers examine their own conduct, its main springs and potential effects on what is taught. (pp. 17-18).

Time Allocation Decisions

Related to the issues involved in content decisions are those decisions about time allocations for subject matter areas. The elementary teacher, as opposed to the junior or senior high school teacher, allocates that most precious of scarce resources—time. The Beginning Teacher Evaluation Study (Fisher and others, 1978; Denham and Lieberman, 1980) is one of the many sources for empirical evidence relating allocated time to achievement. What is important to bring to everyone's attention is the incredible variation in the time allocations that are made by different teachers. While observing fifth grade teachers, it was noticed that one teacher could find only 68 minutes a day for instruction in reading and language arts, while another teacher was able to find 137 minutes a day. At second grade, one teacher allocated 47 minutes a day for reading and language arts, another teacher managed to find 118 minutes a day, or 2½ times more time per day to teach reading and language arts. In mathematics the same variability was shown. One second grade teacher allocated 16 minutes a day to instruction in mathematics, another teacher constrained by the same length of the school day somehow found 51 minutes a day to allocate to mathematics. From such data it is not difficult to infer why this is a management issue of great consequence.

Another time management issue has to do with the ways in which time *within* a curriculum area is scheduled. This decision is of equal importance for those teaching at elementary levels and for those who teach at higher levels where departmentalization often occurs and allocations of time to subject matter areas are fixed. One fifth grade teacher, observed for half the school year, allocated 5,646 minutes to comprehension-type activities such as drawing inferences, identifying main ideas in prose, and paraphrasing what was read (Berliner, 1979). These skills are considered critical for language arts, science, social studies, and any other curriculum areas heavily dependent on prose instruction. This figure stands starkly in contrast with the data from another fifth grade teacher who allocated only 917 minutes to comprehension activities. Such marked variability in time in particular content areas lends, inevitably, to differences in achievement.

Pacing Decisions

Related to choice of content, and time allocations between and within content areas is the issue of pace of instruction. The evidence for the power of the pacing variable keeps mounting. The more a teacher covers, the more students seem to learn. This is hardly shocking news. But again, it is the variability across classes that is most impressive. One teacher adjusts the pace in the workplace and covers half the text in a semester, another finishes it all. One teacher has 20 practice problems covered in a lesson, another manages to cover only 10. One teacher has students who develop a sight vocabulary of 100 words before Christmas, another teacher's students learn only 50. A remarkable finding reported by Shavelson (1983) concerns the teachers' differential treatment of ability groups. Once teachers formed ability groups, they tended to pace the groups differently. That in itself sounds sensible. But the high groups were paced as much as 15 times faster than the low groups, increasing dramatically the difference in what the high and low groups will be exposed to in the school curriculum. The choice of pace, like the choice of content and the decisions about the time to be spent learning particular content areas, determines student achievement. For example, Barr (1980), who has completed a number of studies of pacing, found that 80 percent of the variance in measures of basal reading achievement could be accounted for by the pace of instruction.

Grouping Decisions

Teachers, like any other sensible managers, try to form work groups. Grouping is a very rational response to what Dreeben (1978) pointed out as one of the most salient characteristics of classrooms—their collective nature. But the decisions about the size and composition of the group for various subject matter areas is very complex. We have yet to uncover why many teachers will choose to have no work groups in mathematics instruction, three homogeneous ability groups in reading instruction, and three or four heterogeneously formed discussion groups for social studies. We do know, however, that the size and composition of the work groups affect achievement. For example, Webb (1980) shows how the middle ability child suffers a loss in achievement while the low ability child shows some gains in achievement when they are in mixed ability groups, over what would be expected if they were in uniform ability groups. We have also learned that irrelevant criteria can be used as the basis for group assignment, and that such assignments can be of long duration. Rist (1973) poignantly described how one teacher formed three work groups on the eighth day of kindergarten. It appeared that she used as the basis of assignment those well known correlates of academic ability—clothing, cleanliness, and body odor. The assignments made at the beginning of kindergarten, to what was obviously the group expected to be lowest in achievement, were, in general, still in force three years later when second grade groups were observed. The evidence suggests that the assignment of students to work groups is occasionally like a life-long sentence and always results in students in different groups learning different things while in school.

Decisions About Activity Structures

Activity or task structures, such as reading circle or seatwork or recitation, Doyle (1977) noted, each have *functions* and *operations* (rules or norms) associated with them. The activity structures that are characteristically used by a teacher determines teacher behavior, as well as student behavior, attitudes, and achievement. For example, Bossert (1978) noted that:

> Teachers who relied on recitation were less able to establish close social ties with their students than were teachers who primarily utilized small groups and individualized projects. Recitation places teachers at the center of control. It forces them to rely on equitable, impersonal sanctions (usually short verbal desists) and on the authority of office rather than on more personalized influence mechanisms. By contrast, small groups and individualized instruction increases opportunities for teachers to covertly "bend" classroom rules to handle individual problems and facilitates teacher involvement in, rather than simply teacher direction of, the activity (p. 46).

The difference in rapport between teachers and students is clearly noticeable in the recitation oriented versus the individualized instruction oriented classrooms. Different activity structures in these different classrooms give rise to differences in the behavior and the attitudes of the participants in the activity. Again, as Bossert (1978) noted:

> It was not that the teachers who used recitation were less concerned or less empathic, but rather that recitation precludes the individualization and involvement allowed by other activities (pp. 46-47).

Teachers, who must choose between recitation, lecture, discussion, reading circle, computer-mediated instruction, television, seatwork, and so on, must also learn that each activity structure limits or enhances certain factors that affect instruction (See Berliner and others, 1983). Each structure shows characteristic variations in duration, number of students, opportunity for responding and whether such responding is public or private, opportunities for feedback to students and whether such feedback is public or private, and so on. Teachers do not, usually, know how to make these kinds of cost/benefit decisions when choosing activity structures. They must now learn to do so, since the more we learn in psychology about the operations of behavior settings, ecological settings or contexts, the more we learn how powerful they are in determining the behavior of the participants in that setting.

Summary of Preinstructional Factors

A set of complex decisions must be made, primarily, before instruction takes place. Teachers need to be acutely aware of the power they have when making certain decisions to facilitate or retard achievement, to affect the attitudes of students, and to control student classroom behavior. Among the powerful variables that impact on students are those involved in content decisions, time allocation decisions, pacing decisions, grouping decisions, and decisions about activity structures for instruction. The complexity of the task and the number of powerful variables teachers can control also show up during the teaching performance itself. To that topic we turn next.

During-Instruction Factors

When teachers are working with students scores of factors affect whether or not learning will occur. Among these are few that seem to be powerful and replicable. These include engaged time, time management, success rate, academic learning time, monitoring, structuring, and questioning. These are discussed briefly, in turn.

Engaged Time

As with allocated time, the fact that engaged time or time on task is associated with achievement is not news. The fact that engaged time is so variable across classes is what is now well documented. There are classes where engagement rates are regularly under 50 percent, and those where engagement rates are regularly about 90 percent (Fisher and others, 1978). One hour of allocated mathematics instruction, then, can result in either 30 minutes or 54 minutes of actual delivered instruction to students. In a single week, differences of such a magnitude can yield a difference of about two hours in the amount of mathematics that is actually engaged in by students. It is no wonder that in reading, mathematics, or science, at any grade level, large variations in engaged time by students is a strong predictor of achievement. Rossmiller (1982) recently found consistent and strong relations between time on task and achievement in reading and mathematics as he studied students over a three-year period. The results are shown in Figure 1. The importance of time on task for lower ability children is shown clearly here. The effect is less powerful for students of high ability, but time on task is still a consistent predictor of achievement. Teachers need to be aware of engaged time rates—for individual students and for the class as a whole—in order to ensure that a sufficient amount of time allocated to instruction in a content area is used by students in productive ways.

Time Management

Time must be controlled after it is allocated or it is lost. And it is easy to lose time in the dynamic world of the classroom. For example, transition times (the start up time and time needed to put things away) can mount rapidly. This results in large losses of the time allocated to a content area. In the study of one class (Fisher and others, 1978) where the school day was around 300 minutes, transition times was coded at 76 minutes. The teacher had a listening center, a math facts table, a career education table, a silent reading table, a science center, a cooking station, and more. Students in this class moved in and out of these stations at a rapid rate throughout the day, according to a complex schedule. While trying to be very creative, this teacher actually was losing one fourth of the instructional time each day to commuting.

When given feedback about their behavior, very rapid changes can take place in the ways teachers go about their jobs. Simple management hints can make a big difference. For example, we asked one teacher to write the language arts assignments of her different reading groups on the board at the start of recess, so that the first student into the classroom after recess can start work and the teacher does not have to wait until the last student wanders in to give oral instructions. Savings of six minutes a day in this class occurred with that simple advice. This is not trivial. That adds about 180 student learning minutes a day. It provides a half-hour more of instruction a week, and, potentially, it adds 18 hours of instructional time per year.

Figure 1. The amount of variance in reading and mathematics achievement accounted for by time on task for students of different ability levels over three years.*

Variance Accounted for by Time on Task Variables

Grade and Academic Year	Lowest 25% in Ability		Middle 50% in Ability		Highest 25% in Ability	
	Reading	Math	Reading	Math	Reading	Math
3rd grade 1979-1980	.55	.30	.08	.11	.14	.06
4th grade 1980-1981	.27	.18	.06	.12	.04	.04
5th grade 1981-1982	.73	.12	.16	.19	.16	.16

*Adapted from Rossmiller (1982).

One district that recently tried to audit how time is spent had phenomenal success. They estimated that they added the equivalent of 10-16 days of instructional time per school year. Such time was worth 2-3 million dollars if it had to be purchased. Managing time is serious business in industry and education. In education, however, we probably have not realized how easy it is to lose time through poor management, and do not generally observe teachers long enough and regularly enough to provide them with feedback about this important variable.

Monitoring Success Rate

The Beginning Teacher Evaluation Study provided more evidence in a convincing body of knowledge about the relationship between high success rates and achievement. For younger students and for the academically least able, almost errorless performance during learning tasks results in higher test performance and greater student satisfaction (Marliave and Filby, in press). Rosenshine (1983) has reviewed the data from a number of studies and concluded that during the initial phases of learning, during recitation or small group work, success rate in reading should be at about the 70-80 percent level. When students are reviewing or practicing, as in seatwork, engaging in drill activities, or working on homework, student responses should be rapid, smooth, and almost always correct. Brophy's (1983) recent comments on this issue are relevant:

. . . bear in mind that we are talking about independent seatwork and homework assignments that students must be able to progress through on their own. These assignments demand application of hierarchically organized knowledge and skills that must be not merely learned but mastered to the point of overlearning if they are going to be retained and applied to still more complex material. Confusion about what to do or lack of even a single important concept or skill will frustrate students' progress, and lead to both management and instructional problems for teachers. Yet, this happens frequently. Observational studies suggest that, to the extent that students are given inappropriate tasks, the tasks are much more likely to be too difficult than too easy.

Data from some of the classes of the Beginning Teacher Evaluation Study (Fisher and others, 1978) support Brophy's assertion. Students were coded in some classes as making almost 100 percent errors in their workbooks or during their group work, as much as 14 percent of the time that they were observed. That is, students in some classes were observed to experience total failure in their learning activities for many consecutive minutes of the school day. As might be expected, the percent of time students spent in activities in which they had high error rates was correlated negatively with achievement.

Success rate, then, appears to be another powerful variable with known effects on achievement. Like other such classroom variables, it needs to be monitored, evaluated, and often modified.

Academic Learning Time

A relatively new variable, created after extensive observation and testing of students was completed, is academic learning time (ALT). Virtually all the variables discussed earlier can be related to ALT, which is defined as time engaged with materials or activities related to the outcome measure being used (often an achievement test), during which a student experiences a high success rate. We may visually represent ALT as in Figure 2. The ALT variable is likely to become one of the most useful concepts for judging whether student learning is taking place at a particular point in time in some particular curricular areas. It is appropriate to think of ALT as a proxy variable for student learning: ALT is a variable that can be observed and measured in the classroom, and it has known relations with student learning.

The practical importance of academic learning time in relation to achievement is illustrated by an example from an analysis of reading instruction in second grade (Fisher and others, 1978). Consider an imaginary second-grade student, Sam, whose reading score in October was average among the sample of students under study. That is, Sam was at the 50th percentile. If Sam experiences an average amount of ALT (573 minutes total, or 23 minutes per day in reading), he can be expected to show average reading achievement in December. In other words, Sam will once again be at the 50th percentile. He would have learned quite a bit between October and December, but would not have changed his relative standing in the total sample.

Now let us follow another student, Claire, who also began as an average student. Suppose Claire experienced only 4 minutes per day of ALT (100 minutes total) for the time period between October and December. Claire would be expected to show almost no change in raw score and would decline considerably in relative terms. In percentile terms, Claire would go from the 50th percentile in October to about the 39th percentile in December in terms of relative standing in the sample. If this same average student had experienced very large amounts of ALT, say 52 minutes per day between October and December, then she could be expected to show considerable improvement in reading achievement relative to the other students in the study. Claire would then have started at the 50th percentile in October, and she would be predicted to have moved to the 66th percentile in relative standing by December.

Thus, the student who accrues a large amount of ALT appears to benefit substantially. At least, these are the predictions that researchers have for groups of students who experience these differential amounts of ALT. And these predictions are derived from data collected on hundreds of elementary-school students.

In the example given it may appear that this range of 4 to 52 minutes per day in ALT is unrealistically large. However, these were times that actu-

Figure 2. Defining Academic Learning Time (ALT).

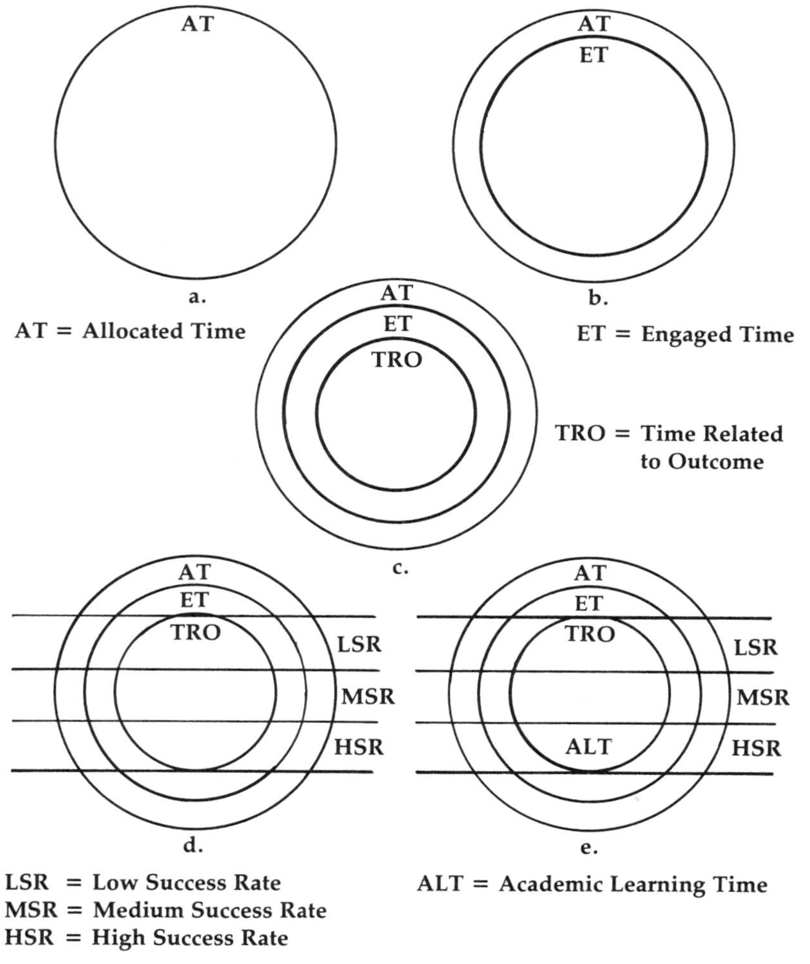

a.

AT = Allocated Time

b.

ET = Engaged Time

TRO = Time Related
to Outcome

c.

d.

e.

LSR = Low Success Rate   ALT = Academic Learning Time
MSR = Medium Success Rate
HSR = High Success Rate

Interpretation: The time allocated for instruction is shown visually in (a). During some of this time, students are engaged, as shown in (b). Some of the time students are engaged is time related to the outcome measures that are used to assess instruction. This is shown visually in (c). The time allocated, whether engaged or not, and whether related to the outcome measures or not, can by yielding low, medium, or high success rates for students (d). That portion of allocated time that is time engaged in activities related to the outcome measures and which provides students with a high success rate is defined as Academic Learning Time, as shown in (e).

ally occurred in the classes studied by Fisher and others (1978, 1980). Furthermore, it is easy to imagine how either four or 52 minutes per day of ALT might come about for a particular student. If 50 minutes of reading instruction per day is allocated to a student who pays attention about one-third of the time, and only one-fourth of the student's reading time is a high level of success, the student will experience only about four minutes of ALT—engaged reading time at a high success level. Similarly, if 100 minutes per day is allocated to reading for a student who pays attention 85 percent of the time and is at a high level of success for almost two-thirds of that time, that student will experience about 52 minutes a day of ALT.

Teachers must learn to keep ALT in mind as they instruct, because large differences in the amount of ALT built up by different students generally result in wide variation in student achievement. Teachers should know the outcome measures that are used for instruction, assign activities related to those outcome measures, see to it that enough time is allocated for students, find ways to keep students engaged, and see to it that the younger or less bright students in particular spend large percentages of time in high-success experiences. Under such conditions students will accumulate a good deal of ALT. Students and classes that accumulate high levels of ALT are those that are likely to achieve more than students or classes with lower accumulations of ALT.

Monitoring

A good deal of classroom work in today's schools is done by students on their own. Students may spend large segments of the elementary-school day in seat work, working individually on a contract in reading, doing the ditto sheets related to a science lesson, or finishing the work-book pages on a topic in mathematics. In three different studies of schooling, examining hundreds of classrooms for students age 8-11, researchers found that students worked privately about 50 percent of the time (Angus, Evans, and Parkin, 1975; Good and Beckerman, 1978; McDonald, 1976). Very little substantive interaction between a student and his or her teachers, classroom aides, or peers, occurs in the schools.

When students are left to work privately and are not monitored by the teacher or classroom aide, they often spend less time engaged in the activities for which they are responsible. In classes where a good deal of work is done by students on their own, the engagement rate in academic subjects usually declines if teachers do not keep their monitoring behavior at a high level. It appears that the classroom in which the teacher moves rapidly about, monitoring students and raising the number of substantive interactions with students, is the class where students do well. A substantive interaction between a teacher and student takes place when the teacher checks to see if the student is doing things correctly, asks questions, gives the student academic feedback, and so on. The greater the number of substantive interactions that take place, the more likely it is that students will achieve academically (Fisher and others, 1978, 1980).

Structuring

During an ethnographic study of more and less effective teachers (Tikunoff, Berliner, and Rist, 1975), the importance of structuring was made manifest. While analyzing protocols of reading and mathematics lessons, sometimes the teacher's intent could not be inferred. That is, the readers did not have a clue about why the lesson was occurring, where it fit in the scheme of things, or what students needed to focus on for success at the task. Almost invariably, the teachers that were judged to be unclear about communicating their goals and giving directions were less effective in promoting academic achievement. Through additional data collection (Fisher and others, 1980), it was concluded that students:

pay attention more when the teacher spends time discussing the goals or structures of the lesson and/or giving directions about what students are to do (p. 26).

Further, it was noted that both success rate and attention were improved when teachers spent more time structuring the lesson and giving directions.

Structuring is especially important in classes where seatwork is used frequently. In those classes children work alone a good deal of the time. Therefore, it is not surprising that children who do not have a clear handle on what they are to do easily find ways to do nothing. Jerome Bruner (1981) has reached a similar conclusion. In visits to schools he saw many children unable to figure out what was expected of them. He felt that some simple attention to this basic management function would easily improve achievement in classrooms.

Structuring affects attention and success rate: It is sometimes not done at all, sometimes it is done only minimally, and sometimes it is overdone. The case of too much structuring was reported by Hassenpflug (1981) of Wisconsin. Her field notes documented how the directions given for many of the worksheet assignments in third grade actually lasted longer than the amount of time needed by most of the children to finish the assignment! In any case, what is worth noting is that structuring is the responsibility of the teacher, it affects performance, and it can be taught.

Questioning

From the time of Socrates to the present, educators have used questioning as an instructional technique. We have learned from research that elementary-school teachers ask many questions—150 per hour when teaching science or social studies (Gall, 1970), and that high-school teachers also ask many hundreds of questions per day. We have confirmed a suspicion long held by observers of schools—that the cognitive level of the questions that teachers ask is very low. A question's cognitive level is that level of thought believed to be required for a student to consider and answer a question. Bloom's taxonomy is one way of categorizing questions (Bloom and others, 1956). Using that categorization system to classify questions asked by teachers in the classroom, we find that most teachers ask lower-order knowledge-level questions (such as, "When did Columbus discover America?). Teachers less often ask higher-order questions that require application, synthesis of knowledge, evaluation, or analysis of information (for example, "Why did Columbus want to reach the East?"). Trachtenberg (1974) analyzed over 61,000 questions in the workbooks, tests, and teachers' manuals accompanying nine world history textbooks. Over 95 percent of those questions were lower-order. These data are not very appealing philosophically, since most of us value the higher-order, more thought-provoking questions. Nevertheless, the lower-order question has been found to serve some positive functions. It promotes participation, establishes a factual data base from which more relevant higher-order discussions can arise, and provides high-success experiences for students. Moreover, in the case of students of lower socioeconomic standing, high levels of lower-order questions seem to correlate positively with achievement (Brophy and Everston, 1976).

Although it is not customary for teachers to ask many higher-level cognitive questions, when they do, another problem arises. They may receive and accept answers that do not match the level of cognitive thought required by the question. An analysis of questions and answers in hundreds of teacher-student interchanges showed that the odds are only about 50-50 that an analysis, synthesis or application-level question will be responded to with an answer reflecting analysis, synthesis, or application (Mills and others, 1980). Thus, teachers would appear to need experience in more than phrasing questions—they need to learn to classify answers as well.

Perhaps the most important point about questions is that higher-order questions do facilitate learning. In a review of the effects of higher-order questions, Redfield and Rousseau (1981) found that teachers who ask more higher-order questions have students who achieve considerably more. The overall effect is such that a typical student exposed to a lesson without higher-order questions may be expected to perform at the 50th percentile on a test related to that lesson. In contrast, if that same student had been exposed to a lesson where many intelligent higher-order questions were asked, the student would be performing at about the 75th percentile on the same test!

Finally, research informs us that we should consider carefully Rowe's (1974) finding that students' answers to questions are of much better quality if teachers wait longer than they usually do between asking a question and requesting a response. This increased wait-time results in increased appropriateness of the response, increased confidence in responding, an increase in the variety of responses, and an increase in the cognitive level of responses. This is not a bad return for a simple adjustment in teaching style—going from the typical one second to the recommended three or more seconds of wait-time. Clearly, there is much to master in this oldest of pedogogical forms—the question. Training is probably not now as extensive in this area as it ought to be.

Summary of During-Instruction Factors

In this section of the review we have noted a number of factors under a teacher's control that can affect student attitude, achievement, and classroom behavior. Mentioned briefly were engaged time, time management, success rate, academic learning time, monitoring, structuring, and questioning. Programs of professional education for teachers should see to it that teachers become familiar with these factors. But teacher educators should *not* make the mistake of presenting each of these factors as single variables that alone will determine achievement. Instructional behavior is multifaceted and it is, no doubt, the interaction of dozens of significant variables like these that affect achievement. If a person makes a change from being a smoker to being a non-smoker, or from being a sedentary person to being on an active schedule, or goes from being on a diet where beef is used a lot to a diet where grain is used a lot, we hope for some improvement in general health and longevity. But any one such change is not expected to make a really big difference. If all the changes in lifestyle noted above were made, marked positive effects on health and longevity are much more likely to occur. The interactive teaching variables are like that. Independently, they may have some slight positive effects, but it will be hard to detect them. When used in combination and when they become a teacher's normal and customary pattern of interactive teaching, these variables are much more likely to affect achievement in noticeable ways.

Climate Factors

For want of a better term, we shall use the term climate to describe characteristics of classroom environments that appear to lead to achievement. Four such factors seem particularly important—the communication of academic expectations for achievement; development of a safe, orderly and academically focused environment for work; quick, fair and sensible management of deviancy; and the development of cooperative environments for learning.

Communicating Academic Expectations for Achievement

The voluminous literature on expectancy effects in education has been reviewed by Brophy and Good (1974) and more recently by Cooper (1979) and by Good (in press). The expectation literature is consistently (though not unanimously) interpreted to show that there are powerful effects on performance when teachers communicate their goals for performance to those they are teaching. If teachers set high but attainable goals for academic performance, academic achievement usually increases. If teachers set goals for performance that are low, academic achievement usually decreases.

The evidence on the differential treatment accorded to high and low ability students is believed to provide clues to the mechanism by which expectancies about performance are communicated. Good (in press) summarized this literature as follows: In comparison to students for whom teachers hold high expectations about performance, the students perceived to be low performers are more often seated farther away from the teacher; treated as groups, not individuals; smiled at less; made eye contact with less; called on less to answer questions; are given less time to answer those questions; have their answers followed up less frequently; are praised more often for marginal and inadequate answers; are praised less frequently for successful public responses; interrupted in their work more often; and so forth. This kind of treatment differential between students for whom teachers hold high and low expectations appears to influence their performance in predictable ways.

The communication of expectations does not just create a classroom climate. The expectations of teachers and administrators can permeate a school, creating a school climate. The work of Rutter and others (1979), as well as Brookover and Lezotte (1977), Edmonds (1979), Vanezky and Winfield (1979), makes this point. Rutter and others (1979) found marked differences in the outcomes of secondary schools attributable to school level variables such as expectations. Their data revealed that "Children had better academic success in schools . . . where the teachers expressed expectations that a high proportion of the children would do well in national examinations" (p. 188). Furthermore, the beneficial effects of high expectations are felt in areas other than academic achievement. Again, from Rutter and others (1979):

The findings showed that schools which expected children to care for their own resources had better behavior, better attendance, and less delinquency. In a similar way, giving children posts or tasks of responsibility was associated with better pupil behavior. The message of confidence that the pupils can be trusted to act with maturity and responsibility is likely to encourage pupils to fulfill those expectations (p. 188).

Thus, the process by which expectations about academic performance are communicated must be learned by teachers if they are to create a positive educational environment for students.

Developing a Safe, Orderly and Academically Focused Environment for Work

The evidence on effective classrooms and effective schools is amazingly congruent. There is always an indication of higher achievement in classes or schools where there is present an orderly, safe environment, a business-like manner among the teachers, and a schoolwide system that reflects thoughtfulness in promulgating academic programs, focuses on achievement, holds students accountable for achievement, and rewards achievement. Where such evidence of order and focus are missing, achievement is lower. Case studies of unusually effective classes in the Beginning Teacher Evaluation Study (Fisher and others, 1978) showed this rather clearly. And Rutter and his colleagues (1979) found similar variables related to achievement when they looked between schools, rather than between classes. Purkey and Smith (1983, p. 445), after reviewing the effective schools literature, comment:

> The seriousness and purpose with which the school approaches its task is communicated by the order and discipline it maintains in its building. . . . evidence exists indicating that clear, reasonable rules, fairly and consistently enforced, not only can reduce behavior problems that interfere with learning but also can promote feelings of pride and responsibility in the school community (p. 41).

Those who train teachers must remember that these findings about order and academic focus do constitute a real and present danger. Literal interpretations of these findings can lead to overcontrol and to such a strict academic focus that it denies the arts or produces debilitating levels of anxiety among students. But a lack of order and a lack of an academic focus have been empirically determined to lead to low levels of achievement and may, therefore, constitute an equally serious threat to the nation.

The power of these variables is clear. The ability to balance these forces is the problem that teachers face. The complexity of teachers is once again highlighted, as teachers must decide how to demonstrate that such things as playfulness and order are not incompatible, and that societal and individual needs must *both* be kept in perspective.

Sensible Management of Deviancy

Jacob Kounin, in an enormously influential work (1970), has given us a set of concepts that help us understand the process of maintaining a workplace free from deviance and in which students attend to their assignments. He gave us *withitness,* describing how effective managers nip behavioral problems in the bud; *overlappingness,* describing how effective classroom managers handle more than one thing at a time; he also described the need for *signals* for academic work; the effects of *momentum* and *smoothness* in lessons on student behavior, and the positive effects on attention of *group alerting, accountability* and *variety* in teaching. These variables have, for the most part, been verified or appropriately qualified in the work of Brophy and Evertson (1976) and Anderson, Evertson, and Brophy (1979), among others. Borg and Ascione (1982) have taken these concepts and developed training materials for teachers. Borg's work provides clear evidence of changed teacher and student behavior as a function of this kind of training. The students in classes where teachers had been taught management skills were markedly more on task and showed less deviant behavior. At the University of Texas, Evertson and Emmer and their colleagues (Evertson and others, 1981; and Emmer and others, 1981) have developed sensible management training programs for elementary and for junior high school teachers. Field tests of these eminently sensible suggestions from research and practice that are designed to help keep management problems to a minimum show that they do work.

This technology for creating learning environments that are relatively free from behavior problems has been developed, primarily over the last decade. (See, for example, Borg and Ascione, 1982; Duke, 1979, 1982). We have only to figure out how to provide the time so that teachers can learn the technology that can be used for controlling the management climate in their classes. Proper control of this climate variable can result in increased achievement through a reduction of time lost due to management problems and by helping to foster a safe and orderly environment in which it is possible for students to learn the school curriculum that was selected for them.

Developing Cooperative Learning Environments

In the last few years, just as we have done in the area of behavior management in classrooms, we have developed technology to help teachers enhance the interpersonal relationships between members of different social classes, races, sexes, or different ability groups. The key element in these approaches to developing cooperative environments is the requirement that every member of a group participate in activities that can be successfully completed only through interdependent and cooperative behavior. In Teams-Games-Tournaments (Slavin, 1980) heterogeneous groups are formed to compete for prizes obtainable through academic achievement. A clever point system is used so that low ability and high ability students can each contribute the same number of points to the team. Over 2,000 schools have tried Teams-Games-Tournaments with some success. The use of this technology usually improves cooperative behavior among students and often improves academic achievement as well.

A different approach is used by Aronson and his colleagues. They required that each member of the group have some of the information needed to solve a problem, thus ensuring that everyone in a group is responsible for success. The techniques used by Johnson and Johnson (1975) and by Sharon (1980) in Israel accomplish similar goals. Technology now exists to create productive and cognitive classroom learning environments. Alas, such technology is not finding its way quickly into programs of teacher education.

Summary of Climate Factors

In this section four climate variables that affect achievement were noted. It was reported that when a teacher communicates high academic expectations, and such expectations become a part of the classroom and school ethos, achievement is positively affected; when teachers create classrooms that are safe, orderly, and academically focused, achievement is increased; when the technology now available to teach sensible management of behavior problems is used, the opportunity for learning increases; and when the technology now available to create cooperative learning environments is used, positive results ensue. Teaching takes place in a context. It can never be decontextualized. The context, that environment for learning that must be developed in order for classrooms or schools to be judged successful, appears to require a press for both prosocial and academically oriented behavior.

Post-Instructional Factors

After an instructional sequence is over, some measure of student learning is usually devised. We have learned, recently, at least two interesting facts about testing that contribute to effective teaching. And we have some new concerns about two other post-instructional factors that have been discussed for years—grades and feedback to students.

Tests

There has been a growing concern that what occurs in classrooms is not represented on some of the standardized tests that are often used to assess student learning and teachers' and school districts' competency. This concern has taken many forms, from concern about whether students have had the "opportunity to learn" what is on the tests used to measure achievement, to content analysis of curriculum and achievement tests to see what degree of overlap or congruence between tests and the curriculum actually does exist. The latter kind of concern gave rise to research that examined each topic in three widely used mathematics textbooks and each test item in five widely used standardized tests (Freeman and others, 1980). In the *best* case, 71 percent of the topics that were on each test were also covered in the text. Thus, in the best case about 30 percent of what was tested had never been covered in school by students. In the *worst* case, 47 percent of the topics that were tested were never covered by the text. That is, the test that is used in some districts to evaluate student learning, teacher competency, and district effectiveness has more than half its items derived from topics never covered by students in that district! The lessons from recent research is clear—if teachers, schools, and districts are ever to look effective, they must learn to use tests that accurately reflect what they teach. The congruence between what is taught and what is tested must be high.

A second issue in testing, especially with the advent of the microcomputer, is that test items can be used to diagnose "buggy" algorithms (Brown and Burton, 1978). J. S. Brown, in particular, has challenged the assumption that a wrong answer shows lack of knowledge. Instead, he has demonstrated convincingly how people may possess the wrong knowledge for a particular task. For example, when a student solves a problem such as 143 minus 28 and answers 125, and then solves 256 minus 179 and answers 123, we see evidence of algorythmic or logical functioning in subtraction. The student subtracts the smaller number from the larger number each time, regardless of which number is on top. The student's solutions show evidence of learning and consistency. They also show, however, that the student has learned faulty or "buggy" algorithms. Hundreds of examples now are being developed to show how teachers can learn what a student knows but is incorrect. Scoring test items wrong is wasteful—items can supply hypotheses about the buggy algorithms in use by students, a first step toward correcting a student's errors.

Grades

The overuse and the coercive power of grades had, in the 1960s, been condemned by many educational reformers. It was thought that learning was lessened when external grading policies were applied. That appears not to be true. In fact, the evidence is persuasive that grades do motivate students to learn more in a given subject area (Gage and Berliner, 1984). The judicious use of grades that are tied to objective performance, as in mastery and some other instructional programs, appears to be related to increased achievement and positive student attitudes.

Feedback

Substantial use of corrective feedback in the academic areas, contingent praise for correct or proper behavior, and the use of students' ideas as a way of letting students know that their contributions are valued, all show positive relations to achievement and attitude (Gage and Berliner, 1984). Such feedback to students is not often found at high rates in classes, despite its logical and empirically determined effectiveness. Criticism, as a form of feedback, if emotionally neutral has been found to be accepted by students, but it has long been recognized that sarcasm and personal attacks are negatively related to achievement and should not be used as feedback for inappropriate behavior. Ignoring inappropriate behavior and other techniques are recommended by behavior modification advocates who have had great success in changing student behavior (see Sulzer-Azaroff and Mayer, 1977).

Summary of Post-Instructional Factors

Briefly mentioned were some teaching practices that typically occur after an instructional episode is completed, and which relate to achievement. It was noted that tests should be used to assess student knowledge, teacher competency, and district effectiveness *only* if the tests and curriculum match. Evidence suggests that our schools are a good deal more effective than is generally recognized, because we seriously underestimate what is learned by students when schools rely on tests that do not measure what is taught. We have also learned that tests need not be designed to be summative, as they so often are. A formative test, designed to systematically diagnose a student's faulty knowledge can be created. Teachers can then more precisely prescribe the kinds of remediation necessary for students with particular needs. Grades and feedback were also mentioned as affecting achievement. Perhaps much of this section can be summarized by the word "accountability." In study after study we learn that when students learn that they are accountable for their academic work because someone gives them feedback in the form of grades, rewards, or criticism for their homework, classwork, or test performance, there is evidence of increased achievement.

Research and the Practice of Classroom Teaching

A good deal of the research cited has been derived from correlational studies or studies of single variables as investigators searched for some effect on student attitude, behavior, or achievement. Teaching—real, live, honest-to-goodness classroom teaching—is extremely complex and extremely dynamic. A very legitimate concern, then, is whether the factors mentioned are found to hold up *in situ*. The evidence, while scanty, is reassuring. For example, the Missouri Math project of Good and Grouws (1979) used training procedures based on the available research (and old-fashioned common sense). Elementary school teachers were trained to

• check the previous day's work and reteach where necessary (this factor is related to the comments on grading and feedback, noted earlier).

• present new content or skills, proceeding rapidly, but in small steps, while giving detailed instructions and explanations (this factor is related to the comments about pacing, success rate, and structuring, noted earlier).

• have students practice the material, while providing feedback and corrections (this factor is related to the comments on questioning, feedback, and monitoring, noted earlier).

• have students do independent practice (this factor is related to the comments about allocated time, engaged time, success rate and feedback, noted earlier).

• provide weekly and monthly reviews (this factor is related to the comments about grades and feedback).

The training program helped teachers to develop a safe and orderly environment for learning. In addition, the teachers developed a climate characterized by an academic orientation. The program was unambiguously successful. Teachers trained by Good and Grouws had students who achieved considerably more than did the students of teachers who did not use the procedures recommended in the training program. Thus, it appears that the dozen or more factors drawn upon by Good and Grouws as they developed training materials proved, in combination, to be effective in regular classroom use. Moreover, the variables that teachers were trained to attend to showed a fascinating pattern when the actual implementation of those variables in classes was studied.

The experimental group of teachers learned to use 15 teaching practices. A comparison of the classroom behavior of the trained and untrained teachers showed that in classroom use, the trained teachers used eight teaching practices at rates different from the untrained teachers (that is, training changed their teaching behavior) and that seven teaching practices were not implemented at rates different than those used by untrained teachers. The interesting pattern shown in the data was that *each* of the eight recommended teaching practices that were implemented by the trained teachers showed a significant relationship with student achievement, and that *none* of the seven recommended teaching practices that were not implemented showed a significant relationship with achievement (Gage and Giaconia, 1981).

The same pattern of relations was shown to hold in the study by Anderson, Evertson, and Brophy (1979). In that experimental study the research on teaching was culled to provide over two dozen recommendations for the teaching of reading in first grade. Teachers who were trained to use the whole set of recommended teaching practices had students who achieved more than did the students of teachers who were not trained. Again, we find evidence that the variables derived from research on teaching can be used to train teachers and in turn, to increase student achievement. Moreover, as in the Good and Grouws study, those teaching practices actually implemented in the trained teachers classes were usually related to student achievement, and those teaching practices that did not actually become a salient part of the teacher's regular classroom behavior usually showed no relationship to achievement. The data from both studies are shown in Figures 3 and 4.

Figure 3. The Relationship between the Implementation of Recommended Teaching Practices and Achievement in the Study by Good and Grouws (1979).*

		Significance of the Relationship between Teaching Practice and Achievement		
		Significant	**Not Significant**	
Recommended Teaching Practices Actually Implemented in the Classroom	Yes	8	0	8
	No	0	7	7
		8	7	15

*Source: Gage and Giaconia (1981).

Figure 4. The Relationship between the Implementation of Recommended Teaching Practices and Achievement in the Study by Anderson, Evertson, and Brophy (1979).*

		Significance of the Relationship between Teaching Practice and Achievement		
		Significant	**Not Significant**	
Recommended Teaching Practices Actually Implemented in the Classroom	Yes	12	2	14
	No	8	9	17
		20	11	31

*Source: Gage and Giaconia (1981).

The implications of these two studies, analyzed in this way, must be made clear: when the research on teaching is used to develop training procedures for teachers, teachers can learn the recommended teaching practices, and if they implement the teaching practices that they have learned they can effect in a positive way student classroom behavior and achievement. That is why, in my opinion, there is cause to be optimistic. The glass is half full.

Other studies that have used research on teaching as guides to improve teaching practice have also been successful. The research team at Stanford did inservice training of elementary teachers and was able to show a positive effect on student achievement (Crawford and others, 1978). In a study with low income Hawaiian children, remarkable increases in reading achievement were noted when a program was instituted using time-on-task, success rate, structuring, monitoring, questioning, and so on. The program worked when it was placed within the Hawaiian cultural context that was familiar to the children (Tharp, 1982). Many of the research variables mentioned above were shown to affect achievement in a study by Stallings, Needles, and Stayrook (1979), and many of these same variables were found to distinguish between effective and less effective secondary school teachers (Evertson, Anderson, and Brophy, 1979). There is good reason to believe that a list of factors such as those presented in this essay, or by Hunter in this volume, or by Rosenshine (1983), or by Good (in press), does represent a reliable knowledge base for the inservice and preservice education of teachers. What will it take to convince the teacher education community to use such knowledge?

Gage (1983) has addressed this problem and his logic will be followed here. When a relationship occurs between a teaching practice and an educational outcome we value, we have "an implication." Implications range along a continuum of strength that may be labeled as going from a *shred* (a glimmer of an insight) to a *suggestion*, to a *recommendation*, to an *imperative*, and on to a *categorical imperative*, where the failure to use certain knowledge would be morally reprehensible. In medicine, extremely small increases in health or longevity due to diet or the use of the new beta-blocker anti-heart-attack drugs become the basis for recommendations and imperatives. Beta-blockers have only a small (though significant) effect on death rate. Yet, a physician who will not order beta blockers for someone recovering from a heart attack could well be sued for malpractice.

There are many variables recently uncovered in educational research that show as strong or stronger a relationship with student achievement and student behavior as variables in medical practice show to longevity and general health. But in medicine such relationships become imperatives, while in education they are treated as shreds—the merest glimmer of an implication. Our research is much less at fault than are our attitudes toward research. Perhaps this essay and this volume will help to change people's opinions about whether in research on teaching the glass is half full or half empty.

References

Anderson, L. M.; Evertson, C. M.; and Brophy, J. E. "An Experimental Study of Effective Teaching in First Grade Reading Groups." *The Elementary School Journal* 79 (1979): 193-223.

Angus, M. J.; Evans, K. W.; and Parkin, B. *An Observational Study of Selected Pupil and Teacher Behavior in Open Plan and Conventional Design Classrooms.* Australian Open Area Project, Technical Report No. 4. Perth, Australia: Educational Department of Western Australia, 1975.

Barr, R. C. "School, Class, Group, and Pace Effects on Learning." Paper presented at the meeting of the American Educational Research Association, April 1980, Boston, Mass.

Berliner, D. C. "Tempus Educare." In *Research on Teaching.* Edited by P. L. Peterson and M. J. Walberg. Berkeley, Calif.: McCutchan, 1979.

Berliner, D. C. "Developing Conceptions of Classroom Environments: Some Light on the T in Classroom Studies of ATI." *Educational Psychologist* 18 (1983): 1-13.

Berliner, D. C., and Rosenshine, B. V. "The Acquisition of Knowledge in the Classroom." In *Schooling and the Acquisition of Knowledge.* Edited by R. C. Anderson, R. J. Spiro, and W. E. Montague. Hillsdale, N.J.: Erlbaum, 1977.

Bloom, B. S.; Engelhart, M. B.; Furst, E. J.; Hill, W. M., and Krathwohl, D. R. *Taxonomy of Educational Objectives: The Classification of Educational Goals. Handbook I: Cognitive Domain.* New York: Longman Green, 1956.

Borg, W. R., and Ascione, F. R. "Classroom Management in Elementary Mainstreaming Classrooms." *Journal of Educational Psychology* 74 (1982): 85-95.

Bossert, S. T. "Activity Structures and Student Outcomes." Paper presented at the National Institute of Education's Conference on School Organization and Effects, San Diego, Calif., January 1978.

Brookover, W. B., and Lezotte, L. *Changes in School Characteristics Coincident with Changes in Student Achievement.* East Lansing, Mich.: College of Urban Development, Michigan State University, 1977.

Brophy, J. "Classroom Organization and Management." *The Elementary School Journal* 83 (1983): 265-286.

Brophy, J. E., and Evertson, C. M. *Process-Product Correlations In the Texas Teacher Effectiveness Study.* Final Report No. 74-4. Austin: Research and Development Center for Teacher Education, University of Texas, 1979.

Brophy, J., and Evertson, C. *Learning from Teaching: A Developmental Perspective.* Boston, Mass.: Allyn and Bacon, 1976.

Brophy, J. E., and Good, T. L. *Teacher-Student Relationships: Causes and Consequences.* New York: Holt, Rinehart and Winston, 1974.

Brown, J. S., and Burton, R. R. "Diagnostic Models for Procedural Bugs in Basic Mathematical Skills," *Cognitive Science* 1 (1978): 155-192.

Bruner, J. "On Instructability." Paper presented at the meeting of the American Psychological Association, Los Angeles, Calif., August 1981.

Buchmann, M., and Schmidt, W. H. *The School Day and Teachers' Content Commitments.* IRT Research Series #83. East Lansing: Institute for Research on Teaching, Michigan State University, 1981.

Carew, J., and Lightfoot, S. L. *Beyond Bias.* Cambridge, Mass.: Harvard University Press, 1979.

Cooley, W. W., and Leinhardt, G. "The Instructional Dimensions Study." *Educational Evaluation and Policy Analysis* 2, 1 (1980): 7-25.

Cooper, H. "Pygmalion Grows Up: A Model for Teacher Expectation, Communication and Performance Influence." *Review of Educational Research* 79 (1979): 389-410.

Crawford, J.; Gage, N. L.; Corno, L.; Stayrook, W.; Mittman, A.; Schunk, D.; Stallings, J.; Baskin, E.; Harvey, P.; Austin, D.; Cronin, D.; and Newman, R. *An Experiment on Teacher Effectiveness and Parent-Assisted Instruction in the Third Grade* (3 Vols). Stanford, Calif.: Center for Educational Research at Stanford, 1978.

Denham, C., and Lieberman, A., eds. *Time to Learn*. Washington, D.C.: U.S. Department of Education, National Institute of Education, 1980.

Doyle, W. "Paradigms for Research on Teacher Effectiveness." In *Review of Research in Education* (Vol. 5). Edited by L. S. Shulman. Itasca, Ill.: Peacock Publishers, 1977.

Dreeben, R. "The Collective Character of Instruction." Paper presented at the meeting of the American Educational Research Association, Toronto, Canada, March 1978.

Duke, D., ed. *Classroom Management*. Seventy-eighth yearbook of the National Society for the Study of Education. Part II. Chicago: University of Chicago Press, 1979.

Duke, D. L., ed. *Helping Teachers Manage Classrooms*. Alexandria, Va.: Association for Supervision and Curriculum Development, 1982.

Edmonds, R. "Some Schools Work and More Can." *Social Policy* 9 (March/April 1979): 28-32.

Emmer, E. T.; Everton, C. M.; Clements, B. S.; Sanford, J. P.; and Worsham, M. E. *Organizing and Managing the Junior High School Classroom*. Austin: Research and Development Center for Teacher Education, University of Texas, 1981.

Everton, C. M.; Anderson, L. M.; and Brophy, J. E. *The Texas Junior High School Study: Final Report of Process-Product Relationships* (R & D Report #4061). Austin: Research and Development Center for Teacher Education, University of Texas, 1978.

Everton, C. M.; Emmer E. T.; Clements, B. S.; Sanford, J. P.; Worsham, M. E.; and Williams, E. L. *Organizing and Managing the Elementary School Room*. Austin: Research and Development Center for Teacher Education, University of Texas, 1981.

Fisher, C. W.; Berliner, D. C.; Filby, N. N.; Marliave, R. S.; Cahen, L. S.; and Dishaw, M. M. "Teaching Behaviors, Academic Learning Time and Student Achievement: An Overview." In *Time to learn*. Edited by C. Denham and A. Lieberman. Washington, D.C.: U.S. Department of Education, National Institute of Education, 1980.

Fisher, C. W.; Filby, N. N.; Marliave, R. S.; Cahen, L. S.; Dishaw, M. M.; Moore, J. E.; and Berliner, D. C. *Teaching Behaviors, Academic Learning Time and Student Achievement*. Final Report of Phase III-B, Beginning Teacher Evaluation Study. Technical Report V-1. San Francisco, Calif.: Far West Laboratory for Educational Research and Development, 1978.

Freeman, D.; Kuhs, T.; Porter, A.; Knappen, L.; Floden, R.; Schmidt, W.; and Schwille, J. *The Fourth Grade Mathematics Curriculum as Inferred from Textbooks and Tests*. East Lansing: Michigan State University, Institute for Research on Teaching, Report #82, 1980.

Gage, N. L., ed. *Handbook of Research on Teaching*. Chicago, Ill.: Rand McNally, 1963.

Gage, N. L. "When Does Research on Teaching Yield Implications for Practice?" *Elementary School Journal* 83 (1983): 492-496.

Gage, N. L., and Berliner, D. C. *Educational Psychology*, 3rd ed. Boston, Mass.: Houghton-Mifflin, 1984.

Gage, N. L., and Giaconia, R. "Teaching Practices and Student Achievement: Causal Connections." *New York University Education Quarterly* 113, 3 (1981): 2-9.

Gall, M. D. "The Use of Questioning in Teaching." *Review of Educational Research* 40 (1970): 707-721.

Good, T. L. "Classroom research: Past and future." In *Handbook of Teaching and Policy*. Edited by L. S. Shulman and G. A. Sykes. New York: Longman, in press.

Good, T. L., and Beckerman, T. M. "Time on Task: A Naturalistic Study in Sixth Grade Classrooms." *Elementary School Journal* 78 (1978): 193-201.

Good, T. L., and Grouws, D. "The Missouri Mathematics Effectiveness Project: An Experimental Study in Fourth-Grade Classrooms." *Journal of Educational Psychology* 71 (1979): 355-362.

Hassenpflug, A. M. *The Use and Understanding of School Time by Third Graders: An Ethnographic Case Study*. Technical Report No. 574. Madison: Research and Development Center for Individualized Schooling, University of Wisconsin, 1981.

Husen, T. *International Study of Achievement in Mathematics: Comparison of Twelve Countries* (Vols. 1 and 2). New York: John Wiley, 1967.

Johnson, D., and Johnson, R. *Learning Together and Alone*. Englewood Cliffs. N.J.: Prentice-Hall, 1975.

Kounin, J. *Discipline and Group Management in Classrooms*. New York: Holt, Rinehart, and Winston, 1970.

McDonald, F. J. *Research on Teaching and Its Implications for Policy Making: Report on Phase II of the Beginning Teacher Evaluation Study*. Princeton, N.J.: Educational Testing Service, 1976.

Marliave, R., and Filby, J. N. "Success Rates: A Measure of Task Appropriateness." In *Perspectives on Instructional Time*, Edited by C. W. Fisher and D. C. Berliner. New York: Longman, in press.

Mills, S. R.; Rice, C. T.; Berliner, D. C.; and Rousseau, E. W. "The Correspondence Between Teacher Questions and Student Answers in Classroom Discourse." *Journal of Experimental Education* 48 (1980): 194-209.

Purkey, S. C., and Smith, M. C. "Effective Schools: A Review." *The Elementary School Journal* 93 (1983): 428-452.

Redfield, D. L., and Rousseau, E. W. "A Meta-Analysis of Experimental Research on Teacher Questioning Behavior." *Review of Educational Research* 51 (1981): 237-245.

Rist, R. C. *The Urban School: A Factory for Failure*. Cambridge: Massachusetts Institute of Technology Press, 1973.

Rosenshine, B. V. "Teaching Functions in Instructional Programs." *The Elementary School Journal* 83 (1983): 335-352.

Rossmiller, R. A. "Managing School Resources to Improve Student Achievement." Paper presented at the State Superintendent Conference for District Administrators, Madison, Wisc., September 1982.

Rowe, M. B. "Wait Time and Rewards as Instructional Variables: Their Influence on Language, Logic and Fate Control. Part one, Wait Time." *Journal of Research in Science Teaching* 11 (1974): 81-94.

Rutter, M.; Maughan, B.; Mortimore, P.; and Ousten, J. *Fifteen Thousand Hours*. Cambridge, Mass.: Harvard University Press, 1979.

Schwille, J.; Porter, A.; Belli, A.; Floden, R.; Freeman, D.; Knappen, L.; Kuhs, T.; and Schmidt, W. J. *Teachers as Policy Brokers in the Content of Elementary School Mathematics*. (National Institute of Education Contract No. P-80-0127). East Lansing: Institute for Research on Teaching, Michigan State University, 1981.

Sharon, S. "Cooperative Learning in Small Groups: Recent Methods and Effects on Achievement Attitudes and Ethnic Relations." *Review of Educational Research* 50 (1980): 241-271.

Shavelson, R. J. "Review of Research on Teachers' Pedagogical Judgments, Plans, and Decisions." *Elementary School Journal* 83 (1983): 392-414.

Slavin, R. "Cooperative learning." *Review of Educational Research* 50 (1980): 315-342.

Stallings, J.; Needles, M.; and Stayrook, N. *How to Change the Process of Teaching Basic Reading Skills in Secondary Schools*. Menlo Park, Calif.: SRI International, 1979.

Sulzer-Azaroff, B., and Mayer, R. G. *Applying Behavior Analysis Procedures with Children and Youth*. New York: Holt, Rinehart, and Winston, 1977.

Tharp, R. G. "The Effective Instruction of Comprehension: Results and Description of the Kamehameha Early Education Program." *Reading Research Quarterly* 17 (1982): 503-527.

Tikunoff, W. J.; Berliner, D. C.; and Rist, R. C. *An Ethnographic Study of the Forty Classrooms of the Beginning Teacher Evaluation Study Known Sample*. Technical Report 75-105. San Francisco, Calif.: Far West Laboratory for Educational Research and Development, 1975.

Trachtenberg, D. "Student Tasks in Text Material: What Cognitive Skills Do They Tap?" *Peabody Journal of Education* 52 (1974): 54-57.

Vanezky, R. L., and Winfield, L. F. *Schools That Succeed Beyond Expectations in Teaching Reading*. Final Report, National Institute of Education, Grant No. NIE-G-78-0027. Newark, Del.: College of Education, University of Delaware, 1979.

Walker, D. F., and Schaffarzick, J. "Comparing Curricula." *Review of Educational Research* 44 (1974): 83-111.

Webb, N. M. "A Process-Outcome Analysis of Learning in Group and Individual Settings." *Educational Psychologist* 15 (1980): 69-83.

A Response to Berliner:
Take Another Look at the Glass

JANE H. APPLEGATE

Two teachers observed a glass left on a table in the teacher's lounge. "You know, people look at glasses like that and argue about whether the glass is half full or half empty. What do you think?"

"I think that is not the real issue," the second teacher responded. "What I want to know is what's in the glass, and who left it on the table."

The second teacher's comments are like those of many educators who read and consider the applications of research on teaching to classroom life. The status of knowledge production is secondary to the substance of the knowledge, the source of the knowledge and the context through which the knowledge is produced and disseminated. Contrary to Berliner's presumptions, educators want to know about "sensible, effective, and efficient teaching practices." They want to know more about what can be done to support and encourage student learning and how to do it. They also want to know the experience base of the researchers and under what conditions the research was conducted. Perhaps another look at the glass is in order.

What is in the Glass?

The intention of Berliner's chapter is twofold: to highlight significant findings from studies aimed at uncovering "effective and efficient teaching practices" and to convince the education profession that such knowledge has merit in the improvement of practice. Berliner has done an adequate job of organizing and summarizing the results from the studies and warns us "not to make the mistake of presenting each of these factors as single variables that alone will determine achievement." Yet, for educators seeking to improve instruction, a list of variables with few clear operational definitions may not be enough to promote change in teacher behavior.

For example, Berliner details the importance of "structuring" as a factor influencing student achievement. Though no definition is given, a reader might infer that "structuring" has something to do with the teacher clearly communicating the goals for instruction or the teacher giving clear directions about what students are to do in a given activity sequence. As

Jane H. Applegate is Director, Educational Field/Clinical Experiences, College of Education, Kent State University, Kent, Ohio.

Berliner notes, "It (structuring) is sometimes not done at all, sometimes it is done only minimally, and sometimes it is overdone. . . . In any case, what is worth noting is that structuring is the responsibility of the teacher, it affects performance and it can be taught."

Assuming, then, that the teacher accepts this responsibility, what should the teacher do? Should the teacher write instructional goals on the board daily? or weekly? or annually? Should the teacher provide a hand-out of plans to students or is it enough to have plans clearly in mind? Should the teacher repeat directions for an activity twice or three times—or five times so all students hear clearly what they are to do? It is not enough to know that "structuring" is important, one must know what it means in the life of the classroom. Questions like those raised earlier require response if the variables listed are to be taken seriously. Whether one is talking about "A.L.T." or "Monitoring" or "Sensible Management of Deviancy," educators expect researchers to communicate the results from their work with clarity and practicality. Right now substance in the glass is cloudy.

Who Left the Glass on the Table?

Educational researchers, translators of research, and consumers of research all have something to gain from the growing attention to research on teaching. So why, then, was the glass left on the table?

As Berliner illustrated, educational researchers have some promising directions for study. Though research on teaching has been difficult to initiate, difficult to undertake, and, in many cases, difficult to understand, educational researchers now have the opportunity to build upon the efforts of researchers like Stallings, Rosenshine, Good, and others to provide solid conclusive recommendations linked to relevant data. As Berliner suggests, researchers have been cautious in their focus, in their designs, and in the interpretations of findings. Wanting to hold true to the cannons of scientific inquiry and yet appear practical and sensitive to the problems of teachers, researchers frequently find themselves caught trying to explain what research is for and what it can and cannot do. Researchers are criticized simultaneously for overgeneralizing from results gleaned from specific research conditions and disclaiming practical applications from studies based upon too little evidence. Too often the effects from research are washed out by arguments from researchers themselves about the value of their efforts. For knowledge from research to be credible researchers must develop a clear sense of purpose.

Translators of research have taken up the challenge of interpreting results from complex studies for knowledge dissemination. The translation function requires the translator to be knowledgeable about both the tenets of research and the practices of teachers. For translators to avoid weak or questionable interpretations, extensive time is needed for reading research and talking with practitioners. Translators' works are usually obvious. In nontechnical journal articles that point to research for substance to undergird these, phrases like, "According to research . . ." or "Research suggests . . ." are cues that a translator has been at work. Sometimes, a translator wishing to have impact upon the research community will write, "No research has yet addressed the problem of . . ." Translators who are program developers will cull research for implications for practice and will adapt those suggestions for program improvement. The program, TESA, for example, has been developed from research on teacher effectiveness to provide a focus for school and teacher improvement.

Translators are often criticized for assuming too much and interpreting research results too broadly. Researchers condemn translators for not understanding research well enough to provide credible interpretation and consumers condemn translators for lack of actual school experience. For translators to be effective in narrowing the theory-practice gap, they should put time and effort into developing their own knowledge bases, research and practice, and into developing skills necessary for linking the two.

Consumers of research are those who look to research on teaching for new insights and suggestions for both practice and future research. They are the knowledge users. Consumers may well be other researchers, translators in search of promising ideas or teachers who want to improve classroom life. The consumers of research take the work of the researcher seriously. Consumers read, think, discuss, and ponder the substance of research be it theoretical or practical. Theoretical consumers look to researchers to continue their lines of inquiry; practical consumers are in search of meaning for the complexities of the teaching-learning process in personal ways. It is also the consumers who challenge the focus and direction of research when clarity of purpose is lacking. If the implications from studies are too simplistic, or if they are too complex, the consumer is likely to respond, "Of course," or "So what?" and continue searching for appropriate information.

Like consumers of other products, research consumers are attracted to results from studies on teacher effects if they have a need for such information, if the information is available and if they have been satisfied with results from similar efforts. The extent to which researchers and translators can meet these conditions will affect research consumption.

What happens to the glass is the responsibility of the teacher education community. "Convincing" the community to use knowledge generated from research may be difficult because the need for this kind of inquiry may not be felt among those who might benefit most from new knowledge about teaching. Perhaps the knowledge generated is simply not available in language or style meaningful to those who want it. Perhaps research results used in the past have not generated hoped-for results in practice. Regardless, educators need to continue looking at the glass, its substance, and its context if instructional improvement is valued.

A Response to Berliner:
on the Lower Half of the Glass

KEN HENSON

In this chapter Berliner has expressed the effects of attitudes toward research on teaching. He insists that most people are pessimistic when it comes to research in teaching. This, says Berliner, is the result of at least three factors. They are: (1) the tendency of earlier researchers to over-sell research to educators, (2) a general mistrust of science and technology, and (3) the newness of the field of research on teaching. While each of these factors obviously contributes to our pessimism, the general mistrust that we have for research runs deeply in our society. In its brief existence America has been blessed with the natural resources needed to outdistance all other countries of the world.

This abundance of wealth coupled with a free, democratic environment that prizes and rewards competition has given each of us an inner drive to succeed. Such practitioners have no time for research. We have proven this repeatedly and the evidence is all around us. Every community has its open schools, many of which are disastrous learning environments, simply because we have rushed in and built buildings attempting to borrow techniques without bothering to try to understand the philosophy that undergirds successful open classrooms, let alone take the time needed to prepare teachers for this drastically different teaching role. Berliner wisely cautions us against repeating this mistake with microcomputers.

The irony of our skepticism for research is exemplified even in the quality that made us a superior industrialized nation: our technology. In fact, it was Frederick Taylor's scientific management style that introduced research in industry leading to close analysis of worker behaviors. The significance of analyzing the worker's behavior and breaking it down into small tasks was quickly accepted in industry. Yet, it was several decades before interaction analysis was used in the classroom and even longer before time-on-task studies began. Yet, as Berliner notes, there is a positive correlation between the time spent on the learning task at hand and the resultant learning. These examples show that while we are prone to rush madly into practice, we are equally prone to shun research even when studies have been proven successful.

Ken Henson is Professor and Head, Curriculum and Instruction, College of Education, The University of Alabama, Tuscaloosa.

Berliner addresses a significant fault in our educational practices today—our failure to recognize political and sociological forces that affect the schools. In particular, I would like to flush out one force that illustrates his point. Part of our society chooses to dismiss research on the grounds that it is unrelated to practice. Another part rejects research on the assumption that it somehow opposes the practical world. How often we hear our colleagues comment, "I don't have time for research since I choose to spend my time preparing my lessons." The implication, of course, is that one must choose between research (either conducting it or reading about it) and practice (becoming a good teacher). Amazingly, these individuals view research and teaching as opposing forces.

This tendency to separate teaching and research has its basis in our society at large which tends to focus on the upper half of the glass rather than on the lower half when it appraises our schools. For a quarter of a century now the American public has focused their attention on the failure of our schools—to teach the basics, to maintain adequate defense, to prepare students to excel on standardized exams, and to discipline our youth. We completely ignore the fact that throughout the years Americans have won more Nobel Prizes than any other nation. In fact, from the time that these awards first began in 1901 til 1980, America had won more than any other nation (166 out of 455)—over one-third of all the Nobel Prizes ever given. Russia has earned 24. It is interesting that the awards won collectively by the three countries whose school systems are so highly regarded, (Great Britain, Germany, and France), together barely exceed the number of awards received by Americans. Yet, we continue to see a half-empty glass.

Surely there must exist somewhere between the exaggerated belief that research will solve all of our problems and the equally absurd idea that research and teaching are unrelated or opposite, the attitude that Berliner reflects in this article. This is the belief that by focusing on the possibilities that research offers and by judiciously applying research to the highly complex teaching process that the result can significantly improve teaching practice.

Never before have our schools suffered such an image problem as they do today. In no other country do the general citizenry feel competent to tell the principal how to run the schools or the teachers how to teach their classes. But this general lack of respect for American educators should come as no surprise since we are so far detached from research. How many current educators would have a ready answer to an education critic—or a substantive response to a voter's demand for evidence that more money would improve our schools? How many could cite even one study that has found that more learning occurs in a class of 10 than in a class of 40? Not only do we fail to conduct research but we tend to fail to read it.

But there is strong reason for hope. The format of Berliner's chapter groups teaching studies into three groups: pre-instruction, instruction, and post-instruction. Such groupings are made essential by the extreme complexity of the teaching process. Recently, studies in education have measured teacher effectiveness in terms of learner attainment based on objectives. State accountability programs are forcing teachers to identify objectives and evaluate accordingly. Education professors are forced to deal with these issues. The use of evaluation is gradually shifting from all summative to include more formative tests, to promote learning. It is time that American educators assume a half-full perspective of research and begin to use research and research findings in their classrooms. Perhaps then, educators at all levels can assume a proactive stance and receive much credit that has long been overdue.

5 Qualitative Research — Another Way of Knowing

VINCENT R. ROGERS

Paulo Freire taught many of Brazil's adult, illiterate poor to read. In order to do so, it was essential that he understand the reality of their lives, the meanings they brought to the events that were a part of their everyday experience. The topics he used as the basis for his reading program had to reflect these meanings; thus he did research in order to discover them. For example, he would show students a picture of a drunken man weaving his way along a city street. Freire believed this picture would evoke notions about alcoholism, its related problems, personal experiences with drinking and drunkards, and so on. Instead, the response was more like, "How lucky he is; he must have a job. How else could he afford to buy alcohol?" (Bogdan, 1982)

Freire had to probe beneath the surface, to ignore conventional assumptions, to move beyond observable behavior in order to understand the meaning of events in the lives of his students.

This attitude, this belief that nothing is necessarily as it appears to be lies at the heart of the research methods we lump loosely together and label "qualitative" or "naturalistic."

Dozens of qualitative* researchers have attempted definitions of these techniques, most with little success. The concept and its accompanying methodologies are so varied and complex that simple definitions aren't adequate. Nevertheless, I think that Rist's (1975) description comes closer

---

*I will use the term "qualitative" rather than "qualitative or naturalistic" during the rest of this paper to conserve space.

Vincent R. Rogers is Professor of Education, University of Connecticut, Storrs.

to the mark than most; it also has the virtues of brevity and clarity. For Rist, qualitative research is "direct observation of human activity and interaction in an ongoing, naturalistic fashion."

While this definition is less than perfect, it does suggest some of qualitative research's most essential aspect. There is so much more to be said, however, about these approaches—so much more flesh to go with the bare bones of Rist's definition—that it would seem useful at this point to go beyond simple definition and list a number of additional characteristics that qualitative researchers associate with their methodology.

Qualitative researchers believe that:

1. Any social entity or institution is enormously complex and subtle. It is difficult to understand what is happening in a first grade reading group or a middle school classroom. The experiences and attitudes of teachers and children both in and out of the school setting all have a bearing on what occurs within the classroom or school. Qualitative researchers accept these complexities, believing that only through their unraveling will anything resembling accurate description result.

2. Intensive study of a given phenomenon over a long period of time is essential for genuine understanding of that phenomenon. Teaching and learning are ongoing processes constantly in flux; to understand what is happening requires sustained, longitudinal study.

3. People and institutions must be studied holistically, and not in isolation from other forces that may influence them. The "wholes" or units may vary in size and complexity, and it may be necessary to study many "wholes" before accurate description of a larger unit emerges. Nevertheless, what goes on in the cafeteria or art studio is indeed related to what goes on elsewhere, both within and outside of the school. The qualitative researcher studies all related and relevant phenomena.

4. The most effective way to study a given phenomenon is through direct, on site, face to face contact with the people and events in question. What people do is often different from what they say. Thus, reliance on paper and pencil tests and questionnaires is often misleading. Rosenthal and Jacobson's classic study, *Pygmalion in the Classroom* (1968) suggested that teachers' expectations bring about dynamic changes in their judgment of children's work. Yet we know little about what actually happened in such classrooms—how teachers treated children, how children responded to such treatment. Only first-hand observation would reveal such subtleties.

5. Knowledge of the behavior of human beings in a given social context is relatively meaningless without some understanding of the meanings those observed give to their behavior. Thus the qualitative

researcher seeks to understand the attitudes, values, beliefs, and underlying assumptions of those being studied, to understand how others view their world. High school students may indeed join informal groups or cliques in school, but such information is relatively useless unless we know why students choose to associate with one group rather than another, what their perceptions are of the values and purposes of such groups. At another level, a field trip to the zoo may be seen by the principal as a learning experience that expands the conventional curriculum. The teacher may view it as "a breather," a day away from the "drudgery of daily classroom life."

6. The basic function of the researcher is *description;* the richest, fullest most comprehensive description possible. Such "thick description" enables the researcher to perceive subtleties in human behavior (is a raised eyebrow a conscious reaction or merely a twitch?) that are vital to full understanding. Such description suggests a basic interest in process rather than product or output. Qualitative researchers describe but do not judge or evaluate—although their data may well be used by others in an evaluative sense. Thus a school may richly document the lives of children as they move through school, including samples of children's work, excerpts from teachers' and children's journals, comments of observers, and so on. Parents, teachers, and others concerned with the quality of children's schooling must then assess this "thick description" and decide for themselves on the adequacy of the school's programs, methods, and activities.

7. The rich description qualitative researchers provide is exactly what it says it is; that is, description of schools, classrooms, children, teachers, parents, counselors, board members, and others connected with schooling *as they are.* Qualitative research is thus non-manipulative, and does not lend itself to "experimental research." The qualitative researcher's "laboratory" is the social setting under question as it is functioning; one does not alter variables or otherwise change the situation under study.

8. Study of a given situation begins without lists of specific hypotheses and objectives, selection of "instruments," and carefully defined areas or categories for investigation. Rather, qualitative researchers use their initial observations and other data to formulate research questions as the study progresses. While one begins with a hunch or a question, it is not until the researcher is involved in the social setting under question that important hypotheses begin to emerge. Thus, a study of ethnic relations among high school students may begin out of a suspicion that various minority groups are isolated socially and academically in a given school. Continued observation

and interviewing may reveal that two or three teachers in a specific program rather than "institutionalized racism" are the source of the problem, and the study may then focus on the behavior of those teachers, their perceptions of their students, students' perceptions of such teachers, and so on. Appropriate techniques will then be chosen to gather the data needed.

9. Generalizable theory emerges from the study of specific settings, rather than prescribing and thus limiting the direction in which a given study may go. A concern for the perceived declining effectiveness of team teaching in a given school district led to a series of interviews with teachers and principals in schools using teaming as a basic organizational device. Ultimately, it became clear that the teaming process per se was not at the root of teachers' problems; rather, the data revealed that the staff was an "aging" group, that many of the problems they identified had more to do with teachers' personal concerns about their lives, status, and careers—in short, many were in the midst of what we have come to call "mid-life crisis." Other studies of older teachers reveal similar patterns of behavior, and it now becomes increasingly possible to generalize about the behavior and problems likely to be encountered by teachers in these age groups. Thus, the study of team teaching contributes to the development of theory, which is referred to by qualitative researchers as "grounded theory."

Qualitative researchers, then, are concerned with the internal life of schools; what is really occurring in classrooms, corridors, cafeterias, and playgrounds. Their task is to look at what we ordinarily take for granted with fresh eyes; to see events, with all of their subtleties and nuances, as they really are.

It would be impossible to list the characteristics of qualitative research as I have done without subtly implying that quantitative research must necessarily be an inferior methodology. Quantitative research techniques are indeed inferior if the researchers goal is to seek answers to the sorts of questions best dealt with by qualitative methods. Obviously, the reverse is also true. Qualitative methodology would be virtually useless if our goal was to gather demographic data about the increase or decline of vandalism or acts of violence in schools; numbers of dropouts or retentions in various programs; racial, ethnic, or socioeconomic makeup of students in alternative schools.

Similarly, experimental research—the study, for example, of the effects of creativity training on the writing performance of six graders—would be best carried out using the conventional, linear approach, which includes problem definition, the formulation of specific hypotheses, the design and selection of instruments, the selection of appropriate, representative sample populations, the matching of experimental and control groups, the manipulation of experimental variables, data gathering, data analysis, and final conclusions.

Both approaches can be rigorous, systematic forms of empirical inquiry—and both can be careless and haphazard, "quick and dirty." Neither is inherently good or bad, superior or inferior. It is vital, however, that both quantitative and qualitative researchers recognize the differences in their approaches to knowing; recognizing the importance (as Gertrude Stein put it) of the *question* before plunging ahead to find the answer. As Elliott Eisner has said, Ken Kesey's play *One Flew Over The Cuckoo's Nest* offers the reader an informed, sensitive view of life in a mental hospital in Oregon as it was experienced by a "participant observer." His perceptions are what we seek—not "the mean view of four writers' observations about a mental hospital in Oregon" Eisner (1980).

Another way of subtly distinguishing between the two approaches is to make use of Everhart's (1975) notion of "how?" vs "how well?" That is, if the researcher wants to know how a new, individualized math program is working in the district's middle school; that is, what it is as students and teachers experience it, one uses the techniques associated with qualitative research. If, on the other hand, he or she wishes to know how well the program is working in terms of some arbitrarily defined standard, quantitative methods are appropriate.

To clarify the difference in still another way, a quantitative researcher's approach to studying the math program described above would undoubtedly focus on certain specific dimensions of the program itself; that is, the teaching materials used, teachers' methods, and the product of these efforts as measured by some form of paper and pencil test after a specified time period of instruction. Qualitative researchers would study what Bogdan (1982) calls the "multiple realities" of such a situation—how students and teachers perceive and experience the program. Qualitative researchers might be interested in the quality of class discussion, who was involved in such discussion, the makeup of various sub-groups that the teacher forms for instructional purposes, the perceptions and expectations teachers hold of certain students or groups, students' views of themselves, their classmates and their teacher, students' attitudes toward schooling itself, and the possible influences that parents, peer groups, and community may have on such attitudes. This is not to say that this becomes an automatic agenda for the qualitative researcher; it is to say, however, that all of these factors represent "realities" or dimensions of the math program that could clarify the question of "how" the program is working. Precisely which "realities" would be studied would only be revealed after a certain amount of broad, preliminary study had been carried out and some tentative hunches or hypotheses identified.

To summarize, the talents of both the qualitative and quantitative researchers are needed if we are to fully understand not only the products of schooling but also its processes.

Rist (1980) has argued that "conventional research has had little impact on teaching and learning in the schools." This is probably an overstatement; certainly schools have changed in a number of important ways during the past 50 years or so; surely some of that change can be attributed to knowledge gleaned from educational research. On the other hand, I think it would be fair to say that schooling has not changed as much as it might have or should have if degree of change can be associated with the quantity of research produced in a given field. Change in the practice of medicine during the last 50 years has been, in many ways, almost miraculous. Certainly a physician who, like Rip van Winkle, might have slept for 50 years and suddenly awakened in the 1980s would find the techniques and methods practiced by his modern day colleagues almost unrecognizable from what he or she was used to. I contend that this would not necessarily be so if the "sleeper" was a classroom teacher. Things have changed—but not that much.

The truth of the matter seems to be that practitioners—teachers and administrators, but particularly teachers—tend to ignore the volumes of research studies and reports produced annually by educational researchers. Why is this so?

Perhaps it is because so much of the research is so badly written. Research reports are often jargon laden, pretentious, and unclear.

A more likely explanation seems to be tied up with the notion of "reciprocity"; that is, most conventional educational research does not involve its subjects in the research itself. They have little to say about the purposes, timing, methods, tests, and so on, to be used in the study. Something is being done to them, but why it is being done is unclear; how it is progressing is a mystery; and the results are often unintelligible. Such research is perceived by practitioners as "hit and run" activity. Researchers appear, administer tests of various sorts, teachers are trained (often against their will or with minimal enthusiasm) to use some new method or set of materials, the researchers appear again a few months later, test again, and are gone. Teachers play little or no role in the development or design of the research, in the data gathering process, in the formulation of hunches or hypotheses, and in the ongoing sharing of tentative results.

Also, many teachers feel that when the research is completed, they do not necessarily understand the problem the researcher came to investigate any better and do not feel equipped to teach more effectively as a result of the research.

Qualitative research, whatever its faults and limitations (and I will deal with these shortly) does usually involve the subjects themselves in the research.

For example, Professor Pertti Pelto (an anthropologist) and I were recently involved in a qualitative study of multiethnic relations in a middle school. Excerpts from the research proposal should make the concepts of reciprocity and involvement clear.

Project Title: Improving Multicultural Teaching and Learning Through a Practical Analysis of Inter-Ethnic Relations in the Fairview* Middle School.

Background: The importance of the development of some sense of understanding of, tolerance for, and respect for those whose cultures differ from one's own hardly needs elaboration. There is ample evidence that schools in general have been less than totally effective in this area; similarly, there is considerable evidence that textbooks, films, and other teaching materials are often biased and inaccurate. Improving multicultural teaching and learning should have a high priority in any school system, and especially in those with multicultural student bodies.

One way to help achieve these goals is through the collaboration of practitioners; that is, classroom teachers, principals, curriculum directors, and others with university specialists in what might be described as curricular improvement through collaborative research.

Methods:

1. Upon receiving the approval of the Superintendent of Schools, Curriculum Director, the Director of Bilingual Education, the Director of the Teacher Corps Project and the Principal of Fairview Middle School, the project will be thoroughly explained to the Middle School staff.
2. A group of from ten to 20 volunteer teachers will be sought to participate in the project as collaborators in both the research and staff development aspects of the project.
3. A series of ethnographic observations will take place by a team of trained observers. Observers will study the nature of inter-ethnic relations in the day-to-day life of children and teachers in classrooms, cafeteria, corridors, and so on.
4. Aspects of the formal multicultural curriculum (for example, textbooks, pamphlets, films, curriculum guides) will be analyzed in terms of factors such as accuracy, bias, and stereotyping.
5. A series of open-ended interviews will be conducted with selected teachers and students to determine their views of both the formal and informal aspects of multicultural education and interethnic relations in Fairview Middle School.
6. A series of follow up, structured interviews with selected teachers and students to seek more detailed information about problems and issues revealed in the open-ended interviewing discussed in #5 above will be conducted.
7. Data from *all* sources will be categorized, organized, and summarized—then *shared* with the volunteer, participant teachers.
8. Planning for improvement in both formal and informal aspects of multicultural education will be based on insights revealed through the various procedures described above. Participant teachers, research team

---

*"Fairview" is of course a fictitious name. It is used to protect the confidentiality of project participants.

members, teacher corps representatives, and others will participate in the design of a suitable staff development program that will build on the strengths revealed in our various analyses and also attempt to deal with whatever weaknesses were revealed.

I have tried to be fair in pointing out the domains of qualitative and quantitative research and in describing some of the essential differences between the two approaches. Given my obvious enthusiasm for what I perceive to be an enormously helpful yet underused set of tools for the better understanding of and improving of education, the tone of the paper has tended to be extremely positive vis-a-vis qualitative methods. It is time now to examine some of the limitations of these approaches. Qualitative research offers some exciting new dimensions to the field of educational research. It is not a panacea or miracle cure for all of the ills that affect us.

For example:

1. Preconceptions, provincialism, prejudice, and other factors can affect one's observations, distort one's findings. Sometimes one sees what one wishes to see. This is particularly so when, for example, white middle class observers are studying problems in a largely black school, or when the observer team does not include women (or men if, for example, one were studying conflict in a girl's juvenile detention home). Similarly, the preceptions of the handicapped, elderly, and other groups might be absolutely vital if genuine insight were to be gained about conditions in nursing homes or other, similar institutions. All qualitative researchers recognize that while it is possible to limit observer bias, it is not possible to eliminate it. The results of such research inevitably consist of both what is out there and what is in the observer.

2. Given the acceptance of the infinite complexity and subtlety of given events, replication is almost impossible for the qualitative researcher. A study of the spontaneous play of a class of kindergarten children simply cannot be replicated. The number of variables is enormous, and each "whole" exists by itself, with all of its nuances. Similar studies can of course be done, but exact replication is not possible.

3. Observers and/or interviewers, no matter how skilled, cannot record everything that they experience. One cannot observe completely; one will never know all there is to know about social interactions taking place, let us say, in a school cafeteria. Usually, selected segments of reality are studied over long periods of time, thus giving the researcher a significant sampling of reality, but never all of it.

4. Since replication is difficult, generalizability is equally so. Rist's (1973) three-year study of a ghetto elementary school class in St. Louis is not representative of all other urban classrooms. It was not

selected at random, it does not represent some broader "population." If a large number of similar studies were conducted, or if the existing literature included much related data, and if that data showed similar results, Rist's study would then add to the strength of this body of work and one might feel comfortable generalizing about such situations. Nevertheless, most qualitative research consists of studies of single cases in limited settings and qualitative researchers are constantly faced with the problem of relating their "micro" studies to the "macro culture" at large.

5. Similarly, qualitative researchers must constantly make arbitrary (though informed) choices about their sources of data; that is, which classrooms should we observe? Which teachers should we interview? Which homes should we visit? There is of course, no guarantee that these choices will always be made wisely.

6. Finally, we must recognize the difficulty of doing field work in public school settings. It is most unusual for a researcher to be a "participant" as was, for example, Jonathan Kozol when he studied the Boston Public Schools while employed there as a teacher. In most cases, the observer is neither a teacher nor a student. Conversely, it is not always possible to behave in completely normal and natural ways as a participant. Phillips (1982) in her study of law schools, *became* a law student. What she did was not out of commitment to the law, but rather out of her curiosity about certain aspects of legal education. Thus, her role as participant-observer was limited. In addition, subjects in school settings may behave differently when an outsider is present, thus masking their true behavior.

Forms of Qualitative Research

Most of us are probably more familiar than we think with the variety of ways in which qualitative researchers work. While the term "ethnography," that is, the traditional participant-observer approach of many anthropologists, seems to come most quickly to mind when one hears the term "qualitative research," practitioners use a number of techniques that do not necessarily fit the classic, ethnographic mode.

Carl Bernstein and Robert Woodward, the authors of *All the President's Men* (1974) employed qualitative research techniques as they sought data from "key informants" involved in the Watergate scandal. So were the investigative reporters who doubted the accuracy of official reports issued during the Vietnam war and so began to conduct intensive interviews with the participants and to observe events on the front with their own eyes. The results of their work were also a form of qualitative research.

The classic, in depth, interviews of children conducted by Jean Piaget and his staff in Geneva as well as Robert Coles (1967) brilliant studies of life among America's neglected children are also examples of qualitative research that do not fit the classic, ethnographic mode.

In addition, one might argue that a novel such as John Updike's most recent work, *Rabbit is Rich* (1981) is not so much a book about one man, Harry Angstrom, as it is a book about all of us who lived through the 1960s and 70s. Surely, Updike clarifies the issues, movements, forces, and attitudes that influenced American behavior during those times. Updike and other artists like him work on a grand scale, illuminating the general through indepth "studies" of people who, though fictionalized, are nevertheless representative of reality. If they were not, the novels in question would not ring true and would be quickly rejected. Instead, most of us recognize at once the reality of the people, times, and places portrayed and often come away from such encounters with a better understanding of ourselves and of our times.

In any case, I choose to use the term "qualitative research" broadly in this chapter. The term suggests to me a wide range of techniques that, if used appropriately, can only increase our ability to study ourselves, our interactions with others, and our institutions.

Rather than use some general, abstract categorization scheme to describe the modes of qualitative research, I think it would be more useful to simply list and briefly describe some of the methods used in a series of sample studies that serve to illustrate the range of approaches used by qualitative researchers. I will not attempt to report the results of these studies but rather will highlight some of the unique methods used by each researcher. Since these descriptions will be incomplete and taken out of context, it is important to remember some of the characteristics that affect all qualitative research; that is, we must keep some of the qualitative researcher's ground rules in mind as we look at segments of isolated studies.

For example, we must remind ourselves that all qualitative research studies tend to evolve, and are constantly reconceptualized; that "instruments" emerge from careful evaluation of preliminary data gathered in the pilot stages of such studies; that situations or people studied should not be altered or changed while the study is under way, and that the most significant "instrument" is always the investigator, since evolving decisions about hypotheses, samples, instruments, and so on, will also depend on the quality of his or her thinking.

Having said all of that, what sorts of techniques do qualitative researchers use? What forms do their studies take?

Item

David Owen (1981) wanted to experience high school again from the perspective of an adult, and compare his experience as a high school student a decade ago with the way high schools function now as social institutions. A youthful 25, he returned to high school as a participant observer, attending classes, taking part in extracurricular activities, attending parties.

Item

Ray Rist (1978) studied the experiences of black children attending a given school during the first year of its integration. He observed the process from the moment the first black child stepped off the bus. He wanted to find out what would actually happen to the children, and reports their reactions as well as those of teachers, parents, and principal.

Item

Harry Wolcott (1973) was curious about the ways in which the principal of an "ordinary" suburban elementary school goes about his or her work, hour by hour, day by day. He thus "followed" his subject (a male) as he carried out his work as principal for a two-year period. Data was also gathered from those who customarily interact with the principal—teachers, other staff members, pupils, parents—but the focus of the study is clearly on one man—the principal.

Item

Heva Varenne (1982) was interested in the nature of social interaction among various groups or cliques in an American high school. While extensive interviews and observations were conducted, Varenne made particular use of the techniques qualitative researchers have come to call "proxemics"; that is, the study of the cultural use of space and how it can affect human interaction. He studied the formal and, more important, informal social functions of spaces such as bathrooms, stairway landings, specific tables in the cafeteria, seldom occupied offices, "back stage" in the auditorium.

Item

Kathleen Wilcox (1978) was curious about the role different kinds of schools play in socializing children for the world of work. Thus, she studied two classes in two different elementary schools. The first school was located in a largely working-class neighborhood, the second in a professional, executive-level neighborhood. The focus of her study was a comparison between the ways in which children are socialized for adult work roles by teachers in two different schools. Thus, through intensive classroom observation, she conducted a "controlled comparison" of children and teachers at work in two different environments.

Item

Frederick Erickson and Gerald Mohatt (1982) were interested in the similarities and differences in the cultural organization of social relationships in two classrooms of culturally similar children who were taught by teachers whose cultural backgrounds differed. Specifically, they studied children in an Odawa Indian Reserve in nothern Ontario, Canada. They wanted to know how white and Indian teachers exercised their authority over their students. In order to do so, they videotaped 18 hours of activity in the two classrooms, and used these tapes as a major source of data.

Item

Frederick Mosteller (Webb and others, 1966) was concerned about the need for new reference books in university libraries. In order to obtain data uncontaminated by the perceptions and opinions of librarians, students, and others, he designed a study of the actual, physical use of certain reference books. For example, he measured the wear and tear on separate sections by noting dirty edges of pages used as markers, the frequency of dirt smudges, fingermarkings, and underlinings.

Item

The "oral histories" collected by Eliot Wigginton (1972) and his students in the now famous *Foxfire* volumes are also examples of qualitative research in action. Wigginton's students interviewed, observed, taped, and photographed the life ways of elderly individuals living in their rural Georgia community in order to preserve the skills and traditions of that community. They recorded hunting tales, ghost stories, recipes, "natural" methods of healing, building, planting, and harvesting techniques. In short, they wrote oral histories of individuals whose stories could only be obtained in that way, since written documents were nonexistent.

Item

Kay Doost (1979) made use of the magnificent collection of student documents stored in the Prospect Archives at the Prospect School in Bennington, Vermont, to study aspects of the development of a single child's thinking over a period of eight years. She examined samples of the child's writing, painting, drawing, work with clay, number work, participation in classroom activities, friendship patterns, and so on.

Item

Schultz and Harkness (undated) were interested in the social contexts in which children spoke English and Spanish in bilingual educational programs. They put a cassette tape recorder in a child's backpack and had each Spanish-speaking child in a bilingual classroom wear it for one half hour, thus recording the child's own natural speech.

Item

Chris Stevenson (1979) was interested in the nature of the transition of 25 adolescents (ages 14-19) from a child-centered elementary school to a variety of types of conventional, traditional, secondary schools. Each student was interviewed at considerable depth in order to arrive at what he calls the "essence" of their values and beliefs concerning the nature of their elementary schooling, secondary schooling, and the transition itself.

Item

Spindler and Spindler (1951) studied the day-to-day professional life of a young fifth grade teacher. Their concerns focused on the self-perceptions of the teacher as teacher, the perceptions of his supervisors and the perceptions of his students. In order to do so, the Spindlers used projective techniques drawn from the discipline of psychology; rating scales, questionnaires and sociograms from sociology; and interviewing and observation techniques drawn from the conventional methods of the anthropologist.

Item

Judith Hanna (1982) conducted a year-long study of a desegregated "magnet" elementary school. She focused her study on various forms of aggression among black and white children. After a series of observations she decided she needed additional data from a representative sample of students. She designed a set of interview questions, then interviewed 120 students in a random sample stratified on the basis of sex, race, and grade.

In summary, qualitative researchers participate and observe, or simply observe; they do concentrated studies of single individuals and studies of groups; they interview, use field notes, audio and videotaped data, film, personal and official documents, photographs, various forms of unobtrusive data as well as quantifiable data. They study the uses of physical space, and they analyze the content of books and magazines. They sometimes use sampling techniques, occasionally compare one group with another, and often combine the methodologies of qualitative and quantitative research. Their studies may last from a few months to five or more years. Their goal remains, however, as it always has been: to observe and study human activity in its natural settings. It should be clear that qualitative researchers must gather vast amounts of data in their work—and that the task of making sense of it all is difficult and time consuming.

The Product of Qualitative Research

So far I have discussed qualitative research in education largely in methodological terms. While I have illustrated consistently with examples drawn from education and child development, I have not dwelt on the substantive contributions of any of my illustrative studies. At this point, I would like to change the emphasis of the chapter from process to product. That is, given the unique methodological contributions of qualitative research, what has such research revealed that may be truly helpful to the classroom teacher, curriculum worker, school administrator, or teacher educator? What are some of the more significant studies of the past ten or 20 years, and what insights and understandings do they reveal?

Obviously, the studies I choose may not be those that others, given a similar assignment, would select. They reflect some of my own interests and biases. The purpose of this section is not, however, to provide a thorough listing and synthesis of the contributions of qualitative research to the field of education. Rather, it is to highlight a few studies that have indeed added to our understanding of the process of education so that the reader will come to better appreciate the present value and potential of qualitative research in education.

- *Fifteen-Thousand Hours,* Michael Rutter, Barbara Nauhn, Peter Mortimer, and Jeanette Ousten (1979.)

  Subtitled, "Secondary Schools and Their Affects on Children," Rutter and his colleagues studied 12 secondary schools in London's inner-city over a three-year period. Their basic research question was, "can a good school help its students overcome the adverse effects of economic disability and family adversity?" Since the investigators were interested in both school processes and products, they used techniques drawn from both qualitative and quantitative methodologies. Nevertheless, considerable use was made of classroom, playground, and other observations as well as open and structured interviews with students and staff. Their fundamental conclusions were that:

1. Secondary schools in London do differ markedly in the behavior and attainment of pupils despite similarities of socioeconomic, racial, intellectual, and other factors among their pupils.

2. Outcome differences were associated with factors such as degree of academic emphasis, use of praise rather than severe punishment, high expectations of teachers about children's work and behavior, positive behavior modeling on the part of teachers, immediate and direct feedback in terms of praise and approval, development of schoolwide values and norms of behavior, staff concern for individual pupil needs, teacher and pupils working together in shared

activities toward common goals, and allowing children to hold positions of responsibility in the day-to-day functioning of the school.

Fundamentally, *Fifteen-Thousand Hours* suggests that schools can indeed make a difference in the lives of children, and that earlier, largely quantitative studies of the effects of schooling masked many significant, influential factors.

- *The Urban School: A Factory for Failure,* Ray Rist (1973)

Rist was concerned with the fundamental question, "How do teacher assumptions about children's academic and other abilities manifest themselves in the classroom?" In order to answer that question he observed a single class of black children and their black teachers in a St. Louis elementary school from their first day of kindergarten through the third grade. As early as the eighth day of kindergarten he noted academic segregation based on factors such as children's physical appearance, use of language, and family socioeconomic status.

Groups were labeled "slow" and "fast." "Fast" learners received more encouragement, attention, and privileges than did slow learners. Rist found that a number of shared assumptions dominated teachers' thinking: for example, "middle class students can learn, lower class cannot; white schools are good, black schools are bad; control was necessary, and freedom is anarchy; violence works, persuasion does not; teachers can save a few but will lose many; the school tries, the home will not."

Therefore it appears as if public education may perpetuate rather than break down social and economic inequalities found within the system.

- *School Teacher,* Dan Lortie (1975)

Lortie is concerned with what might be called, "The Culture of the Teacher." His basic research question is, "What forces influence teachers' self-concept, the images of their social purpose, and their understanding of their role as teachers?" Lortie conducted hundreds of interviews with classroom teachers and used a number of other data sources as well. Among other findings, Lortie concluded that American teachers are often lonely, neglected, isolated professionals. They receive little support, less constructive criticism, few rewards. Above all, they would seem to need more contact with other adults in their day-to-day classroom work as well as more opportunity for genuine interaction and dialogue and with their peers in the course of their professional lives.

- *A Phenomenological Study of Perceptions About Open Education Among Graduates of the Fayreweather Street School,* Christopher Stevenson (1979)

During the past decade, parents, teachers, principals, and others have frequently raised the question, "What happens to students who have attended child-centered, experience-based, open schools when they make the transition to more conventional schools?" Stevenson addressed himself to this and other related questions such as, "To what extent can the humanistic values of a particular open school (Fayreweather Street School in Cambridge, Massachusetts) become part of the lasting values of its students? What are the educational beliefs of students who have experienced programs with varied and sometimes contrary emphases?"

Stevenson, using in-depth interviews and phenomenological analysis as his basic methodological approaches, found that differences in teaching styles and curriculum between the schools caused little difficulty for students in transition. Instead, satisfactory adjustment was largely a matter of the nature of "interpersonal dynamics" in the new school; that is, the extent to which students were helped to feel secure, trusted and respected, to develop a sense of "belonging." Stevenson's subjects advocated schools where teachers accept students as they are and try to develop the unique abilities and talents of every person. They valued teaching and learning responsibility and involvement in life in the world outside the school. Most important, they have come to think that education, at its best, is deeply concerned with the students' individuality; all other considerations are secondary in their eyes.

- *A Child as Thinker: One Child's Thought as it Reflects Intentionality,* Kay Doost (1979)

In a most unusual study, Doost traced the development of a single child's thought in a classroom setting over an eight-year period from 1971-1978. The child was five when the study began. Doost's basic source of data was the documents produced by the child during this period, including painting, drawing, building, and other three-dimensional work, and writing. A fundamental question was, "Is there continuity and coherence in the meaning of the work produced over an eight-year period?" Doost described in great detail the themes, motifs, and mediums as they were presented in "Neil's" work. His motifs range from vehicles to structures, his themes from "battles" to "search."

Doost observed that "all of the motifs and themes that are present in the collection of work are introduced by the second year; no new themes or motifs emerge after 1972-73. His drawings, writing, and building reflect the *restatement* and *elaboration* of the same motifs and themes." While the form of Neil's work changes, the meaning is continuous. His work is rich and complex. It implies that "curriculum" does not have a single, objective content, but rather is full of meaning and of potential relationships that should be open for *individual* interpretation and exploration.

- *Life in Classrooms,* Philip Jackson (1968)

    Jackson was concerned with describing what most of us would call the quality of life in elementary school classrooms. His lengthy observations and interviews resulted in a description of a number of issues affecting teachers and their pupils. For example, children must learn to adapt to a number of situations that are new to them; that is, associating with large numbers of children, adjusting to new conceptions of power and authority, dealing with a lack of privacy, coping with a series of adult strangers who will have profound influence and control over them, judgment by peers and teachers, learning to wait for things (teacher's help, a drink, to be called upon). A child's "success" in school is then largely a function of his or her ability to "accommodate" or adjust to a series of new psychosocial demands. Perhaps most important, children appear to accept these changes with quiet resignation; like prison, one must do one's time until the day of release.

Qualitative research does have something to tell us. Its insights are not limited to descriptions of esoteric, isolated "simple" societies. On the contrary, scholars such as Rist, Jackson, and Lortie, as well as dozens of others whose work was not included here, have addressed themselves to educational questions that, while complex, subtle, and difficult, are often among the most important questions facing educational practitioners.

Kathleen Wilcox's (1982) perceptive description of the application of qualitative research to the study of schooling includes a number of conclusions that will serve well as a summary to this section. Among those that seem most significant and relevant to the research I have described in this section are the following:

1. American elementary and secondary schools serve largely as instruments of cultural transmission. Despite the dreams and aspirations of those who view schools as agents of social change, schools do not appear to perform this function. Instead, they socialize children in the life-ways, values, attitudes, and ideals of the culture as it is, rather than as it "ought" to be. The schools are essentially instruments of the wider society.

2. Schools are a powerful influence on the lives of children; they are "effective"; they do make a difference. The effects of schooling, however, are as indicated in #1 above, largely to socialize children to take their places in the society as it exists.

3. Many attempts at "reform" in schooling have been more superficial than substantive. In-depth, longitudinal analysis reveals again and again that schools remain largely authoritarian, controlling, routinized, regimented, competitive, time-dominated institutions

in which individuality is largely suppressed. This again, does not so much reflect a conscious effort on the part of educators to shape schools in this image; rather schools function as elements of the broader society.

4. Schools also serve to perpetuate the existing social-economic hierarchy of society as a whole. That is, not only do they reflect the values and traditions of society in a larger sense, they also serve to teach students where they belong in that heirarchy, and they appear to do this very efficiently.

5. Many qualitative researchers have focused their work on the problems caused by the conflict of cultures within schools and classrooms. Their work continues to suggest that learning improves when teaching methods, materials, and styles incorporate elements of the learner's culture.

6. Qualitative research demonstrates over and over again that education is an exceedingly complex phenomenon; that there are many "curricula" in the school or classroom, some of them explicit, others implicit or hidden; that there are indeed, "educations" rather than education.

A few years ago, I put together, what was for me at least, a fascinating collection of essays. The material was eventually published in the *Phi Delta Kappan* (1980) under the title, "What We Don't Know About Education." The series was an attempt to identify some of the gnawing questions that still prevent us from providing children with a genuinely effective education. The series included pieces by John Goodlad, Courtney Cazden, Elliot Eisner, Paul Brandwein, Maynard Reynolds, John Downing, Vincent Glennon, Joseph Renzulli, Barry McPherson, and myself.

Rereading the series today, I am struck with the number of questions raised by each contributor that seem to call for more qualitative, more naturalistic forms of research. In my section on the social studies, for example, I raised questions like these:

We know little about the effects of certain aspects of the school environment on the social and political attitudes of children and youth. How does one begin to think about oneself and about others when physically disabled children become a part of the school milieu, when a new program for gifted children is begun, when the reward and punishment systems are changed, when new dress codes are established? How do disabled and gifted children think of themselves and of others when such programs are begun? What are the effects of academic standards (such as competency tests) for promotion and high school graduation on student self-concept and attitude toward others?

John Goodlad's piece was entitled "What We Don't Know About Schooling" and was more general in nature than was mine or any of the others. I have chosen, therefore to reproduce the most significant of Goodlad's questions, not only as examples of areas of vital concern to children, teachers, parents, and others but also examples of questions that virtually demand qualitative research procedures. Goodlad asked:

1. What do 5-and 6-year-olds think about as they approach and enter "school" for the first time? I clearly remember that first day of school, with children converging from all directions (we walked to school in those days), suddenly panicking and running home. Was it the number of others? Was it sudden realization of freedoms about to be lost? Was it fear of the unknown? What meanings do young children derive from their first few days in school? How do these meanings influence what follows?

2. What meanings are children deriving from the succession of words, intonations, and expressions surrounding them in classrooms? What the teacher thinks is "perfectly clear" is—perhaps more often than not—meaningless or interpreted differently by most students. It was years after their younger son stood ankle-deep in the foam peering into the waves, before Garp and Helen realized Walt's interpretation of the warning, "The under*tow* is bad today." Walt had been dreading a giant *toad*, lurking offshore, waiting to suck him under and drag him out to sea. For many children, much of school may be very much akin to Walt's fear, at the water's edge, of the undertoad.

3. What about the cumulative impact of 13 years of schooling? Do they add up to those behaviors of critical thinking, appreciation of others' views, compassion, independent work habits, sound judgment, and the like extolled in the aims of education? or does schooling tend more to instill those values of conforming, seeking right answers, and following rules or instructions that so many segments of society also value?

   Such a question should remind us that we have precious little knowledge of the total array of subject matter, instruction, and activities encountered during the 13-year trip through school, to say nothing of students' perceptions of these. The dominant rhetoric addressed to schools throughout the 1970s has been to get back to the basics. Such data as we have suggest that we have been back there for some time, if the basics mean the three Rs.

4. Some school reformers commend tracking for handling pupil diversity and correcting low achievement in schools. But how many schools already are tracked and in what ways? Should we track? Evidence of the impact of tracking on student achievement is so mixed that one wonders whether it is worth the effort to track. But how about the impact on students' self-concepts and desire to learn? Do teachers in tracked classes provide more or less for individual

differences than when they think their classes are more heterogeneous?

5. There are many areas of schooling about which we make assumptions that may not accurately reflect much of what goes on in any
given school. For example, in planning programs of general or
liberal education, educators and others almost always assign differ-
ing attributes to the major domains of knowing. The social sciences
presumably promote critical inquiry regarding forms of government, right of citizens, economic orders, and the like. The
humanities teach appreciation for literary style, how to consider
issues of right and wrong, the meaning of truth, etc. The arts not
only cultivate our aesthetic sensibilities but also promote individual
creativity. Mathematics and the physical sciences develop both appreciation for and skill in ordered thinking, as well as a basic understanding of what humankind has learned about this planet and the
universe.

Are these the understandings, appreciations, and processes developed in schools? I have observed no more creative expression in
music classes than in others. Social studies teachers appear to me to
be as consumed with instilling facts as are other teachers. Reading
and answering questions orally or in writing appear to characterize
both science and social studies more than do problem solving and
high-level cognitive processes. Do fact-oriented examinations in
literature classes turn students' attention away from what Shake-
speare has to teach us about human beings?

6. It has been said that the prime goal of schools should be to teach
students how to learn. Consequently, it seems to me that children
and youth should be exploring a variety of ways of knowing, not
necessarily with one teacher or several teachers stressing the same
approach but with different teachers in a variety of learning settings.
Are they? Does a single way of approaching school tasks begin to
dominate early, or are several alternatives maintained and refined
for most of precollegiate schooling?

The turbulent 60s acted as a catalyst, a stimulant to our interest in
qualitative research in education. We wanted to know what was really
happening to black and other minority children in their schools. Since
that time, interest and activity have grown steadily. Murray Wax's studies
of desegregated schools were supported by the National Institute of
Education as were the qualitative studies of the "Experimental Schools
Project." The National Science Foundation has funded similar studies,
and the AERA now encourages the submission of papers describing
qualitative studies for reading at its annual and regional meetings.

Although change is coming slowly (some say with glacier-like speed)
doctoral research at schools and colleges of education is no longer nar-

rowly quantitative in nature. A number of the studies described in this chapter were completed by doctoral students at the University of Connecticut, and the changes that have occurred here are taking place at other universities as well.

Most important, the strident conflict between qualitative and quantitative researchers has softened. People are talking to each other, listening to each other, accepting the need and desirability of both approaches, and recognizing that if we are to answer questions as fundamental as "do schools educate?" we shall have to make intelligent and sensitive use of all the tools at our disposal.

References

Bernstein, C. and Woodward, R. *All the President's Men*. New York: Simon and Schuster, 1974.

Bodgan, R. and Biklen, S. *Quantitative Research for Education*. Boston: Allyn and Bacon, Inc., 1982.

Coles, R. *Children of Crisis*. Boston: Little, Brown, Inc., 1967.

Davis, C.; Back, K.; and MacLean, K. *Oral History*. Chicago: American Library Association, 1977.

Doost, K. "A Child as Thinker: One Child's Thought As It Reflects Intentionality." Unpublished Doctoral dissertation, University of Connecticut, Storrs, 1979.

Eisner, E. "On the Difference Between Scientific and Artistic Approaches to Qualitative Research." Paper presented at the AERA Annual Convention, Boston, April 1, 1980.

Erickson, F., and Mohatt, G. "Cultural Organization of Participation Structures in the Classrooms of Indian Students." In *Doing the Ethnography of Schooling*. New York: Holt, Rinehart, and Winston, 1982.

Everhart, R. "Problems of Doing Fieldwork in Educational Evaluation." *Human Organization* 34, 2 (Summer 1975), p. 208.

Goodlad, J. "What We Don't Know About Schooling." *Phi Delta Kappan* 61 (May 1980): 591-592.

Manna, J. "Public School Policy and the Children's World." In *Doing the Ethnography of Schooling*. New York: Holt, Rinehart, and Winston, 1982.

Jackson, P. *Life in the Classrooms*. New York: Holt, Rinehart, and Winston, 1968.

Kesey, Ken. *One Flew Over the Cuckoo's Nest*. New York: Penguin, 1976.

Lortie, Dan. *School Teacher: A Sociology Study*. Chicago: University of Chicago Press, 1975.

Owen, D. *High School: Undercover with the Class of '80*. New York: Viking Press, 1981.

Phillips, S. V. "The Language Socialization of Lawyers: Acquiring the 'Cant.' " In *Doing the Ethnography of Schooling*. Edited by G. Spindler. New York: Holt, Rinehart, and Winston, 1982.

Rist, R. "Ethnographic Techniques and the Study of the Urban School." *Urban Education* 10, 1 (April 1975).

Rist, R. *The Invisible Children*. Cambridge: Harvard University Press, 1978.

Rist, R. *The Urban School: A Factory for Failure*. Cambridge: MIT Press, 1973.

Rist, R. Speech delivered at the University of Connecticut, April 1980.

Rogers, V. and others. "What We Don't Know About Education: A Symposium." *Phi Delta Kappan* 61 (May 1980): 591-606.

Rogers, V. "What We Don't Know About the Social Studies." *Phi Delta Kappan* 61 (May 1980): 596.

Rosenthal, R. and Jacobson, L. *Pygmalian in the Classroom*. New York: Holt, Rinehart, and Winston, 1968.

Rutter, M. and others. *Fifteen-Thousand Hours*. Cambridge: Harvard University Press, 1979.

Schultz, J. and Harkness, A. "Language Use in the Bilingual Classrooms." Harvard Graduate School of Education (unpublished paper).

Spindler, G. and Spindler, L. "Roger Harker and Schonhausen: From Familiar to Strange and Back Again." In *Doing the Ethnography of Schooling*. Edited by G. Spindler. New York: Holt, Rinehart, and Winston, 1982.

Stevenson, C. "A Phenomenological Study of Perceptions about Open Education Among Graduates of the Fayrweather Street School." Unpublished Doctoral dissertation, University of Connecticut, Storrs, 1979.

Updike, John. *Rabbit is Rich*. New York: Knopf, 1981.

Varenne, H. "Jocks and Freaks: The Symbolic Structure of the Expression of Social Interaction Among American Senior High School Students." In *Doing the Ethnography of Schooling*. Edited by G. Spindler. New York: Holt, Rinehart, and Winston, 1982.

Webb, E.; Campbell, D.; Schuartz, R.; and Sechrest, L. *Unobtrusive Measures*. Chicago: Rand McNally and Co., 1966, p. 9.

Wilcox, K. "Ethnography As a Methodology and Its Implications to the Study of Schooling." In *Doing the Ethnography of Schooling*. Edited by G. Spindler. New York: Holt, Rinehart, and Winston, 1982.

Wilcox, K. *Schooling and Socialization for Work Roles: A Structural Inquiry into Cultural Transmission in an Urban Community*. Doctoral dissertation, Harvard University, Cambridge, 1978.

Wigginton, E. *Foxfire*. New York: Anchor Books/Doubleday, 1972.

Wolcott, H. *The Man in the Principal's Office*. New York: Holt, Rinehart, and Winston, 1973.

A Response to Rogers

WILLIAM D. CORBETT

If you don't know where you are going, any road will get you there.

The Talmud

The direction of education should be based on the proven successes of the past and present. Identification of proven success, however, is not as clear cut as it would appear to be because of the complexity of the educational process and the diversity of the constituencies we serve. It is from the multitude of components that contribute to good education and the variety of efforts made by innovators that we expect researchers to assist us in mapping our course.

Since educational research affects the lives of practitioners as well as the students served, it is valuable to have lucid description of the two major types of research by a person who is a recognized leader in the field. Vincent Rogers has depicted the strengths and weaknesses of both quantitative and qualitative research and offered cogent examples of each technique. The chapter should be excerpted from ASCD's Yearbook and placed on the required reading list of those who are preparing for teaching and administrative careers. Current practitioners should also read the chapter with care.

Those of us who are public or private school practitioners have been both beneficiaries of sound research and victims of poor research. The very word "research" tends to lend authority to headlines, however outrageous, to meet the public's appetite for news:

Class Size a Factor in Reading Success
Class Size Not Important in Educational Achievement
Open Education Proves Successful in Affective Education
Research Shows Traditional Approaches Best for Basics
Reading Scores Improving
Study Shows High School Graduates Are Illiterate

Headlines like these confuse the public and frustrate educators. They indeed embarrass serious researchers.

Much of the questionable research that gains wide attention is "so called" hard data research. It is often dependent upon the results and analysis of multiple choice, fill-in, machine-scored tests. Deductions drawn from this type of research are statistical with seldom a careful look at the instruments used, not to mention the effects these instruments

William D. Corbett is Principal, James Russell Lowell School, Watertown Public Schools, Watertown, Massachusetts.

have on the educational process. The more the multiple choice, fill-in instruments are used to draw educational conclusions, the more the emphasis is placed on them at all levels. Education, at least in the United States, is correspondingly diminished to serve these evaluation procedures.

Qualitative research is much more expensive and requires unusual sensitivity and experience in both process and analysis.

Let it be said that meaningful educational research of all kinds is costly and needs talented and perceptive directorship. Let it also be said that a great disservice to both education in general and to conscientious researchers in particular is done by the several who engage in shallow research.

Perhaps it is time for serious researches like Vincent Rogers, John Goodlad, and others to call for a permanent blue-ribbon research monitoring committee to rank educational research according to its integrity. The committee would be ready to analyze and answer authoritatively the shoddy pieces of research that appear periodically in the news media. In this manner the word "research" would reacquire the respect it deserves and those affected by research would give it the attention necessary to chart the direction of education.

The Price of Everything, the Value of Nothing

ANNE RONEY

In his essay, Vincent Rogers defends qualitative research. Perhaps his need to do so points more to certain predilections in ourselves than to deficiencies in qualitative methods. We are as entranced by numbers as crows are by shiny objects. How do we explain this attraction? Our delight with numbers probably goes back to the very moment when, as young children, we first counted six cookies on a plate or 23 cows alongside the highway or 15 days until Christmas. What precision and economy of expression! What power it was to realize that an unknown— that pile of cookies—could be counted and thus controlled, manipulated to divide the pile or to win the game or to sequence time itself. So we began to attack unknowns with numbers, using ever more sophisticated calculations. In a society with competing traditions, populated by people from many nations, and striving to move forward, we encountered many unknowns or, at least, questions for which previous answers no longer sufficed. This faith in the quantitative was reinforced on every hand as our penchant for problem-solving bloomed into technology.

For some of us the faith occasionally dimmed. As a new teacher, I was dismayed when the librarian stopped at my door, form in hand, and inquired as to my circulation total for the month. I had not kept any circulation figures, I told her, searching about in my mind for a way to construct a number. I stammered something about having 32 students and having been to the library two or three times. She said, "Oh, that's all right. I'll just put down '150' for you. That's close enough." She went on her way. With her went my incorrect number, wafting its way through the bureaucratic channels, making wrong every other number it touched. Realizing how often such estimates are entered on forms, I became skeptical about numbers. They are very nearly all ball-park figures, used more for their economy of expression than for their precision.

Of course researchers are not as naive about the precision of numbers as I was. They have devised all sorts of safeguards and hedges: the standard error of measurement, Type I and Type II errors, levels of significance, degrees of freedom, random selection, and so on. Each safeguard fulfills a necessary function and in so doing, makes the resultant numbers more authoritative than ever. But, transformed in analysis, the original bit of data has been so far removed from its origin as to be unrecognizable even to its mother.

Anne Roney is Elementary Supervisor, Department of Public Instruction, Knox County, Knoxville, Tennessee.

In addition to the seduction of numbers, we must contend with both a predilection for method and the unwise application of quantitative designs. Apparently, pioneer educational researchers came from agriculture and psychology and were constantly glancing with envy at the laboratory experiments of chemists and physicists. Using these models in education, we have applied spelling treatments to classroom groups as if we were applying fertilizers to plots of corn; and we have counted the responses of students in class discussions as if they were rats in a maze. We have thus removed the variables under study from their setting—the school or the social group, such removal being a condition of the quantitative design.

Researchers have not set out to isolate their problems from context. Ideally, each problem worthy of inquiry is derived from both a situation and a review of related research and literature. But in doctoral dissertations, Chapter Twos are often deadly; and the lines of thought connecting them to problem, methodology, and findings are likely to be less than clear and direct. In other research reports, the space devoted to the review of the literature and the rationale for the study is usually much less than the space given to metholodogy. Preoccupied with design rather than utility, the researcher is compelled to explicate his/her mathematics for the benefit of other researchers; that is, to share the recipe whether or not the pudding is worth eating. Quantitative designs *are* often precise and elegant. We get caught up in their tight beauty in the same way that we admire an architect's elevation drawings, whose delineated grace may obscure the clumsiness of the resulting structure. It is lack of attention to context and overemphasis on the means instead of emphasis on the ends that make the use of research discouraging to the practitioner.

Even if early educational researchers had derived their methods from sociology, anthropology, and history, we probably could not have escaped the American romance with quantitative methods. And would we want to? Oh, no. As Rogers pointed out, quantitative methods are effective and useful. The power of numbers is particularly persuasive, as I found on a winter morning when the heater in a portable classroom had been turned off the night before. The teacher had complained to me (her principal) about the cold, but it was only when she sent a note saying "It is 42° in here" that I jumped up and arranged for her class to occupy the cafeteria. Numbers give substance and specificity to description; they support or fail to support our judgments and our hunches; they enable us to evaluate reported information. Indeed, a school leader would be lost without his/her quantitative litany: How soon? How many? How often? Out of how many chances? At what cost?

Quantitative approaches stem from our logical and analytical ways of knowing. What they do not give us is the context, the setting, the framework of meaning that surrounds each problem and that would enable us to assimilate the findings and thereby enlighten our work.

Qualitative methods permit the scrutiny and analysis of individual variables while preserving the setting under study. The reports of qualitative research are written as narratives, which have the advantage of accessibility of meaning to the reader, being full of concrete references and identifiable characters. If we deal only with quantitative data, like Oscar Wilde's cynic, we know "the price of everything and the value of nothing." Numbers cannot tell the whole story. It is qualitative information that arises from and addresses the holistic and intuitive ways of knowing that the true scientist does not fear.

References

Mead, Margaret. *Coming of Age in Samoa.* Laurel Edition. New York: Dell Publishing Company, 1961.
Wilde, Oscar. *Complete Works of Oscar Wilde.* London: Collins, 1981, p. 418.

6 Democracy in Evaluation: The Evolution of an Art-Science in Context

ASA G. HILLIARD, III

*T*o some extent, the practice of systematic evaluation in education and the practice of teaching, administration, and policymaking have developed in isolation from each other. For the most part, official evaluators have been psychologists or educators whose prime orientation has been toward developing competence in statistics and formal research designs. Few, if any, notable evaluators are also recognized as top educational leaders or teachers. An exception to this rule would be B. F. Skinner, who combines research, evaluation, and pedagogy into a valid and harmonic, if philosophically controversial, whole. His behavior modification approach is widespread in education. But, such an interrelationship between evaluation and instruction is rare. In many school districts, for example, the formal organizational structure effectively seals formal evaluators off from meaningful communication with instructional staff. But, even here there are notable exceptions, such as where criterion-referenced tests are created by the joint efforts of teachers and evaluation personnel, and where the lines of communication between them remain open.

Generally, teachers and educational leaders have a great deal of freedom to select and employ their methodologies, or even to employ no particular methodology at all. Educators are seldom called to be articulate

Asa G. Hilliard, III, is Fuller E. Callaway Professor of Urban Education, Georgia State University, Atlanta.

about their practices. Perhaps this is why it would be difficult, if not impossible, to develop a malpractice suit against an educator. To date, there is no equivalent in education to "standard procedures" in medical practice. I do not argue for or against this. I merely use this as an example to illustrate the common disconnection between evaluation, which is highly developed and systemized, and educational leadership and instruction, which is much less so at any general level. This means that precision testing cannot inform precision teaching. The popularly assumed connection between teaching and testing can be nothing more than imaginary. Teacher education curricula, to the extent that they share a common content, do not prepare teachers to make decisions based on data from standardized tests! It almost seems that evaluation is the science and that leadership and teaching are the art of education. This is not the case. The reason for this de facto conceptual segregation stems from a lack of agreement and a lack of clarity concerning the purposes of evaluation in schools. More will be said about this later.

Because of the tendency to operate with formal evaluation separated from leadership and teaching, it has been difficult to meaningfully integrate systematically developed evaluation data into important instructional decision-making processes. For example, many school districts report academic achievement results for students once a year as citywide grade-level averages. Sometimes the averages for each school in the district are given, yet such information does not provide much guidance for educational leaders or teachers. The following categories of information are left out of traditional school evaluation efforts:

1. What achievement *gains* do *individual* students make month by month or over the course of the academic year?
2. What are the *gains classroom by classroom?*
3. What are the *gains* according to the length of time students were enrolled in a given classroom? (This recognizes the problem of transiency.)
4. What are the *gains* related to *teacher turnover* in assignment?
5. What *empirical* information shows that academic achievement test content matches the content of the actual curriculum offered in the schools?
6. What *empirical* information enables school district leaders to compare the achievement of students to *external achievement standards,* such as nationally standardized achievement tests?
7. What specific provisions are made for educational decision makers (including teachers) to become familiar with the results of evaluation activity?

If test results aggregated at the individual school level, are generated only once a year, and come from tests that are not content-valid, then educational leaders and teachers are left with no alternative but to fall back on informal or unconscious processes.

Ideally, testing is far from the whole of evaluation. Yet, to say this is to present even greater problems. There is less shared thinking about the non-test parts of evaluation than there is about formal standardized testing. For example, socialization goals are stated but are seldom systematically evaluated and reported.

Vast energy and resources are expended on testing and on reporting test results. This enterprise seems to have face validity. That is, tests and test reports "look scientific" and "valuable" in themselves. Conversations about numbers or scores and their patterns are plentiful. For example, the rise or fall of Scholastic Aptitude Test (SAT) Scores alone is often sufficient to start long conversations about the *reasons* for the changes, but not about the *meaning* of the scores. Many who receive information about SAT scores are not familiar with the actual test content. How else can we explain the surprise of educators in California, for example, at declining SAT scores, when many of those same educators made the decisions about curriculum content, which seem largely responsible for the decline? Such decisions included less math and English requirements in the high school curriculum.

In evaluation, both art and science are useful to educators. The primary issue is not one of either art or science, it is also not one of either quantitative or qualitative data. The primary issue centers on the ultimate *utility* of any data and the nature of the purposes of the evaluation enterprise, which are tied to the nature of the education enterprise itself. If democracy in education is a goal, then democracy in evaluation should follow. It is in the context of democracy or its alternatives that the question of evaluation in education as an art-science is situated.

I believe there is a real crisis in educational evaluation. This crisis does not stem from a technical deficiency in information-processing systems, or even from the absence of fully developed, clinical observation-oriented systems of data gathering. The crisis stems from competing philosophies and theories of education, which cause choices to be made along a continuum of democracy to autocracy in education. All other discussions about evaluation are tied to this issue in one way or another.

Basic Assumption: Evaluation Can and Must Contribute to the Improvement of Instruction as Determined by the Quality of Student Achievement.

No matter what the philosophy, evaluation activity should be undertaken with the goal of learning how to guarantee a high quality of education for students. We may evaluate in order to describe what is going on. We may also evaluate in order to learn why things happen and to learn what must be done in order to intervene effectively for better results. In the process, many detours and dead ends are possible. For example, educators frequently become fascinated by evaluation procedures, to the extent that the procedures become ends within themselves. Educators may also become fascinated with popular teaching methods and techniques to the extent that these methods and techniques become ends in themselves, even if they cannot be shown to produce any particular quality of academic achievement in children.

Most formal data collection procedures focus on the *status* of children or the *status* of systems at a given time. Yet, it is information and perspectives on the *process* that will enable decision makers to become involved in more appropriate ways. It is not *that* School A received test scores "one grade level below the national average in arithmetic"; it is that the educators must know *why*.

It has not always been, and is not yet explicit, that the primary purpose of evaluation is the improvement of education. It was a major innovation at the national public policy study level (Holtzman, Heller, and Messick, 1982) that this precise goal was articulated. The consequences of accepting this simple assumption are enormous. With this acceptance, the entire character of the evaluation enterprise is forced to become dynamic and functional. To say that evaluation is dynamic and functional is to say that the information derived from the process is a prerequisite for the implementation of instruction and leadership for instruction. If evaluation in a given school system, usually testing, could be stopped without affecting classroom and school practices, we may conclude that evaluation activity is *pro-forma*. On the other hand, if the teaching-learning process is impeded due to the absence of formal evaluation data, we may conclude that evaluation activity is *essential*.

If present evaluation activity is directed toward the goal of improving student achievement, then there is not much evidence that the goal is being achieved as a consequence. In fact, some of the most dramatic successes in teaching and learning do not appear to be connected to traditional formal education at all (Boehm, 1979; Freire, 1973). More important perhaps is the fact that, until recently, successful educational programs or schools were not usually the subject of researcher or evaluator interest. It was the decade of the 1970s that saw widespread attention to the study of effective schools. In fact, much of the conventional wisdom, stemming in part from evaluation studies (Coleman, 1966; Jencks, 1972; Moesteller and Moynihan, 1972; Covant, 1959), was characterized by varying degrees of pessimism that schools could do much to "make a difference." Even where studies of school effectiveness support the hypothesis that schools make a difference, the indices of "success" tend to be a minimum criteria, such as basic-skills achievement.

Millions of dollars have been spent on school evaluation. However, the fruits of such efforts are not clearly evident or impressive. Theories, methodologies, and techniques become evermore complicated and proliferate almost exponentially. I hope the future holds surprises.

A comprehensive model of the assessment program is needed.

The separation between evaluators and educators mentioned earlier is often exacerbated by another level of fragmentation within the two categories. Evaluators are seldom utilized in a way that allows them to develop a comprehensive view of the entire educational process. Similarly, educators are seldom in a position to view the total educational effort comprehensively. But, such a comprehensive view is imperative in both cases.

The education setting may be thought of as *situated* in a larger ecosystem. The education setting itself is also an ecosystem. Appropriate evaluation must be designed with the whole in mind. Figure 1 illustrates a way of thinking about the scope of the formal testing and evaluation process as presently practiced in most educational systems.

Effective evaluation requires evaluators and users to be clear about the tasks they are performing in terms of the *purpose* for evaluation, the *type* of data-gathering procedures to be used, and the *audience* to which the results are to be directed.

It is a major and common source of confusion when the features of each of the three categories are mixed haphazardly. For example, for what audience is I.Q. data meaningful and necessary? Is a good (content-valid) test for academic achievement as beneficial as a meaningful predictor of student performance? Do the same achievement test results have meaning for all possible audiences?

The model of test types, audiences, and purposes may also be simultaneously applied to parts of the ecosystem. Systematic information is needed about the following:

1. Students
2. Teachers
3. Administrative leadership
4. Support service staff
5. Educational organization, facilities, and resources
6. External social system factors.

For example, is the acadmic achievement of teachers and administrators related to the level of academic achievement of students? What audience should receive information from an investigation of such a question? Why collect such information?

It should be clear from a review of the history of evaluation in schools that much more work has been done to develop procedures for examining student behavior than with any other category of school personnel. For example, although most school systems regularly evaluate their professional personnel, data from such evaluations are not normally aggregated, analyzed, and used to explain the achievement levels of students.

Figure 1. Scope of the Formal Testing and Evaluation Process.

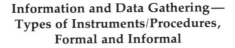

**Information and Data Gathering—
Types of Instruments/Procedures,
Formal and Informal**

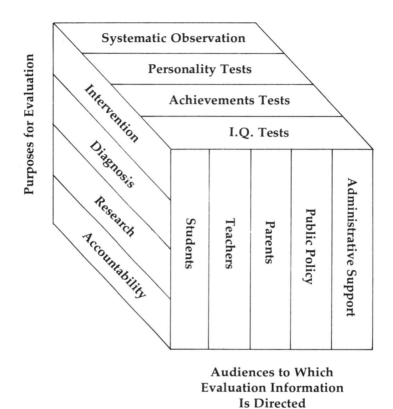

**Audiences to Which
Evaluation Information
Is Directed**

There are some exceptions; however, such data are extremely sensitive. Similarly, the broader social system within which the school is located receives little attention as a source of data to explain student achievement. Yet, all of these things are tied together in the real world. Student academic achievement results can be understood only in reference to a broader perspective on how the various parts of the whole system interact. For example, high and persistent levels of unemployment among parents of school children affect motivation, hope, nutrition, health, experiental opportunities, and many other factors.

Prerequisites for the Establishment of Educational Evaluation as an Art-Science

Four things are required if the art-science of educational evaluation is to reach its full potential:

1. A comprehensive model of the evaluation process, which reflects the complexity of the educational ecosystem, must be made explicit. When such a model is developed, it will be easy to see that some parts of the educational process receive disproportionate attention, while other parts of the process are not examined systematically at all. It is the balanced and comprehensive systematic examination of all parts of the educational process that will help us to understand it. I refer to this as "ecological" evaluation.

2. Explicit, articulated, and valid pedagogies must be available for application and for use. The evaluation process will make no sense whatsoever if pedogogical remedies for its deficiencies cannot be described. Without standard pedagogies, testing for classification or testing for the purpose of describing present levels of academic performance can be done; but testing for the improvement of instruction cannot. For example, it would be useless to collect data to show that reading achievement among students is low and then, on the basis of those data, take steps to change instructional practices unless *valid remedies* were available for educators to implement. Unfortunately, what exists on the pedagogical side is a veritable supermarket of potential remedies, some of which have little more value than patent medicine. Clearly, progress in evaluation is tied to progress in the development of valid teaching strategy.

3. Valid testing and assessment procedures must be available. It is not enough that testing and assessment procedures are reliable. It is not sufficient to establish certain types of validity for tests, such as face validity and predictive validity. What is required is "prescriptive" or "instructional" validity (Holtsman, Heller, and Messick, 1982). In other words, testing and assessment procedures must focus on educational interventions that can improve achievement outcomes for children.

4. Theoretical and philosophical clarity is essential. It is not enough to express commitment to democracy or to its alternatives (Hilliard, 1982). Confusion and disorder in professional practice are the consequences of the absence of a clear commitment to well-defined theoretical and philosophical principles.

Who Evaluates and Why

Educational evaluation in a democratic society must be based on a special view of the person and his or her relationship to others and to the environment. Each student has a unique environment that influences and that can be influenced by that student. The environment includes culture, social class, history, family, and political condition. Each person in an environment actively interacts with it in a way that transforms reality. The natural relationship between people and their environment is a reciprocal. Evaluation in education (which is based on recognizing and understanding active learners within a context in a reciprocal relationship between person and context) is evaluation that fits the real world and makes it possible for evaluation to serve democratic needs.

By a democratic philosophy of education, I refer to those assumptions, beliefs, and values that support the quest for equality of educational opportunity and that support viewing learners as subjects rather than objects in the educational process. Students are more than the passive recipients of canned knowledge. They are students to the precise degree to which they join in *the creation of knowledge.* Not all educators have such aspirations for students, especially the masses of students. The character of our evaluation efforts will definitely be shaped by our view of the aims of education for all students.

San Francisco's Project Literacy used the following motto: "For it is through action that words gain their power and meaning . . . and through critical words that action gains its clarity and effectiveness." This means that evaluation is a process that requires the meaningful and complete participation of all parties in the education process. It is not, and cannot be, a process that is managed by a few for the benefit of many.

Present practices in evaluation are often limited because evaluation tends to be:

- Ahistorical
- Acultural
- Acontextual
- Apedagogical.

History, culture, context, and pedagogy do exist as real influences on education, but educators must decide if they believe they are important in education. If not, they can be ignored, but, if they are important, then they cannot be ignored in teaching or in evaluation. It is a false representation of reality to ignore the historical, cultural antecedents to educational events, to ignore the social forces that impinge upon those events, and to fail to relate the event appropriately to the state of the art in pedagogy. Such an approach devalues the individual child in favor of a mythical average child. Such an approach also fails to recognize the place of the evaluator as a part of the teaching-learning process.

We learn from observing mothers and infants that teaching and learning is a natural process. During the first two years of their lives, children learn some of their most difficult tasks with no formal instruction. For example, children learn to speak their native language, a highly complex cognitive operation; yet they do this naturally, almost without apparent effort. This natural teaching-learning process can become distorted as a consequence of attempts conceptually or in practice to separate teaching from learning and/or to submerge the reciprocal nature of the process. For example, teachers establishing goals and teaching strategies in isolation from learners, who are unknown to the teachers at the time, will result in a distortion of the natural teaching-learning process. I call this a distortion, not because nothing will happen between teacher and learner, but because what will happen in such a case will be drastically reduced in terms of meaningful communication between teacher and learner. The resulting condition has been referred to as a monologue by the teacher and participation in the "culture of silence" by the learner (Freire, 1973).

Paulo Freire has worked on the problem of adult literacy in many parts of the world, and has done so with singular success. The principles indicated are rooted in a concept of democracy and extend to democratic pedogogy. He described the common denominator among many people who are illiterate and uneducated as follows:

> Gradually, as part of the "culture of silence," they come to view their lowly position not as a matter of culture (or man-made) but as a matter of nature (God-made or Fate). They come to assume the role of spectator viewing the vital processes of society as if they (the students) were on the outside looking in. Regarding their condition as natural, they grow more and more inactive, trusting primarily to fate and becoming dependent upon others for leadership and direction.

Perhaps with no segment of the human population have education problems seemed so intractable as with adults who have not learned such "basic skills" as literacy, numeracy, and how to be active effectively on their own behalf. Yet, it it precisely with such seemingly retarded and, in fact, dormant populations that some educators have been able to generate remarkable results. For example, if we take the work of Paulo Freire and his associates in Brazil, Africa, and America; the work of Allen and Lottie Marcus in their *English on Wheels* program in California; and the work of Septima Clark, originator of the Freedom Schools Literacy Program in the South, we will have three outstanding examples among many positive changes that have occurred rapidly.

For example, with Paulo Freire, non-reading adults in abject poverty have been taught to read their daily newspapers in 30 hours of literacy training (Brown, 1975). In the case of the Marcuses, migrant farm workers in California were taught to speak English fluently in a few months. In the case of Septima Clark, nearly 12 million illiterate African-Americans read well enough to pass the state literacy tests, which were established to keep them from voting. Material for reading instruction was not taken from primers in this case but from state constitutions.

An important common element in each of these three teaching approaches with adults was the democratic, pedagogical goal of "waking up the learner" as the precondition for educational success. What is meant by "waking them up," as expressed by Septima Clark, is allowing learners to see themselves as taking an active role in the design, execution, and evaluation of their educational activities.

In large bureaucratic systems, with the need to standardize for efficiency and with external demands for evaluation data, it is sometimes hard to remember that the active and critical participation of the learner in the education process is most typical of democratic education.

A democratic evaluation process is one that concerns itself with the active, critical initiative of the learner and not simply with the academic outcomes of the learning process as reflected in standardized achievement tests. The power of such an orientation can be illustrated by following the line of thinking that has been expressed in at least one alternate view of impediments to the teaching-learning process. Generally, impediments to learning are believed to be due to the absence of intellectual power in students. The educability concept so prevalent in education today is linked to this assumption. If the educability of students is a major factor in teaching, then the question of *who* evaluates and *how* evaluation will be done will take one direction. In all probability, the evaluation process is totally outside the learner and seeks little more than data for rough global classification. At least, this is what we observe in present evaluation processes in many public schools, but is there an alternative? Naturally, there may be many.

The oldest recorded view of education was framed thousands of years ago (James, 1976) as a part of the Egyptian "mysteries system" (University). In this system, the expected impediments to learning were not matters of intellect but of virtue. A person could become virtuous by study in all the liberating (liberal) arts of grammar, rhetoric, and logic (the trivium in Greece during later years), and arithmetic, astronomy, geometry, and music (the quadrivium later in Rome). The study of these intellectual disciplines was designed to produce a person who was virtuous in the following ways:

1. Control of thought
2. Control of action
3. Steadfastness of purpose
4. Identity with the spiritual life
5. Evidence of having a mission in life
6. Evidence of a call to spiritual orders
7. Freedom from resentment

8. Confidence in the power of the teacher
9. Confidence in the power of the learner
10. Readiness for initiation.

In this view, impediments to learning rather than due to the absence of intellectual power were seen as the absence of one or more of the ten virtues. Thus, the absence of a purpose or mission in life would impede learning, probably through the loss of motivation and energy for focused attention. The absence of patience could also be seen, interestingly, as an impediment. "Confidence in the power of the learner" anticipates our more recent concept of "locus of control."

This way of thinking locates the source of learning impediments strictly in the reciprocal relationship between a person and his or her broader environment. It should be clear instantly that we have little or no evaluation technology that can assist us in analyzing possible learning impediments that are thought to be tied to questions of virtue or character. We do not even use theoretical or philosophical positions that lead us to ask such questions. Perhaps it is less evident that, if one holds such a view of learners and of learning, the major focus of "evaluation" efforts is on circumstances within the learner. The learner will feel the weight of the impediment and will feel the weight lifted when the virtuous life is learned. The "mysteries" and "secrets" were not hidden by teachers or custodians of knowledge. In this view, the absence of virtue leaves the student blind to obvious things because of negative ideas that compete for energy and attention. The quest for meanings is at the center of a student's efforts to learn in this system. In general, students who failed were not thought of as lacking in intellect; they simply lacked a *voice* to "speak their word." They had become *unconscious* rather than retarded.

In a democratic education system, evaluation is not merely a technical exercise, nor can it be limited merely to those who possess technical expertise in evaluation technology. Such experts may assist all parties in the evaluation process to frame the questions, collect the data, analyze the data, and determine their meaning. An example of this process operating partially in a commercial setting will be cited later in the chapter.

In summary, there are those who see the role of educators as one of managing all the elements of the instructional process for the benefit of students, who are expected to have little, if anything, to say about that process. On the other hand, there are theories and philosophies of education that may place learners at the center of educational decision making where they become collaborators in the educational process. In such a point of view, it is clear that the question of *who* is to do evaluation and *for whom* evaluation is to be done takes on different meanings as we move from one pole to the other.

The State of the Art in Educational Evaluation: Some Samples of Exemplary Activity

The field of educational evaluation is a hotbed of activity. Many evaluation activities and procedures are still in the developmental stages and are not ready for practical application. Others are tried and true. In some cases, promising new developments in evaluation have received very little attention from professionals in the field. Frequently, dependable measures of mental activity have been developed and validated, even though no practical pedagogical use for these well-developed procedures has been discovered. In such cases, research utilizing new instruments can and should proceed. However, the educator should not be confused about the utility of impressive procedures. For example, many instruments have been developed for research in cognitive psychology. Piagetian principles can be demonstrated using such instruments. Yet, it is not yet known precisely how such instruments can be used to assist educators in changing their teaching practices for the benefit of students.

There is a tendency for educational practitioners to demand more of evaluation than the state of the art will allow it to deliver.

Earlier, I alluded to the fact that much more refinement and sophistication have been shown in data collection on learning than in data collection on any other part of the school's ecosystem. As a result, while the models for thinking about evaluation may be explicit in terms of categories of data needed, the state of the art itself is such that the bulk of the categories within which data are needed are categories where valid instrumentation and procedures have yet to be developed. In spite of such limitations, the evaluation process and the developmental activity necessary to produce appropriate evaluation tools will and must continue.

In the past two decades, notable developments have occurred in the practice of educational evaluation. During the past few years, unique approaches to evaluation have surfaced. Among them are approaches that focus on the interaction between a teacher and a learner as the primary unit of analysis, approaches that focus on the interaction between teachers and individual classrooms as the primary unit of analysis, and approaches that utilize whole schools as the primary unit of analysis. Interestingly enough, all of these approaches appear to be emerging simultaneously. it is also interesting that in each case the success of the approach appears to be due to the development of increasingly sophisticated methods of systematic *observation* of live behavior in a more or less natural context. Examples of these three evaluation approaches follow.

Interaction Between Child and Teacher as the Primary Unit of Analysis

Reuven Feuerstein, an Israeli psychologist, has worked for nearly three decades to develop a detailed understanding of the teaching and learning process (Feuerstein, and others, 1979; Feuerstein, and others, 1980). His mentors were Jean Piaget and Andre Rey. Much of Feuerstein's work is based in the cognitive psychology of Piaget and Rey, but Feuerstein carries their work much further. Far from being content to describe cognitive processes, Feuerstein has been interested in their modification. Feuerstein's system to modify cognition is divided into two parts: the Learning Potential Assessment Device (assessment) and Instrumental Enrichment (remedial teaching).

Based on long years of clinical observation and attempts to develop systematic remediation for difficulties that students experience in learning, Feuerstein has developed a "cognitive map." Included in the cognitive map is a part that describes the domains within which learning difficulties are likely to occur. Further, it describes the specific difficulties that are likely to occur within each of three domains. Feuerstein's research has shown that learners experience difficulty when they attempt to collect information in order to solve problems when they attempt to process information using problem-solving strategies, and when, having solved the problem, they attempt to express the results. These three phases of the cognitive map are called the *input phase,* the *elaboration phase,* and the *output phase.* There are eight typical cognitive difficulties or "deficiencies" that occur in the input phase, eleven in the elaboration phase, and eight in the output phase. The validity of assessment can be judged in part by the degree to which there is agreement among assessors regarding the difficulties for a given learner in these three phases. But, the highest level of validity for the system will occur, if, as a consequence of identifying the difficulty, appropriate remedial strategies can be applied. This is precisely what has happened with thousands of teachers and learners in Israel as a result of Feuerstein's work.

Feuerstein's work departs from traditional individual assessment in several ways. The focus of the assessment practice is on an analysis of the act of learning, while learning is taking place, as opposed to an analysis of the achievement of learners based on test results that are analyzed long after the learning act has actually occurred. Feuerstein's approach differs also in its conception of the assessor's role. In Feuerstein's system, the assessor is both tester and teacher—not merely a forecaster but a specialist in the remediation of learning as well. Further, the role of the assessor extends to that of consultant with teachers, instructional leaders, and other partners in the learning process. Assessors generate a highly specialized and sophisticated level of valid knowledge in this system that makes them more valuable to teachers and instructional leaders.

Feuerstein's approach may be contrasted with that of David Wechsler whose system is essentially designed to yield information about learner *rank* in academic achievement. It may also be contrasted with the recent system of assessment developed by the Kaufmans, who also had worked earlier on Wechsler's test. The Kaufman test changes the basis of the assessment from one that looks at academic achievement to one that looks at learning. However, in the Kaufman assessment (Kaufman Assessment Battery for Children—K-ABC), the focus of *ranking* students with numbers is preserved. The Feuerstein system is the most developed of all the systems in that the assessment and remedial teaching strategies are highly integrated. But, the best part of the system is that solid academic achievement results for students can be demonstrated when the Feuerstein system is applied. This stands in sharp contrast to any competing system at present.

Interaction Between Teachers and Individual Classrooms as the Primary Unit of Analysis

Researchers and evaluators have developed highly systematic and sophisticated ways of analyzing the interaction that takes place between teacher and students in the classroom. Among those researchers and evaluators, David Berliner and others at the Far West Laboratory in San Francisco stand out. Like Brophy and Good (1968), and Stallings and Travers (1976), Berliner and others chose to initiate their investigations of classroom behavior by designing observation systems. In the case of Berliner, 40 classrooms were identified and ranked according to the academic achievement of children in those classrooms in given subject matter areas. The ten top classrooms were then contrasted with the ten bottom classrooms. Berliner and others utilized *ethnographic* observation approaches. Based on the ethnography, it was discovered that superior and inferior classrooms could be distinguished from each other along a number of dimensions. There were 21 generic features that distinguished between superior and inferior classrooms no matter what the subject matter. Then, there were a number of other distinguishing features between those classrooms depending on the academic area within which academic achievement was tested.

It is through the work of such evaluators that much more has been learned about the ways teacher behavior influences student outcomes. In fact, it may be said that greater professional confidence now exists in the principle that teacher behavior can be *expected* to influence student outcomes. For many years, educators and psychologists have suggested that factors inside the student were primarily responsible for the level of academic achievement obtained by students. The knowledge of how teachers affect student learning will be important in the design of professional programs for teacher education and supervision as well.

Using the Whole School as the Primary Unit of Analysis

During the past decade, researchers have been interested in the development of more sophisticated ways of analyzing the total school environment in order to determine if school factors can be identified that contribute to academic achievement in children. Notable among such researchers is Ronald Edmonds (1979). Previous researchers asked "if *school* worked" (Coleman, 1966; Jencks, 1972; Moesteller and Moynihan, 1972). Ron Edmonds raised the question in a different way. Instead of asking if all schools "worked," he simply asked, "Do *any* schools work?" He was interested especially in large urban schools where children are normally expected to fail. Edmonds was able to identify hundreds of secondary schools where academic achievement for students was considerably higher than would have been predicted given the typical urban environment that included high degrees of poverty. Edmonds was able not only to identify schools that "worked," but, having identified them, he applied carefully developed, systematic observation procedures and was able to identify key features of those schools. Then, Edmonds went one step further and attempted to consider the key features as operating principles and to apply them in one of the largest public school systems in the nation, the New York City Public School System. Initial reports are favorable.

Using Evaluation as a Teaching Tool

Some years ago, "Sesame Street" was developed in an attempt to improve the academic performance of low socioeconomic-status children by giving early academic educational opportunities through television programming. Through interviews with LaMarion Hayes, an educational researcher employed on the "Sesame Street" evaluation team, I learned of a number of innovative uses of educational evaluators by the television network (Lesser, 1974).

Obviously, the nature of television as a medium is such that gaining the attention of the audience must be accomplished through the appeal of the stimuli that are presented on the screen. This means that programming has been designed in such a way that it captures and sustains the attention of the audience. According to Hayes, "Sesame Street" program designers sought to accomplish this by producing programs with a high level of activity, which operated on the assumption that learning could be enjoyable, provided repeated messages to be learned by varying the format but maintaining the message, and carefully avoided the use of negative images, among other things. Each program lesson was self-contained for the simple reason that the television audience varied from day to day. Many things can be said about the initial work in the development of "Sesame Street." However, what interested me most was the use of educational evaluators by program staff.

Simply put, "Sesame Street" program staff determined whether the messages sent were received by the children, and if not, why. As soon as such simple questions were engaged by evaluators, traditional educational evaluation activity became almost obsolete. It was clear that a very close interaction between program writers, performers, and evaluators would have to be maintained, which, in fact, was the case. Performers and writers needed to know almost immediately whether or not a particular segment, as well as the whole program, would "work." A great deal was at stake if segments or programs did not work since a lot of money was involved. To avoid risking large amounts of money, innovative evaluation practices were required. The essential evaluation innovation was the integral involvement of evaluators on a day-to-day basis. Perhaps it is testimony to the validity of the evaluation effort that "Sesame Street" gained early recognition as an outstanding children's program and has been able to maintain audience loyalty and children's achievement results for more than a decade.

Conclusion

During the coming years, we may expect a rapid proliferation of activity in evaluation, including the use of numerous innovative processes, materials, and practices. New uses for data processing, new types of statistical procedures, new developments in observational technology, and so on, will be made available to educational evaluators. But once again, *the fundamental issues in evaluation are not ones of technology but ones of theory and philosophy and, perhaps, politics.* In a democratic society with democratic goals for education, there is a set of evaluation processes that fit the general goal. That set of processes must include attention to the situation within which evaluation occurs. This means the development of systematic attention to history, culture, pedagogy, and theory. It also means that evaluation must be utilized to improve the instructional process.

The capacity to accomplish these things is with us now, although refinements of practice will continue.

References

Allen, V. F. *What Does A Reading Test, Test?* Philadelphia: Temple University, College of Education, "TTT" Project Monography Series, No. 1, USOE Contract No. OEG-0-70-2046 (721), 1974.

American Psychological Association, American Educational Research Association, and National Council on Measurement in Education (Joint Committee). "Technological Recommendations for Psychological Test and Diagnostic Techniques." *Psychological Bulletin* 51, 2 (1964): Part II.

American Psychological Association, American Educational Research Association, and National Council on Measurement in Education (Joint Committee). *Standards for Educational and Psychological Tests,* 1974.

Baller, W.; Charles, D. C.; and Miller, E. L. "Mid-Life Attainment of the Mentally Retarded: A Longitudinal Study." *Genetics Psychology Monographs* 75 (1967): 235–329.

Berliner, David C. "Impediments to the Study of Teacher Effectiveness." *Beginning Teacher Evaluation Study Technical Report Series,* Report No. 75-11-3. San Francisco: Far West Laboratory for Educational Research and Development, November 1975.

Boehm, G.A.W. "How to Teach the Esoteric Mathematical Principle of Infinite Convergence—And Make Any 6th Grader Eat It Up." *Think* (Sept./Oct. 1979): 10–14.

Brophy, J. E. and Good, T. L. "Teachers Communication of Differential Expectations for Children's Classroom Performance: Some Behavioral Data." *Journal of Educational Psychology* 60 (1968): 365–374.

Brown, Cynthia. *Literacy in Thirty Hours: Paulo Friere's Process in Northeast Brazil*. London: Writers and Readers Publishing Cooperative, 1975.

Buros, O. *Seventh Mental Measurements Yearbook*. Highland Park, N.J.: Grayphon Press, 1972.

Ceja, M. V. Letter to Gerald Klein, Aircraft Engine Group, General Electric Company, Cincinnati, Ohio. (A summary of California State Department of Education evaluation data on Project SEED). From M. V. Ceja, Assistant Superintendent of Public Instruction for Compensatory Education, February 13, 1975.

Chase, Allan. *The Legacy of Malthus: The Social Costs of the New Scientific Racism*. New York: Knopf, 1977.

Cohen, R. "The Influence of Conceptual Role Sets on Measures of Learning Ability." *Race and Intelligence*. Anthropological Association, 1971.

Coleman, J. S. and others. *Equality of Educational Opportunity*. Washington, D.C.: U.S. Government Printing Office, 1966.

Conant, J. B. *The American High School Today*. New York: McGraw-Hill, 1959.

Edmonds, R. "Some Schools Work and More Can." *Social Policy* (March/April 1979): 29–32.

Federal Trade Commission. *Effects of Coaching on Standardized Admission Examinations*. Washington, D.C.: Bureau of Consumer Protection, FTC, 1979.

Feuerstein, R. *The Dynamic Assessment of Retarded Performers*. Baltimore: University Park Press, 1979.

Feuerstein, R. *Instrumental Enrichment*. Baltimore: University Park Press, 1980.

Freeman, D. J.; Kuhs, A. C.; Porter, A. C.; Floden, R. C.; Schmitt, W. H.; and Schivelle, J. R. "Do Textbooks and Tests Define a National Curriculum in Elementary School Mathematics?" *The Elementary School Journal*, in press.

Freire, Paulo. *Education For Critical Consciousness*. New York: Seabury, 1973.

Hilliard, Asa G., III. "The Strengths and Weaknesses of Cognitive Tests for Young Children." In *One Child Indivisible*. Edited by J. D. Andrews. Washington, D.C.: The National Association for the Education of Young Children, 1975.

Hilliard, Asa G., III. "Democratizing the Common School." *The Proceedings of the Conference on the Common School in a Multi-cultural Society*, College of Education, University of California at Los Angeles, June 1982.

Hirsch, J. "To Unfrock the Charlatans." *Sage Race Relation Abstracts* 2, 6 (May 1981): 1–67.

Holtzman, W. H.; Heller, K.; and Messick, S. eds. *Placing Children in Special Education: A Strategy for Equity*. Washington, D.C.: National Academy Press, 1982.

Houts, Paul, ed. *The Myth of Measurability*. New York: Free Press, 1977.

James, G. G. M. *Stolen Legacy*. San Francisco: Julian Richardson, 1976.

Jencks, C. *Inequality: A Reassessment of Family and Schooling in America*. New York: Basic Books, 1972.

Jenson, Arthur. "How Much Can We Boost I.Q. and Scholastic Achievement?" *Harvard Educational Review* 39 (1969): 1–123.

Jenson, Arthur. *Bias in Mental Testing*. New York: Free Press, 1980.

Jones, Reginald, *Standardized Testing in the San Francisco Public Schools*. Report to the San Francisco Public Schools Commission, 1976.

Kamin, L. *The Science and Politics of I.Q.* New York: John Wiley, 1974.

Kaufman, A. S. and Kaufman, N. L. *K-ABC: Kaufman Assessment Battery for Children—Interpretive Manual*. Circle Pines, Minn.: American Guidance Service, 1983.

Lesser, G. S. *Children and Television: Lessons From Sesame Street*. New York: Vintage, 1974.

Mercer, Jane R. "I.Q.: The Lethal Label." *Psychology Today*, September 1972, pp. 44–47, 95–97.

Messick, S. *The Effectiveness of Coaching for the SAT: Review and Reanalysis of Research from the Fifties to the FTC*. (ETS RR 80-8). Princeton, N.J.: Educational Testing Service, 1980.

Moore, W. "Florida's Standardized Testing Program: A Tool or Weapon?" In *Testing and Evaluation in Schools: Practitioner's Views*, 19–26. Edited by C. B. Stalford. Washington, D.C.: National Institute of Education, 1980.

Mosteller, F. and Moynihan, D. P. *On Equality of Educational Opportunity.* New York: Vintage, 1972.

National Association for the Advancement of Colored People. *NAACP Report on Minority Testing.* NAACP Special Contribution Fund, 1790 Broadway, New York, N.Y. 10019, May 1976.

Ramsbotham, A. *The Status of Minimum Competency Programs in Twelve Southern States.* Jackson, Miss.: Southeastern Public Education Program, 1980.

Schragg, P. and Divoky, D. *The Myth of the Hyperactive Child and Other Means of Child Control.* New York: Random House, 1975.

Slack, W. V. and Porter, D. "The Scholastic Aptitude Test: A Critical Appraisal." *Harvard Educational Review* 2, 50 (1980): 154–175.

Stallings, J.; Wilcox, M.; and Travers, J. *Phase III, Instruments for the National Day Care Cost-Effects Study: Instrument Selection and Field Testing.* Menlo Park, Calif.: Stanford Research Institute, 1976.

Trusheim, D. and Crouse, J. "The ETS Admissions Formula: Does the SAT Add Useful Information?" *Phi Delta Kappan* (September 1982).

Wechsler, D. *The Measurement and Appraisal of Adult Intelligence,* 4th edition. Baltimore: Williams and Wilkins, 1958.

White, D. M., ed. *Toward a Diversified Legal Profession: An Inquiry into the Law School Admissions Test, Grade Inflation, and Current Admission Policies.* San Francisco: Julian Richardson Associates, 1981.

Wigdor, A. K. and Garner, W. R., eds. *Ability Testing: Uses, Consequences, and Controversies,* Vol. I and II. Washington, D.C.: National Academy Press, 1982.

A Review and Extension of Hilliard's Proposals for Reforming Educational Evaluation

DANIEL L. STUFFLEBEAM

When leaves begin to fall, one pays little heed to any particular one. But as they accumulate, their common message cannot be ignored. So it is with critiques of evaluation. Educators have been hearing or reading them for two decades (Cronbach, 1963; Cronbach, and others, 1980; Eisner, 1975; Glass, 1975; House, 1973; Patton, 1978; Scriven, 1967; Stake, 1967; Stufflebeam, and others, 1971; and Suchman, 1967). The recent one by Hilliard (in press) adds little that has not been charged or recommended before, and it is far from a comprehensive review. But its familiar, if restricted, message is nonetheless valid.

The benefits from investments in educational evaluation *have* been disappointing. Evaluations that are known or even claimed to have had a positive impact on policy development, program administration, teaching, and learning are rare. Charges of irrelevant, narrow, and/or untimely findings are common. And not infrequently, critics have charged that evaluations have exacerbated and failed to correct inequities in society (Stake, 1981).

In postulating reasons for the failure of educational evaluation, Hilliard touched on a number of recurrent themes. Too often, evaluations have not been integral to the programs under review. They have not been collaborative, improvement-oriented enterprises. Instead, they have often been mechanical exercises confined to administering, scoring, and interpreting standardized tests, not because these are pertinent to key questions, but because they are available and easy to use. Often, evaluations that have focused on end products have had little to say about the involved process and, in general, have been narrow. Usually, they have not taken into account the relevant historical, cultural, and organizational contexts; neither have they drawn effectively from pertinent pedagogy and the findings from educational research. Finally, they have frequently failed to embody the principles of democracy in how they are designed, interpreted, and reported. For example, they have often been used as instruments of the privileged and powerful for maintaining an advantage over the underprivileged.

As for progress, Hilliard mentioned a few developments that he admires and that give some reason for optimism. These include: integrating

Daniel L. Stufflebeam is Director, The Evaluation Center, College of Education, Western Michigan University, Kalamazoo.

assessment and feedback in the learning process; identifying factors outside the learner that potentially distinguish between superior and inferior classrooms; using studies of school effectiveness to identify variables; and employing ongoing formative evaluations to guide program development. I am glad for the opportunity to underscore the potential usefulness of these thrusts.

Overall, Hilliard charged that those concerned with educational evaluation have failed in their evaluations and have not as yet reached a consensus about how to reform their practice. While I won't refute this charge with a sweeping claim of reformation in the field of evaluation, I do believe that Hilliard omitted mentioning some pertinent and significant advances. In the spirit of building on—as opposed to refuting—his thesis, I will mention a few developments that I believe are responsive to the problems he identified.

After five years of extensive development, the Joint Committee on Standards for Educational Evaluation—a 17-member body appointed by 12 professional societies (including ASCD)—issued a book of 30 standards by which to guide and assess evaluations of educational programs, projects, and materials (Joint Committee, 1981). These standards call for evaluations that are useful, feasible, ethical, and accurate, and they embody democratic principles. This development, at least, is a significant step in the direction of consensus about what constitutes sound evaluation.

Also, a number of groups have articulated comprehensive views of the criteria that should be considered in assessing educational programs. Especially pertinent to the Hilliard critique is a proposal by the Irish educator, Thomas Kellaghan (1981). Arguing that equality of educational opportunity is a basic value that should undergird education throughout the world, he proposed seven basic criteria for assessing success. An educational institution should:

1. Provide an adequate range of educational opportunities
2. Make its service accessible to all potential students
3. Involve students from all segments of society in the full range of provided opportunities
4. Assist students from all segments of society to aspire to high levels of achievement in education and life
5. Help students from all segments of society to attain the full sequence of offerings in an educational institution
6. Demonstrate that students from all segments of society have achieved acceptable levels of skill and knowledge
7. Demonstrate that the institution has had a beneficial impact on all parts of the society it serves.

Use of the full range of these criteria would place evaluation in an instrumental role of helping society to educate all its people equitably and comprehensibly.

Another pertinent effort to expand evaluative criteria is embodied in a joint effort by the Toledo, Ohio, Public Schools and the Western Michigan University Evaluation Center (1980a, 1980b). They prepared two manuals that, respectively, array and define criteria for assessing student growth and development and criteria for assessing all administrative aspects of an educational institution. The first of these sets of criteria (Stufflebeam, 1978) is organized to assess student growth and development in each of the following categories: intellectual, emotional, physical and recreational, moral, aesthetic and cultural, vocational and social.

A second set of criteria for assessing the administrative aspects of an educational institution concern the adequacy of means necessary for achievement of goals, such as sound policy, qualified faculty, adequate facilities, up-to-date materials, excellence of program offerings, enthusiastic and effective teaching, use of evaluation for program improvement, extent of library holdings and services, safe transport to and from school, safety in the institution, staff morale and communication, community support, sufficient finances, and efficient management. Both sets of criteria are soon to be published by the Kluwer-Nijhoff Publishing Company (Nowakowski, in press). Like the familiar *Roget's Thesaurus*, they should be of great assistance to groups as they plan studies to provide comprehensive assessments of students' developmental needs and achievement and of the institutionalized educational offerings that are provided to serve these needs and attain the desired outcomes.

Also, such heuristic listings of criteria are consistent with the view that evaluation should be an ongoing, cooperative, and dynamic process that is oriented to fostering improvement. Educators will not solve the problems that Hilliard has identified by replacing the sets of standardized tests that now dominate evaluation practice with another supposedly more valid set. Validity is a relative concept, since an information-gathering device is valid or invalid depending on its pertinence to the questions to be answered. Such questions must be derived by close consideration of the program to be assessed and of its context, by consultation with those who bear responsibility for its effective operation and use, and by consideration of the basic values of the broader society. I could not agree more with Hilliard's fundamental position that evaluations must be designed and conducted as collaborative ventures aimed at diagnosing and helping to serve the educational needs of all our citizens.

At present, I believe the best guide that educators can use to fulfill this purpose is embodied in the Joint Committee *Standards* (1981). They contain widely shared principles and technical advice that are aimed at ensuring that evaluations will be useful, feasible, ethical, and technically sound; and they call for a democratic process in designing, conducting, and reporting evaluations. Moreover, these standards are being subjected to an ongoing process of review and revision to ensure that they will continue to promote and not stifle the services of evaluation to education and society.

References

Cronbach, L. J. "Course Improvement Through Evaluation." *Teachers College Record* 64 (1963): 672-683.

Cronbach, L. J.; Ambron, S. R.; Dornbusch, S. M.; Hess, R. D.; Hornik, R. C.; Phillips, D. C.; Walker, D. F.; and Weiner, S. S. *Toward Reform of Program Evaluation: Aims, Methods and Institutional Arrangements.* San Francisco: Jossey-Bass, 1980.

Eisner, E. W. "The Perceptive Eye: Toward the Reformation of Educational Evaluation." Stanford: Stanford Evaluation Consortium, December 1975.

Glass, G. "A Paradox About Excellence of Schools and the People in Them." *Educational Researcher* 4 (1975): 9-14.

Guba, E. G. "The Failure of Educational Evaluation." *Educational Technology.* (1969): 29-38.

Hilliard, A. G., III. "Democracy in Evaluation: The Evolution of an Art-Science in Context." In *Research and Practice in Education.* Edited by Philip Hosford. Alexandria, Va.: ASCD (in press).

House, E. R., ed. *School Evaluation: The Politics and Process.* Berkeley: McCutchan, 1973.

Joint Committee on Standards for Educational Evaluation. *Standards for Evaluations of Educational Programs, Projects, and Materials.* New York: McGraw-Hill Book Company, September 1981.

Kellaghan, Thomas. Speech presented at Javeriana University in Bogota, Columbia, November 25, 1981.

Nowakowski, J., ed. *Toledo Inventory of Educational Variables: Handbook for Teachers and Administrators.* Boston: Kluwer-Nijhoff, in press.

Patton, M. Q. *Utilization-Focused Evaluation.* Beverly Hills: Sage, 1978.

Scriven, M. "The Methodology of Evaluation." In *Curriculum Evaluation.* Edited by R. E. Stake. American Educational Research Association Monograph Series on Evaluation, No. 1, Chicago: Rand McNally, 1967.

Stake, R. E. "The Countenance of Educational Evaluation." *Teachers College Record* 68 (1967): 523-540.

Stake, R. L. "Setting Standards for Educational Evaluators." *Evaluation News* 2 (1981): 148-152.

Stufflebeam, D. L. *Philosophical, Conceptual, and Practical Guides for Evaluating Education.* Kalamazoo: Evaluation Center, Western Michigan University, 1978.

Stufflebeam, D. L.; Foley, W. J.; Gephart, W. J.; Guba, E. G.; Hammond, R. L.; Merriman, H. O.; and Provus, M. M. *Educational Evaluation and Decision-Making in Education.* Itasca, Ill.: Peacock, 1971.

Suchman, E. A. *Evaluative Research.* New York: Russell Sage Foundation, 1967.

Toledo Public Schools and the Evaluation Center. *The Toledo Catalog: Assessment of Students and School Administration, Volume 1—Students.* Kalamazoo: Evaluation Center, Western Michigan University, June 30, 1980a.

Toledo Public Schools and the Evaluation Center. *The Toledo Catalog: Assessment of Students and School Administration, Volume 2—School Administration.* Kalamazoo: Evaluation Center, Western Michigan University, June 30, 1980b.

A Reaction to Hilliard

ROBERT J. MUNNELLY

Hilliard does a nice job of raising our professional consciences about the gaps that exist between evaluation practices and instructional methodology. It is a professional problem that deserves more attention from college faculties, school district staff, and R and D center researchers.

Much professional effort has already been devoted to identifying this problem. So, for me, the value of the chapter lies in the presentation of examples of professional practice in which democratic and humanistic principles of education are conjoined with evaluation technology and instructional pedagogy to help students grow and improve.

I wish, however, that Hilliard had included more about developments or projects "where criterion-referenced tests are created by the joint effort of teachers and evaluation personnel, and where the lines of communication between them remain open." I am just now becoming aware that in many school districts teams of teachers are tackling the task of building tests to indicate how well students are performing relative to a defined body of content. Many of us in local schools and school districts are finding that criterion-referenced and domain-referenced tests give descriptive lucidity about student performance, which can then be used by teachers to plan instructional sequences targeted directly at the skill or content needs. This effort strives to make evaluative testing congruent with instruction. A recent, easily obtainable booklet by the National Council for the Social Studies gives step-by-step help on how local school district staff can work on this important task of translating curriculum goals into performance criteria and then developing criterion-referenced evaluation (Williams and Moore, 1980). Note that the booklet uses social studies rather than the sequential skill subjects of math and reading as its source of ideas about the relationship of evaluation and instruction.

As one segment of a systemwide curriculum evaluation effort, the Reading, Massachusetts, Schools have used items and data provided by the National Assessment of Educational Progress to construct evaluation instruments that help us to know more about student attainment. From a wide variety of test questions in an inexpensive item bank, we constructed criterion-referenced tests that correlate with our goals and objectives. We then used the results to make instructional adjustments and curricular refinements.

Robert J. Munnelly is Assistant Superintendent, Reading Public Schools, Reading, Massachusetts.

We also administered tests developed by the Massachusetts State Assessment Project to give data about student performance. The project sampled students around the state, but we gave the tests to our own students and then used performance data from these domain-referenced tests to compare our students as a group to students in other reference groups in the state. Making criterion-referenced tests, such as the State Assessment tests, do norm-referenced duty has been helpful in explaining to the public how our students are doing academically (Popham, 1976). A report of this curriculum evaluation effort was recently described in a newsletter of AASA's National Council for the Improvement of Instruction (Munnelly, 1982).

Engaging instructional staff in the process of bringing evaluative testing and instruction closer is a practical way of clarifying what Hilliard calls the "theoretical and philosophical confusion of professional practice." I do want to point out that as teaching faculties develop curriculum and prepare instructional activities that are congruent with evaluative information, the school staff does not commit itself to a mindless concept of precision teaching wherein long lists of narrow objectives, unimaginative teaching, and computer-assisted recordkeeping are the features. Instead, the process may be our best hope for implementing humanistic and democratic principles, which both Hilliard and I believe are important.

References

Munnelly, Robert J. "Public Confidence Through Curriculum Evaluation." *The School Administrator* 39 (July-August 1982): 34-35.

Popham, W. James. "Normative Data for Criterion-Referenced Tests?" *Phi Delta Kappan* (May 1976): 593-594.

Williams, Paul, and Moore, Jerry (eds.). *Criterion-Referenced Testing for the Social Studies, Bulletin 64.* Washington, D.C.: National Council for the Social Studies, 1980.

An Extension of Hilliard's Thesis

GILBERT N. GARCIA

Schools and schooling are daily activities. As such, they demand dynamic evaluation paradigms that capture the character of the activities and make sense of them. Hilliard's paper addresses the evaluation issues of the day aptly.

Rules and Regulations issued by federal agencies for the purpose of implementing legislation vary on a number of critical points, one of which is the set of evaluation criteria used to select quality proposals and to monitor the progress of funded programs. Notwithstanding the ambiguity of some of the Rules and Regulations regarding evaluation plans, designs, and reporting formats, they have influenced extent and quality of evaluations carried out in education contexts. Regulations issued by the U.S. Department of Education, especially those issued in response to ESEA, Title VII, the Bilingual Education Act, are one example. Since 1969, Rules and Regulations have addressed the prevailing assessment issues, though not always from psychometric or even pedagogic perspectives. Rather, they have reflected political expediencies. On the other hand, since 1979, the climate has changed for the better.

Today, issues of assessment are based on a more comprehensive understanding of (or at least, concern for) the complexity of schools and schooling. Thus, as Hilliard notes so clearly, the question posed in the past with regard to bilingual education programs for limited English-proficient students was, "Does the federally funded program work?" Attempts to respond to the question from either side lead to misinterpretation and significant distortion of the services provided for and the benefits derived by students and schools. Slowly the question has evolved into one that asks, "What effects do the services have on particular students in particular contexts?" I agree with Hilliard that this is a much better question. It implies a number of points that are critical in determining student growth in terms of the development and enhancement of skills that appear necessary for effective participation in "all-English classrooms." The points are:

- A full understanding of the instructional and non-instructional services to be provided to students

---

The point of view expressed in this commentary is that of the author and does not reflect the policies of the U.S. Department of Education.

Gilbert N. Garcia is with the Office of Bilingual Education and Minority Languages Affairs, Washington, D.C.

- A comprehensive set of entry, placement, promotion, and exit criteria with which to structure the services that match student skills, abilities, and motivations
- Realistic understanding of the human resources characteristics needed to serve students
- Detailed material resources and program management systems plan
- Thorough understanding of school policies and community practices regarding the educational goals and objectives of each.

Education programs that reflect this level of planning are programs that can succeed in educating students, who, for a number of personal and extra-personal reasons, are not equipped to participate effectively in all-English classrooms. The limited English-proficient students served by Title VII programs are but one example of the broader student population in need of school services so structured. The cost benefits to the country are self-evident.

Section III.
Using Knowledge

7 *The Art of Applying the Science of Education*

PHILIP L. HOSFORD

*T*he title of this chapter implies the use of one's intuitive faculties and accumulated knowledge in efforts to impart knowledge, skills, and values. What is the magic or artistry that some teachers demonstrate while providing students with a superior education? Why do some teachers have these qualities and others lack them? How are these traits identified and acquired? Is it possible for the education profession to select, train, and maintain only high-quality personnel?

The Major Premise

Most teachers are good at their job. They usually get a little better every year. The word competent comes to mind.

Some teachers are unbelievably good at their job. They are truly superior. The word genius comes to mind.

A few teachers are bad at their job. They should never have become teachers in the first place. The word deplorable comes to mind.

The Minor Premise

Superior teachers have a sound foundational knowledge base. They are well informed in their subject-matter teaching fields; understand the basic concepts of human growth and development; are familiar with basic principles of learning, and understand the purpose and value of lesson planning, curriculum development, diagnostic procedures, and a variety

Philip L. Hosford is Professor, Department of Curriculum and Instruction, College of Education and Department of Mathematical Sciences, College of Arts and Sciences, New Mexico State University, Las Cruces, New Mexico.

of evaluation techniques. They are competent consumers of current educational research.

Moreover, superior teachers fully understand and believe that *how* they teach is as important as *what* they teach. They organize and provide instruction for their learners with artistic grace, and society profits from the intelligent, healthy citizenry produced. Others may provide instruction with a vengeance, and society must later deal with the havoc produced. The genius of the artistic teacher is not predetermined by genetics. To be sure, genetics may preclude some, but the superior teacher is not "born." Training and experience make essential contributions to the development of the functioning superior teacher. Superior teachers must *become* what they are.

The Conclusion

What a wonderful world an educational organization would provide for its learners if there were no bad teachers and only superior ones. And what a wonderful world that would be for the teachers if they had no bad administrators and only superior ones.

Obviously, the achievement of such a wonderful world is the joint responsibility of teacher preparation and inservice training and supervision. Selective-retention programs in the undergraduate preparation of teachers should screen out most of those destined to be ineffective, and the remainder should be identified during the first years of teaching and never achieve tenure. All others should be afforded programs to help them rapidly join and remain in the ranks of those recognized as superior teachers.

Today only potentially superior teachers graduate from the ideal teacher preparation program. Graduates of such programs demonstrate the requisite knowledge base. Graduates demonstrate process skills in simulated and laboratory settings with children of appropriate ages. The people who know these graduates would be happy to have them as teachers for their own children or relatives. In short, they have the accumulated knowledge and intuitive faculties that enable them to impart desired knowledge, skills, and values to their students. Such a teacher preparation program may not be typical. Yet, the knowledge, skills, and facilities are generally available to make such a program typical throughout this country.

Similarly, the ideal inservice training program today results in a tenured faculty of only superior teachers, or those of imminent promise of joining that category. But, again, such a school district is probably not the typical district. Yet, the knowledge, skills, and facilities are generally available to make it so.

In both cases, the prerequisite study of education is guaranteed and is capped with demonstrated skills in applying the science of education in admirably artistic ways. The ultimate effect of such an achievement would be manifested in the implementation of initial certification and in the granting of tenure. The following outlines of the science and art of education are designed to lead to the final consideration of certification and tenure as affected by such teacher preparation and inservice training programs.

The Science of Education

For economy of discussion, I will limit the number of aspects to be considered under the rubric of the *science of education*. I accept the definition of science as the "accumulated knowledge systematized and formulated with reference to the discovery of general truths and the operation of general laws."

For my purposes, only the following two aspects of the science of education will be presented:

1. A synthesis of some of the important research accomplished during the past ten years, which highlights the differences between effective teachers and ineffective teachers on the basis of student achievement scores, self-concept, and attitude tests
2. A knowledge and understanding of our most valued goals of education, which will be discussed under the topic of the Silent-Curriculum.

Process-product research of the past decade has confirmed many aspects of what superior teachers in prior times knew only intuitively. Such teachers provided instruction in artistic ways based on that intuitive knowledge. They had no research base on which to resist bandwagon movements or new theories that seemed incongruent with their intuitive knowledge. The findings of the past ten years have received extensive exposure in the literature. To aid in the organization of the research I use the acronym TEMPO:

T = Time-on-Task (utilization of time by learners)
E = Expectation (learner perceptions of teacher expectation)
M = Monitoring (corrective feedback, teacher awareness of learner progress)
P = Problems assigned (difficulty level of assigned work)
O = Organization (classroom management, climate, and time allocations)

As with much research, each element of TEMPO has been presented in the past few years in varying and sometimes conflicting views. Each has been challenged; but taken as a group, the components of TEMPO formulate a systematic approach toward improving instructional effectiveness.

The superior teacher has welcomed the overall impact of the knowledge and recognized that the omission of any element creates a less successful learning atmosphere. Each element of TEMPO will be discussed in turn so that they may be easily referred to in our discussion of artistry in instruction.

T = Time-On-Task

In 1954, the school district in which I had taught and served as principal created a new position entitled the Director of Instruction. I received the assignment along with instructions to produce a course of study for each grade and subject in the school district. To identify the actual curriculum in grades 1-6, all teachers were asked to complete a form indicating the amount of time they allocated to each subject during an average week or day. The results were dismaying. In grade two, the average allotted time per day for reading ranged from 30 to 150 minutes. In grade five, the average time allotted for art ranged from none to two hours per day. When this information was reported back to all those involved, the common goal became the achievement of a mutually agreed upon balance in our time allocations. We had no trouble perceiving that students provided with no time for art learned very little about the subject compared to students allotted two hours a day for this subject.

Today, time-on-task research goes well beyond consideration of differences in time allocations per subject, important as they may be. Rosenshine and Berliner (1978), and many others since, have reported that students taught by effective teachers spend a significantly greater amount of time actually involved with reading and arithmetic than do students being taught by ineffective teachers, even though the *allotted* times for instruction are exactly the same in both cases.

Consequently, gains in achievement test scores reflect this difference. *How* effective teachers achieve the higher rate of time-on-task for their students without seriously damaging other aspects of education will be examined in later sections dealing with the artistry of the superior teacher.

E = Expectations

Effective teachers consistently project a high expectation of learning for each of their students. These expectations are within the student's learning limits and are fully understood by teacher and student. Goals are reached through mutual understanding, cooperation, and work. This gets well beyond any Pygmalian effect and becomes a major element in creating the climate of a classroom. Consistent student perception of realistic, relatively high teacher expectations builds a recognized and rewarding climate for learning.

M = Monitoring

Effective teachers employ a variety of routines to monitor student progress. They have different routines for homework collection, feedback, grading and recording, discussion, seat work, and committee work. Each routine provides the teacher with knowledge of student progress and opportunities for providing timely corrective feedback. The teacher continuously updates the diagnosis of learning problems, achievements, and appropriate feedback for each student. Effective teachers predict student performance with a high degree of accuracy.

P = Problems Assigned

Psychological theory, as well as common sense, supports the knowledge that effective teachers assign problems and homework at such a level that the students can perform most of the assignments successfully on their own. The climate and routines established in the classrooms of effective teachers permit early, accurate, and helpful feedback to the learners regarding their performance on assignments.

O = Organization

Effective teachers manage well. Coping is rarely an issue. The students are so busy at task-related activities, following sensible routines, and striving toward clearly understood objectives that situations with which teachers must "cope" seldom have an opportunity to arise. Through management skills superior teachers achieve what has commonly been labeled "preventive discipline" in the professional literature. They are not automatically superior teachers. They plan, worry, and work hard. I have never known superior teachers who "took it easy." But the real secret to their success—what sets them above the good teachers who also work, plan, and worry—is their process of management. They have learned (and firmly believe) that process affects product; that how they manage their classroom significantly affects the climate, motivation, and goal achievement in their classrooms. In short, their knowledge base includes a thoughtful understanding of the importance of the Silent Curriculum.

The Silent Curriculum

The Silent Curriculum is created only as we teach. Unquestionably it varies from day to day depending on the procedures and problems our students bring to class, but over a period of time we create with our students our own unique Silent Curriculum.

My first insight into the critical importance of what I was to label the Silent Curriculum some ten years later came during the end of a school year when we were in the process of "failing to re-employ" ten teachers. We had conscientiously lived through all due-process procedures; identified the problem with the teacher, offered help in all possible ways, summoned support services, and scheduled extra classroom visits by appropriate supervisors. All summative evaluations confirmed the negative decision. The final consensus was that we had had in our employ for a full school year, ten *ineffective* teachers. Ten ineffective teachers, each with an average of 30 students, meant that at least 300 students that year were subjected to an inferior education.

That ugly thought prompted close examination and review of the files, records, and reports of the ten teachers to obtain clues that could help us avoid employing ineffective teachers in the future. Principals and supervisors reported that all ten teachers were sufficiently knowledgeable in the subject matter areas they were employed to teach. All ten were being released because of deficiencies in human relations skills. Students, parents, colleagues, and supervisors sought support from one another in attempts to identify just what was wrong. Students of these ten teachers were absent more than others, did not seem interested in school, or rather openly expressed a hatred of it. We found no other explanation as to why the ten teachers were ineffective except the conjecture that they had little awareness or understanding of the Silent Curriculum and its impact on classrooms.

Through subsequent years, I observed highly effective teachers who were "traditional" or "democratic"; those who ran an "open" classroom, "individualized," or used the "learning center" approach; those who "grouped" and those who didn't; those who used the basic reader and those who used the language experience approach; those who were white, black, brown, red, and yellow; those who were religious and those who were not. I also observed *ineffective* teachers who fit many of the categories above, but in each case the Silent Curriculum created in their classrooms was simply unacceptable to those in governance positions.

During those same years a more operational definition of the Silent Curriculum was developed through an entirely different activity.

An Operational Definition

In the late 1960s, I formulated a list of 26 objectives of education taken from the literature. Through trial and error, and responses from many groups of practicing educators, the list was reduced to the following 12 objectives:

1. Wise use of leisure time
2. Knowledge of world problems
3. Skill in use of the three Rs
4. Improved self-concept
5. Sense of patriotism

6. Preparation for college
7. Desire for learning
8. Physical and mental health
9. Respect for others
10. Preparation for employment
11. Multicultural understanding
12. Spiritual and moral values.

Throughout the 1970s hundreds of teachers and administrators participated in forced Q-sortings of the 12 objectives and consistently selected the same four most important objectives that the schools should accomplish. Although they did not always emerge in the same rank order, their separation from the fifth objective selected by the group was always clear and distinct. Hence, no rank order is assigned to them here, as shown in Figure 1.

If these four are the most desirable objectives of education, then where do three of them fit into our curriculum planning, lesson planning, and materials design? Many of the ten ineffective teachers we released showed good planning in the area of Skill in Use of Three Rs, but all of them had troubles in the other three areas. They either ignored three-fourths of the curriculum or were unaware of their existence and importance because of the heavy silence surrounding them.

The Silent Curriculum can be defined as the three-fourths of the desired curriculum about which we have had so little to say in education, namely: the desire for learning, respect for others, and improved self-concept. To be sure, many of us on campus and in the field have exhorted all to be good human beings in classrooms and schools and to behave in ways that would help achievement in the three Silent Curriculum areas. But not until the 1970s did we see many determined, empirical research efforts seriously examining the Silent Curriculum areas.

Research and the Silent Curriculum

Aspy and Roebuck (1977) addressed the problem squarely. Their research showed us that teacher behavior in the areas of interpersonal

Figure 1. Four Most Valued Objectives of Education as Selected by Groups of Professional Educators.

Desire for Learning	Skill in Use of Three Rs
Improved Self-Concept	Respect for Others

relations can indeed be changed through inservice training. Furthermore, the closer the training is to the desired specific behaviors, the greater becomes the probability that the behaviors will be used in the classroom.

Following the training period, Aspy and Roebuck pursued the question of whether such changed teacher behaviors affected their students in significant ways. They reported positive and significant relationships between levels of teacher interpersonal functioning and attendance, achievement, and self-concept. That is, in rooms where teachers sustained the use of their interpersonal skills, which they had been trained to use, attendance was significantly higher, gains on achievement test scores in reading and arithmetic were significantly higher, and significant improvement in self-concept took place. Moreover, a strong relationship was found between principals' levels of interpersonal functioning and the tendency on the part of their teachers to employ the same interpersonal skills in the classrooms.

Much of the research reported along these lines has focused on the elementary school level. However, the importance of the Silent Curriculum at the secondary level cannot be denied. One of the most noticeable results obtained from improving the Silent Curriculum is that of increased student motivation. Motivation has been identified by secondary teachers as their single most important problem (Hosford, 1978). That finding was later re-examined in a large school district in Texas. Over 120 high school teachers were asked to identify the one problem that they would most like to have help in solving. The synthesis of these problem statements was the same as that obtained from different groups 14 years earlier in the same city:

1. How do I get students to want to learn?
2. How do I motivate capable students who lack the desire to apply their knowledge and skill?
3. What methods can I use to cause students to want to do outside work?

These questions do not relate to the teaching of any special subject matter or grade level. They do not deal specifically with teaching the three Rs. The questions can only be answered through an improved Silent Curriculum.

Another View

From the Referent Theory of Instruction (Hosford, 1973) two of the hypotheses generated included:

Differences in teachers will explain a significant portion of learner differences in the "non-content" areas of improved self-concept, desire for learning, and respect for others.

The X quality that marks the fine teacher and the Y quality that marks the poor teacher are most easily observed in the process of human interaction commonly recorded in a micro-teaching situation.

Several studies (Hosford and Schroder, 1974; Hosford and Neuenfeldt, 1979; Hosford and Martin, 1980) designed to examine the two hypotheses provided still a different view of the Silent Curriculum and its impact on teacher evaluation. Groups of teachers and administrators were found to achieve high consensus levels after viewing four-minute segments of several teachers in the act of teaching. In each case the viewers were asked to respond to the question, "Would you want this teacher for your child or little brother or sister next year?" Response categories were limited to *yes*, *maybe*, and *no*. Viewer evaluators were limited to those who had no acquaintanceship with the teacher being viewed. High positive correlations were found between all viewing groups, and the following findings were reported by Hosford and Martin (1980):

1. The teaching experience and grade level of the viewing professional educator make no difference.
2. The subject matter teaching field(s) of the viewing professional educator makes no difference.
3. Six professional educators will provide an adequate sample for obtaining general consensus.
4. Professional educator consensus will be reliably obtained from one year to the next.

The Beginning Teacher Evaluation Study, Phase II, a research project (Sandoval, 1976) on effective teacher behavior based on videotaped recordings, confirmed that teacher behavior recorded on tape appeared to be consistent with teaching style over a period of time.

This small but increasingly important body of literature relating the use of videotape recording to evaluation of teacher effectiveness is growing. But in the meantime, perhaps it raises more questions than it answers. On what bases are viewers responding with such confidence? What exactly is it that they are evaluating? Are their evaluations confirmed by judgments in the field over a period of years? Can these objectively gained judgments be confirmed by measurements of student growth?

One answer to the first two questions is that viewers are responding to the Silent Curriculum they see being created by the teacher. Instructional theory, the Neuenfeldt study (1978), elements of the Aspy-Roebuck study (1977), and experiences like those with the ten ineffective teachers imply a definite "yes" answer to the third question of confirmation of judgments in the field. The same sources would imply a probable affirmative response to the last question regarding student growth.

Applying the Science of Education

Superior teachers have a sound and basic knowledge of the curricular elements commonly found in teacher preparation programs. They are also intelligent consumers of research, knowing well the meaning of time-on-task, expectations, monitoring, problems assigned, and organization (TEMPO). Moreover, superior teachers understand that creating a facilitating Silent Curriculum pays high dividends in student growth in all four of the major curricular areas: desire for learning, skill in the use of the Three Rs, respect for others, and improved self-concept.

Although this knowledge and understanding is essential to becoming a superior teacher, it is not sufficient. Skills in the application of the knowledge and the ability to create a desirable Silent Curriculum are also necessary. Knowledge of the various elements of TEMPO, for example, tells us nothing about *how* to achieve high rates of time-on-task or *how* to create the climate of expectation. The gap between knowledge and practice must be bridged.

Measuring the Elements of TEMPO

As with any skill-development process, improvement depends on knowledge of results. One's skill in hitting the tennis ball into the correct section of the opposite court has little chance for improvement if one practices only in the dark and can receive no feedback as to where the ball is landing. In each of the TEMPO areas, we also need measurements of success fed back to us if we are to improve our skills.

Objectively measuring results and providing the necessary feedback are major obstacles to bridging the gap between knowledge and practice. The research that assured us of the veracity of the TEMPO knowledge was costly and required years of controlled activity. As individual teachers, supervisors, and principals, we cannot wait three years nor spend a million dollars to measure our achievements in TEMPO areas as we seek to improve our skills. We need measurement procedures that cost little in terms of money, time, and effort; provide us with objective assessments regarding our performance; and yield clearly understood data against which we may easily test our future performance, progress, and growth.

The following procedures for measuring elements of TEMPO deserve our consideration because they are practical, objective, and cost-effective. Some may view them as too simplistic and yearn for more sophisticated procedures of measurement. But the real value and importance of simple procedures like these may lie in the discovery that individual teachers, teams, or faculty can create such measurement tools, entirely acceptable to themselves, which can then be used for self-evaluation and improvement or inservice training. Moreover, local data norms or criteria may then be cooperatively developed for assessment purposes.

Measuring Time-on-Task

This procedure is a modification of one suggested by Research for Better Schools (1981). Information gathered using this procedure yields a time-on-task rate for the number of students present. An observer-recorder is needed to complete the form during the time period designated. If teachers wish to use the procedure for self-evaluation, they designate a time and then ask a colleague, supervisor, or student to complete the rating form as illustrated in Figure 2.

The only decision the observer must make is how many students at any one minute are clearly not on-task. If there is doubt as to whether a student is daydreaming or giving serious thought to the subject at hand, the doubt is always resolved in favor of being on-task. At one point during each minute of observation the observer records the number of students present and the number who are unquestionably not on-task.

In the example given in Figure 2, 22 of the 25 students enrolled were present during the first three minutes of observation. When another student returned to the room during the fourth minute, seven of the 23 students then in the room were observed as being off-task. By the seventh minute of observation, only one student was off-task. Simple subtraction in each column then gives the number of students on-task for each minute and for the total seven-minute observation time. The computations for the on-task-rate (.86) can then be made as shown.

Is .86 a "good" time-on-task rate if you use the data gathering procedure just described? Well, it is nothing to brag about according to two pilot studies involving 140 observations in the classrooms of 70 different teachers in grades 1-12 in Texas and New Mexico. Both studies found a median time-on-task rate of .93 based on "middle of the lesson" observations. Furthermore, no significant differences were found among rural,

Figure 2. Time-on-Task Observation Form.

Teacher _____ Date _____

Observer _____ Subject _____

Number enrolled _____ 25 _____

Min.:	1	2	3	4	5	6	7	Total
Present	22	22	22	23	23	23	23	158
Not on-task	2	3	1	7	5	3	1	22
On-task	20	19	21	16	18	20	22	136

$$\text{On-task rate} = \frac{\text{Total on-task}}{\text{Total present}} = \frac{136}{158} = .86$$

suburban, and urban schools, or among grade level and subject variables as described in the following conclusions:

1. Elementary reading teachers' rates were essentially the same as those of junior high school reading teachers (.96).
2. Elementary mathematics teachers' rates were essentially the same as those of junior high school mathematics teachers (.96).
3. Reading teacher rates in urban schools (.94) were similar to mathematics teachers rates in rural schools (.96) in spite of demographic, cultural, and subject matter differences.

Principals, supervisors, and teachers performing the observations reported that a five-minute observation was sufficient to gain time-on-task ratings with which they would concur as professional observers. All agreed that a rating below .90 indicated an *ineffective* situation. When challenged with questions related to quality of time-on-task or student involvement, all reported they observed no classroom where the task at hand did not directly relate in a valuable way to the prescribed curriculum during their middle-of-the-lesson coding time.

Perhaps the most important outcome of the two studies was the successful translation of knowledge to practice. The observers reported that many of the teachers they had observed began searching for more efficient ways of passing out papers, taking roll, getting out books, and generally examining management procedures that could be shared with students to increase time-on-task.

Measuring Expectation

The following procedure for measuring teacher expectation shows that: (1) it is possible to gather indicators of this TEMPO element; and (2) teachers, principals, and school districts can devise a procedure acceptable in their own context.

Since the expectation element of TEMPO is keyed to the image of the teacher's expectations *as perceived by the students*, a questionnaire completed by the students can provide valuable assessment data. Some preliminary findings have emerged from data gathered from over 600 students in grades 5-12 responding to two questionnaires; the first is shown in Figure 3.

The second questionnaire differed from Figure 3 only in that students responded for the entire class, rather than just for themselves. For example, the first item was changed to "The Teacher expects all, most, some of us, to learn." No differences in response patterns were found between the two questionnaires when they were distributed randomly among students in the same class.

More interesting, these data indicate that student achievement level did not influence response within a class. That is, perceptions of students earning high grades in a class did not differ from those who were earning

Figure 3. A Questionnaire for Assessing the Expectancy Factor of TEMPO.

Questionnaire

Circle the letter in front of the statement that most closely states your answer to the following question:

What does your teacher expect of you?

I.   A. The teacher always expects me to do my assignments.
    B. The teacher sometimes expects me to do my assignments.
    C. The teacher never expects me to do my assignments.

II. A. The teacher always expects me to enjoy learning.
    B. The teacher sometimes expects me to enjoy learning.
    C. The teacher never expects me to enjoy learning.

III. A. The teacher always expects me to cooperate and help others learn.
    B. The teacher sometimes expects me to cooperate and help others learn.
    C. The teacher never expects me to cooperate and help others learn.

---

low grades. However, students in low-ability *classes* (as described by the teacher) perceived lower teacher expectations than those in high-ability classes with the same teacher. Generally, the teachers involved were poor predictors of student response. A better set of predictions was obtained for question 1 (assignment completion) than for questions 2 and 3 (learning enjoyment and cooperation). Finally, these data indicated that although most of the 600 students understood that they were expected to learn; they did not think that their teachers expected them to enjoy their classes.

All teachers involved in this assessment participated in much of the analysis and debate of the findings. This kind of action research involving teachers can lead to valuable research evaluation at the essential level for bridging the gap between knowledge and application.

Measuring Monitoring

Measuring this element of TEMPO involves obtaining objective data regarding the accuracy of teacher predictions of comparative student performances, as well as the accuracy of teacher prediction of difficulty types that will be displayed by individual students. Consistency in data treatment procedures is needed to aid in detecting teacher skill development in monitoring for use at the district level, building level, or simply for individual teacher self-evaluation.

One such monitoring index (M-1) may be obtained by analyzing teacher-predicted scores for students on a test, either teacher-made or standardized. A sample of teacher-predicted scores, actual scores, and the differences between those two scores is shown in Figure 4 for a classroom of 20 students.

The simple arithmetic computations required to arrive at the score of .88 for the first monitoring index (M-1) are also shown in Figure 4. How "good" is an M-1 score of .88? One might believe that it will depend on the subject, grade level, type of test, and students. However, data derived from 32 participating teachers, grades 1-12, from both public and private schools show an M-1 average score of 89 percent, but differences could not be explained by grade level or by subjects, including English, civics, mathematics, history, and spelling. The procedures were used in spelling lessons in grades 2-12 by 20 of the teachers, who found no indication that grade level influenced accuracy of prediction.

Other monitoring indexes can be developed by teachers to determine their accuracy of prediction in many other areas such as student preferences regarding testing (objective, subjective), free-time activity, or type of error each student will make on a given test. In any case, teachers can establish current average monitoring scores based on several such predictions, which can later point to indications of improvement in monitoring skill. At the building or district level, if the same procedure is used in all classes at a given grade level or for a given subject, comparisons of teacher monitoring indicators become possible. Over a period of time, such indicators could well identify inservice training needs for selected teachers.

Measuring Problems Assigned

Here we seek a procedure for objectively gaining a problem assignment score to provide a consistent basis for assessing our skill improvement in this area of TEMPO. The goal is for students to be able to complete accurately at least three-fourths of the assigned work without further instruction. The procedure should not impose on instructional or teacher time; it should yield the problem assignment score with minimum computation and effort, and concomitantly increase awareness of the importance of assigning work only after sufficient instruction has been provided.

For consistency of measurement, problem assignment scores should be obtained only from assigned work done in class. One indicator of problem assignment ability can be obtained by systematically examining such student scores. To illustrate, we examine the following scores made by ten students on an assignment where 20 is the maximum score possible: 18,

16, 17, 12, 20, 19, 18, 20, 14, 18. Eight of the ten scores (80 percent) show satisfactory completion of at least three-fourths of the work assigned. Also, the average of the ten scores is 17.2, or 86 percent of the maximum score of 20. Using just this set of scores, the first indicator, then, is that 80 percent of the students were able to successfully complete the assigned work. Second, as a group, the students averaged an 86 percent completion rate.

Figure 4. Tabulations and Computations for the First Monitoring Index (M-1) for a Classroom of 20 Students.

| | Test Scores | | |
Student	Teacher Prediction	Actual Score	Difference
a	18	19	1
b	10	7	3
c	16	16	0
d	20	17	3
e	12	16	4
f	14	17	3
g	15	10	5
h	17	20	3
i	18	18	0
j	19	13	6
k	11	14	3
l	16	17	1
m	17	14	3
n	18	16	2
o	16	12	4
p	19	18	1
q	20	18	2
r	20	20	0
s	18	17	1
t	17	14	3

Total Differences = 48

$$M - 1 = \frac{(\text{No. of Students}) \times \text{Perfect Score} - \text{Total Differences}}{\text{No. of Students} \times \text{Perfect Score}}$$

$$\text{or } M - 1 = \frac{(20 \times 20) - 48}{20 \times 20} = \frac{400 - 48}{400} = \frac{352}{400} = .88 \text{ or } 88\%$$

181712

One group of teachers using the preceding procedure gathered results from grades 6-9 in different subject areas and ability levels. Their first data indicated an average assignment completion rate of 73 percent. However, they noted that many student questions had involved failures in listening and reading directions, rather than requests for help in substantive ways. They changed their procedures to include a five-minute period immediately following the announcement of the assignment during which time no additional help was provided and no procedural questions were answered. This change resulted in an increase in assignment performance from 73 percent to 81 percent. After several weeks of using the five-minute rule, many of the teachers involved reported improved reading and listening behaviors among their students, especially among those who had previously and persistently asked trivial questions. Several reported a strong intuitive feeling that their Silent Curriculum had noticeably improved.

Examination of scores as given in the preceding example is not a new procedure for most teachers. But the systematic record keeping of results may be. A careful record of the percent completing at least three-fourths of several assignments, as well as the group average score, can provide a new view of problem assignment skills. We can discern percentage differences by subject, topic, and student groups, which we otherwise might miss. Such differences, once identified, can lead to valuable changes and improvements in the design of our assignments as well as their administration.

Measuring Organization

Problems of validity and reliability can be confounding when attempts are made to gain objective measurements of organizational skills. Specific skills are difficult to isolate, and the general organization skill is inseparable from the concepts of the Silent Curriculum as well as from the other four elements of TEMPO. Some important questions that need answers include: Do our established routines enhance desire for learning and accuracy of self-concept? Do our management procedures increase time-on-task, build respect for others, and enhance the learning climate?

Some objective measurements can be made. Our time allocations for subject matters can be determined and compared to those recommended by the district. Loss of time-on-task minutes can be compared for structured and unstructured learning activities or for two different routines used in collecting and returning homework or other materials. Different strategies for opening and closing a period of instruction can be compared so that the value of time saved by one strategy may be assessed against its impact on the Silent Curriculum. Attendance rates can be noted from grading period to grading period. We can have four-minute videotape segments of our teaching viewed by peers who do not know us personally.

The Value of Measurement

A few simple time- and cost-effective procedures have been outlined for measuring elements of TEMPO and the Silent Curriculum. At least three reasons point out the value of such nonstandardized procedures at a local level to help bridge the gap between theory and practice.

1. When practitioners develop and test data gathering procedures based on research findings, the procedures take on a high level of acceptance among those involved.
2. When practitioners analyze results and modify data gathering procedures, the related research base takes on new meaning for those involved.
3. When practitioners relate their analyses, both the knowledge and the procedures tend to diffuse among faculty and schools within the district.

Perhaps involvement of practitioners in the development, analysis, modification, and testing of procedures is the key to quickening the pace toward acceptable, sound teacher evaluation procedures. Even at the higher education level, a clear call for an action-oriented view of quality assessment has been made by Astin (1982):

Education needs a new approach to quality measurement, an approach that is conceptually simple and yet consistent with what is already known . . . and—most important—that offers some reasonable hope of significantly improving the quality of education (p. 13).

Among other things, Astin argues that the adoption of such procedures in a college or university would signal to all members of the academic community that the institution is concerned about improving the quality of teaching.

But much is yet to be done. Valid and reliable procedures and measurements based on the science of education are essential for developing sound teacher evaluation procedures. Without procedures that accurately measure the Silent Curriculum, even valid measures of TEMPO elements could become sterile and mechanistic. Although increased instructional skill in the TEMPO areas probably promotes a better Silent Curriculum, creating the needed valid measurement procedures for the Silent Curriculum might well be the most difficult bridge we have yet to build between knowledge and practice.

Without such procedures, the Silent Curriculum will continue to be that vague aspect of the classroom that "no one can measure," forever buried in the shadow of easily measured gains in achievement test scores.

Without such measures we revert to the historic procedure of gathering a number of supervisor judgments over a sufficient time period to finally render a governance decision. And at the college level, students will continue to graduate who may or may not prove effective in the field.

With the needed valid and reliable assessment procedures, much advancement can be made. The three elements of the Silent Curriculum could be assessed along with their counterpart—the Three Rs. Inservice training programs could be based on objective assessment of faculty development needs. Graduation from teacher preparation programs could signify a knowledge base in the science of education as well as a demonstrated potential in the art of applying that knowledge. In short, the science of education identifies the important elements of teacher effectiveness. Measurement permits assessment of those elements and points the direction to strategies for improving the art of application.

The Supervisory Problem

All that precedes this section adds only a small page to the literature of our profession unless it is followed by a call to action that makes sense at the levels of teacher preparation and inservice training prior to tenure acquisition. This call to action must confront the supervisors and administrators of both programs with their responsibilities in its implementation. These responsibilities cannot be abrogated or delegated. The connection between knowledge and practice must be achieved at both levels.

The College Level

All instructors and supervisors active in teacher preparation programs throughout the country must accept, and be required by their peers and administrators to accomplish, the necessary procedures to guarantee graduation of only those students who have the potential to become superior teachers. Selective-retention procedures throughout the undergraduate programs must identify those who do not demonstrate either the knowledge of the fundamental science of education *or* the ability to create a desirable Silent Curriculum in their classes.

Minimum competency tests in the areas of mathematics and communication skills must be prerequisite to formal entrance to such preparation programs. There is no moral persuasion possible to do otherwise for the benefit of future students of these prospective teachers. Following appropriate remedial efforts, those demonstrating a lack of either the necessary cognitive or process abilities must be counseled to other areas of endeavor. They cannot be permitted to graduate from an accredited program.

This requires careful and accurate monitoring of students in both cognitive and process areas. If we could graph one's knowledge of the science of education (with an emphasis on TEMPO) against one's art in applying that science (with an emphasis on the Silent Curriculum), prospective teachers would fall into one of the four areas shown (Figure 5).

Based on these concepts, we can now draw another illustration showing three areas of demonstrated abilities in which students in teacher preparation programs would fall. These three areas are shown by draw-

Figure 5. Four Quadrants of the Science and Art of Education.

	(HL) High Science Low Art	(HH) High Science High Art
The **Science** **of** **Education** **(TEMPO)**	(LL) Low Science Low Art	(LH) Low Science High Art

The Art of Application (Silent-Curriculum)

ing two arbitrary curves representing predictions of teacher success based on all data available at the preparation level. These three areas, shown in Figure 6, are (1) predicted superior teachers, (2) predicted potentially superior teachers, and (3) those who did not demonstrate the required minimum performances in the science and art of education areas (the shaded area).

Figure 6. Three Areas of Predicted Teacher Performance.

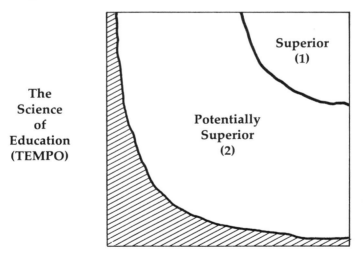

The
Science
of
Education
(TEMPO)

Superior
(1)

Potentially
Superior
(2)

The Art of Application
(Silent-Curriculum)

The Pre-Tenure Level

Assuming teacher preparation programs graduate only potentially superior teachers, the inservice training programs of schools during the pre-tenure years must be based on careful diagnosis of TEMPO and Silent Curriculum measurements obtained in the field. During the college preparation, some can be screened out who are diagnosed as not having the potential, but there is little opportunity to measure how a student will perform when in charge of 30 students, or five classes in a secondary school, for an entire school year.

For the first time the novice must take full responsibility for lesson planning, classroom organization, control, management, grading, parent conferences, faculty activities, and the thousands of decisions made by a teacher each day. For the large group of first-year teachers who fall in the area of potentially superior teachers, the inservice training programs must be positive, purposeful, and rewarding. Valid measurements of the TEMPO and Silent Curriculum areas need to be obtained carefully by principals and supervisors for comparison with previous scores of each teacher against scores of superior teachers in the same area and level. Growth goals may then be mutually established and sought. During this three-year period, healthy feelings of helpfulness, pride, and appreciation can develop between supervisor and teacher and between experienced colleague and beginner.

During this same period, a few beginning teachers may fall back to the shaded area of Figure 6. This may be expected, but must not be accepted. These teachers need immediate support, assessment, and help in the areas in which they are falling short. Even with such support, some will still fall deeper into the shaded area of Figure 6 and will voluntarily withdraw themselves from the profession. Others must be advised to do so, and those few who remain in the shaded area, but dispute the measurements and judgments of the supervisors and administration, must be treated fairly and firmly in being informed that their contracts will not be renewed.

Summary

The standard categorical syllogism opening this chapter contained the conclusion that the knowledge and abilities are available today to ensure teacher preparation programs that graduate only potentially superior teachers. Similarly, it is in the power of school districts today to mount inservice training programs that result in tenured faculties of only superior teachers, or those of imminent promise of joining that category.

Selected aspects of the science of education were considered under the acronym TEMPO. Definitions and the impact of the Silent Curriculum were reviewed. Selected nonstandardized procedures for measuring elements of TEMPO and the Silent Curriculum were outlined.

Such objectively gained measurements in the areas represented by TEMPO and the Silent Curriculum were viewed as essential to achieving the connection of knowledge to practice.

Those responsible for teacher education at both the college and pre-tenure levels must provide for the valid measurements, analyses, goal setting, and facilitating provisions needed to guarantee the quality of teachers awarded tenure. The massive, long-term improvement effect of such action will be the steady growth toward faculties composed of superior teachers. Then, students in every grade, in every school, in every subject or activity, will have teachers who are well informed in the science of education and who have become artists in its application. What a wonderful world that will be!

References

Aspy, D. and Roebuck, F. *Kids Don't Learn from People They Don't Like.* Amherst: Human Resource Development Press, 1977.

Astin, A. W. "Why Not Try Some New Ways of Measuring Quality?" *Educational Record* (Spring 1982): 10-15.

Hosford, P. L. *An Instructional Theory.* Englewood Cliffs, N.J.: Prentice-Hall, 1973.

Hosford, P. L. "The Silent Curriculum: Its Impact on Teaching the Basics." *Educational Leadership* 36 (1978): 211-215.

Hosford, P. L. and Martin, J. V. "Prospective Teacher Evaluation Via Videotape." *Action in Teacher Education* 2 (Winter 1979-80): 16 (per p. 17 of chapter 7), 45-47.

Hosford, P. L. and Neuenfeldt, J. C. "Teacher Evaluation Via Videotapes: Hope or Heresy?" *Educational Leadership* 36 (1979): 418-422.

Hosford, P. L. and Schroder, A. "Can the X-Factor of Teaching Be Used In Research?" Las Cruces: New Mexico State University, 1974. (ERIC Document Reproduction Service No. ED 100 920).

Neuenfeldt, J. C. "An Investigation of an Alternative Method of Evaluating Classroom Teaching." Doctoral dissertation, New Mexico State University, 1977. *Dissertation Abstracts International* 38 (1978): 7121A-122A.

Rosenshine, B. and Berliner, D. "Academic Engaged Time." *British Journal of Teacher Education* 4 (1978): 3-16.

Scandoval, J. *The Evaluation of Teacher Behavior Through Observation of Videotape Recordings. Beginning Teacher Evaluation Study: Phase II, 1973-74, Final Report: Volume III 3, 1976.* (ERIC Document Reproduction Service No. ED 127 368.)

Huitt, W.; Caldwell, J.; Traver, P.; and Graeber, A. Classroom Observation System for Student Engaged Time." In *Leaders Guide for Student Engaged Time.* Edited by Helms, A., Graeber, J., Caldwell, J., and W. Huitt. Philadelphia: Research for Better Schools, Inc., 1981.

The Silent Curriculum:
More than Intuition

JOHN J. KOEHN

One of my favorite pastimes as a school administrator is to conduct exit interviews with high school seniors. Just before they graduate, I ask randomly selected students to comment about their high school experiences: what they liked, what they disliked, how much they felt they had learned, where they were heading in life. Usually, the question that "grabs" them most is, "Who was your favorite teacher?" and "Why?"

I generally get an instant response with a lot of enthusiasm. Almost without exception students choose to describe their favorite or most memorable teacher in terms of the Silent Curriculum. Seldom, if ever, do students recall or praise their favorite teacher for being superior at teaching subject-verb agreement or the use of mathematical equations. Rather, students say he or she "really cares" or "really respects us as people" to describe the truly memorable teacher. So Hosford is correct when he places such high importance on the Silent Curriculum. Managing the Silent Curriculum effectively is a real skill—comparable to managing one's life in an artistic and sensitive way. As Hosford states, "Superior teachers must become what they are."

The next time you have the chance, ask adults to recall their most memorable teacher. Note how they choose to describe those special individuals. I'll bet they will picture their favorite teachers just like the seniors in the exit interviews. First and foremost, they will recall the person as being "human." Inevitably, they will use such words as "warm," "caring," "tough as nails," "demanding," or other descriptive words that denote human characteristics. Seldom do adults recall what was being taught in the course. They do remember with amazing clarity *how* the teacher taught—whether the teaching skills were good, bad, or indifferent.

The Silent Curriculum is a potent one. Of all the curricula—official, real, and silent—it is the one best learned by students. They "read" it instantly and draw conclusions just as quickly. If the teacher does not possess a desire to learn, students will not want to learn. If the teacher has a poor self-concept, the self-concepts of the students will suffer. If teachers do not respect themselves and others, students will not show respect.

John J. Koehn is Director of Instruction, Oconomowoc Area School District, Oconomowoc, Wisconsin.

Hosford refers to the "intuitive feelings" teachers have that the Silent Curriculum is either improving or deteriorating. Intuition, while sometimes appropriate, is not sufficient to manage the Silent Curriculum. Handling the Silent Curriculum effectively places a significant responsibility on supervisors and other administrators. As a practitioner involved with teachers on a daily basis, I offer the following suggestions for supervisory behavior, which may create a favorable impact on the Silent Curriculum being delivered in the classroom and the school:

- Create and maintain an awareness of the Silent Curriculum—how it works and how it impacts on learning.
- As a supervisor, be willing to spend time with teachers to help them discover and reflect upon their human qualities. Teachers must discover the choices they have in teaching—to be strict or permissive, group-oriented or individually directed, and so on.
- Eliminate criticism as a way of providing feedback from administrator to teacher, and from teacher to student. Strive for a truly failure-free school. Make the absence of failure the major ingredient of the Silent Curriculum. Self-concept is nourished in the absence of failure.
- Develop and nurture an appreciation for "action research" on the part of teachers. Make data gathering and analysis a high priority. Also, make the process of data gathering simple and convenient. Use your noncertified staff to reduce the burden on teachers; train secretaries and aides to organize the data for teachers.
- Help teachers to understand that good motivational procedures require attention before, during, and after learning experiences. As high levels of motivation are stimulated, student desire to learn will flourish.
- Assist teachers in identifying their needs in order to improve instruction. Guard against making your needs theirs. Use data and evidence to show results or change in teaching and learning as teachers strive to grow.
- Develop a reward system for staff members who devote themselves to the art of teaching.

By following the above procedures, the matter of implementing a positive Silent Curriculum will not be "intuitive." Rather, we will ensure that our students are being exposed to a curriculum that is no longer silent, but that speaks loudly to their sense of human values.

A Response to Hosford

PATRICIA B. ALLEN

Hosford's thoughts were refreshing to read. Most of the ideas are not new. Instead, as he stated, they are "common sense" things that effective teachers have always done intuitively. But it is encouraging to find research backing up "common sense."

The process-product studies completed in the last ten years are correlational studies. Everyone knows that correlation does not establish causation. Nevertheless, it is easy for teachers to accept the results and incorporate them into their teaching repertoire when the research supports their intuitive beliefs regarding effective teacher behavior.

Experimental studies are also being conducted that do establish a casual relationship between specific teacher behaviors and student achievement. One example is "The Missouri Mathematics Effectiveness Project: An Experimental Study in Fourth-Grade Classrooms" conducted by Good and Grouws (1979). Their purpose was to examine the effectiveness of a prescribed teaching program on student achievement. The program they developed evolved from their earlier process-product study (1977). Here you see a process-product study backed by an experimental study. The beauty of the present situation is that superior teachers now have the research base needed to resist bandwagon movements that refute their intuition/artistry.

With the elements of TEMPO, Hosford provides a framework in which teachers can structure and control their classrooms by implementing specific teacher behaviors. The five elements are all variables that are under the teachers' control, and they are all technical skills that teachers can work on to improve.

I don't believe anyone can "tell" teachers how to teach because teaching is truly an art. But even an artist must have some basic skills. An artist knows how to mix primary colors to produce secondary colors, knows what kind of brush to use, which brush strokes are most effective, and how to draw using perspective. Teachers must also have certain technical skills. Today we can provide teachers with knowledge of skills that are backed by both "common sense" and research findings—skills that can assist them in improving student achievement.

Time-on-task, along with the content covered, has produced the highest and most consistent correlations with student gain in achievement of any of the variables studied in the process-product studies. The key here

---

Patricia B. Allen is Social Studies Consultant, Lee County District School Board, Fort Myers, Florida.

is not allocated time for a task, but instead the actual number of minutes engaged in the task. Again, in some of the moves toward school reform in the 60s, the idea of open-space schools, individualized instruction using learning activity packets, learning centers, and programmed instruction came to the forefront. These types of activities are not suitable for elementary and most middle school students because student ability and skill to manage time has not yet matured and developed. Students who are allowed to choose the learning activities they engage in are usually lower in time-on-task and therefore in achievement.

Anyone with "common sense" knows that the more time-on-task a student has, the more opportunity that student has to learn. What was apparently not obvious to some was that when a teacher is instructing a small group, the rest of the class is usually off-task or doing busy work.

Superior teachers know that substantive teacher-student interaction in a small group is effective in producing student achievement. But they also face the reality that the rest of their unsupervised students are not on-task. Therefore, the next best solution to prevent off-task behavior and promote achievement is to provide whole-group instruction along with guided practice/reinforcement activities, and immediate feedback. It is during guided practice sessions, as teachers circulate among students, that they can provide individualized, one-on-one teaching.

Along with the five elements of TEMPO, Hosford provides a sample method for measuring each one. As he said, the measuring methods may be viewed simplistically by some, but they are indeed a beginning! He indicates that the methods in his paper should merely serve as examples. The measuring methods are an attempt to stimulate self-evaluation by teachers. Developing additional methods for measuring the elements would be an appropriate area for further educational research by those who have an interest and expertise in teacher effectiveness. The elements of TEMPO and the concept of measuring them assuredly have direct implications for supervisors who work with teachers in formative evaluation. They provide a plausible framework for assisting teachers to grow professionally.

Research indicates that when your goal is to increase student achievement in the basic skills, you can reach your goal by practicing the skills contained in TEMPO. Teachers in elementary and middle schools should aid students by correcting wrong performance and insisting on repetition of the correct performance until the student achieves mastery. Students need a solid foundation of basic skills before they can move on to critical thinking. This lack of drilling and overlearning of basic skills to the point of the skills becoming second nature may account for the deficiencies of many high school students. They can't analyze, synthesize, and/or discriminate: that is, they can't think critically unless they have something to think about (content plus skills).

Some of the criticism aimed at this research is that the results are only applicable to elementary students. No doubt this is true, and continued research with secondary students at all levels of ability should be done to alleviate this problem. Already there is evidence that the elements of TEMPO might be appropriate for low-ability secondary students, secondary students from low socioeconomic backgrounds, and secondary students who are anxious or dependent. Do remember that the elements of TEMPO should not be viewed as a fixed model of teaching. Instead they are a framework to be modified based on the student and the subject being taught.

A word of caution—we should never become so "scientific" that we lose sight of the human element, namely, the "art of teaching." But because a data base is rapidly being developed that correlates specific teacher behaviors with higher levels of student achievement, it seems logical that teachers and supervisors should focus some of their energy on the premises found in this data base. Phil Hosford appears to be on the right track.

References

Good, Thomas L. and Grouws, Douglas A. "The Missouri Mathematics Effectiveness Project: An Experimental Study in Fourth-Grade Classrooms" *Journal of Educational Psychology* 71 (1979): 355-362.

Good, Thomas L. and Grouws, Douglas A. "Teaching Effects: A Process-Product Study in Fourth Grade Mathematics Classrooms" *Journal of Teacher Education* 28 (May-June 1977): 49-54.

A Response to the Art of Applying the Science of Education

SIDNEY H. ESTES

"Monitoring" is a weakness of our educaton system. The aerospace industry "tracks" missiles as an essential part of that program. It *must* be done in the launching of rockets into space as they move along a given trajectory and return to another site. "Tracking" is an absolute necessity, and "correctives" must be applied. The act of teaching and learning requires the "tracking" of students along a given trajectory, leading to an ultimate destination. During the course of that "flight" correctives should normally be made of necessity. Unfortunately, that is generally not done.

Hosford is right when he says *effective* teachers assign problems in homework "at such a level that the students can perform most successfully on their own." In the Atlanta school system a telephone "Homework Hotline" has revealed some interesting information. Most students calling in for assistance do not necessarily lack the ability to do the assignment. In most cases they simply do not understand the assignment; it has not been clearly explained to them. Once clarified by hotline staff, the student is then able to progress successfully with the homework. Hence, attention *does* need to be given to the matter of in-service and/or teacher preparation, which specifically addresses that particular act of teaching.

I cannot avoid giving attention to an item in the questionnaire used to measure expectations that states, "The teacher always expects me to enjoy learning." Referring to the research, Hosford reports that "these data indicated that although most of the 600 students understood that they were expected to learn, they did not think that their teachers expected them to enjoy their classes." That is absolutely unfathomable, but probably true nonetheless. My observations and association with others would support that revelation. We all know that learning is not always fun, and that it requires time and effort. Nonetheless, there are teaching techniques and approaches that suggest that under the direction of a competent and empathetic teacher, learning *can* be fun.

I support the selection retention procedures suggested by Hosford in regard to undergraduate programs. Prospective teachers should be "screened" before entering teacher preparation programs, and monitored as they proceed through them. The screening should be coupled with observations and evaluations relating to the work of the student in

Sidney H. Estes is Assistant Superintendent, Division of Instructional Planning and Development, Atlanta Public Schools, Atlanta, Georgia.

specific courses and simulated or laboratory experiences. If such procedures were employed, the Student Teaching period would simply be the "icing on the cake." Once the person has completed the undergraduate program and joined the ranks of a school system in the role of teacher, further in-service experiences should relate to that person's role in a particular setting, associated with the person's needs as they relate to the needs of the learner. Such in-service would be a "honing" of the superior teacher, graduated by a creditable institution of higher education, to perform the needed work of educating our youth. When coupled with other techniques, such as program planning, monitoring, and/or management systems, it seems tenable that society would reap rewards by those facets in the teaching-learning arena. The process would yield productive, efficient, contributing high school and college graduates who would partcipate effectively and efficiently in our society, maintaining personal dignity and an attitude of sharing and serving, while producing for mankind on a global, national, and local basis.

8 Knowing, Teaching, and Supervising

MADELINE HUNTER

*T*eaching seems to be one of the last professions to emerge from the stage of "witch doctoring" to become a profession based on a science of human learning, a science that becomes the launching pad for the art of teaching. Only recently, however, has long-established research in learning been translated into cause-effect relationships of use to teachers. Only recently have teachers acquired the skills of systematically using these relationships to accelerate learning. Only recently have we accepted that *all* students and, in fact, *all* people can learn. No one denies that differences exist in genetic endowments. The quality of teaching, however, has the power to accelerate or retard an individual's learning; therefore, professional expertise in both art and science becomes our most powerful school factor.

Current findings are in direct contrast to the former fatalistic stance that regarded I.Q. and socioeconomic status as unalterable determinants of academic achievement. Gone also should be the notions that different ages, ethnic derivations, or content to be learned require a completely different set of professional skills, or that effective teachers must be born and can't be made. While the *form* may be different, the *substance* of excellence in teaching remains the same. Discoveries that dispelled these previously held educational myths are not entirely new, but recent translation from theory into teaching practice has effected the metamorphosis from a reactive to a proactive profession of education.

Teaching is a Science and an Art

Teaching, as it is used in this chapter, is defined as the constant stream of professional decisions that affects the probability of learning: decisions

Madeline Hunter is Academic Administrator, University of California at Los Angeles.

that are made and implemented before, during, and after interaction with the student. While highly related, teaching is distinct from determining curriculum. Curriculum building involves setting long-term goals that are based on beliefs and values. Teaching involves factor-analyzing those goals into dependent and independent sequences of learning, diagnosing students to determine what each has achieved in that sequence, and employing psychological principles that contribute to the speed and effectiveness with which each student acquires new learnings in those sequences. Curriculum building and teaching are equally important. To teach exquisitely that which is not worth the effort or to set worthwhile goals that are never achieved are both manifestations of poor educational practice.

Both science and art are essential to effective teaching. Teaching is a manifestation of science because:

1. Identifiable cause-effect relationships exist between teaching and learning.
2. Those relationships hold for all teaching and learning regardless of content, age, and socioeconomic and ethnic characteristics of the learner.
3. While many of these relationships were identified in the static purity and potential sterility of the research laboratory, those relationships seem to hold in the dynamics inherent in the vitality of a functioning classroom.
4. Those relationships are stated in terms of probability not certainty.
5. The deliberate, intuitive, or inadvertant use of those cause-effect relationships can be observed and documented in the process of teaching.
6. The principles derived from those relationships should also be incorporated in the process of planning and evaluating before and after teaching.
7. The science of teaching can be taught and predictably learned by most professionals who are willing to expend the required effort.

Effective teaching also can be (not invariably *is*) an art that goes beyond proficiency because:

1. An aesthetic quality can exist in planning, in teaching, and in the evaluation of teaching performance.
2. Those aesthetics can be observed, identified, labeled, and acquired but, with our present state of knowledge, cannot predictably be "taught."

This chapter will focus on the present state of the science of teaching, which is generalizable to all goals in all content and always mindful that an art exists beyond that science.

The Science of Teaching

Teaching is an applied science derived from research in human learning and human behavior: an applied science that utilizes the findings of psychology, neurology, sociology, and anthropology. The science of teaching is based on cause-effect relationships existing in three categories of decisions that all teachers deliberately make, intuitively or by default. Any of these decisions may be delegated to the learner. While students' assuming responsibility for their own learning is a major goal, accountability for students' learning remains with the teacher.

1. *Content decisions.* Regardless of whether a long-range goal is set by school district, state mandate, parents, students, or teachers, the teacher must task-analyze that goal to decide which component learning will be taught "tomorrow morning." This decision is based on what the student knows now and what he or she is next ready to learn, as well as the degree of intellectual complexity of the new learning that each student, with reasonable probability, can achieve.

   Examples:

   The long-range goal may be sophistication in quantitative relationships. The teacher determines whether each student has mastered the simpler concepts and skills that make the next learning possible, whether it be adding with regrouping *or* proceeding to the next unit in calculus. The teacher must also decide on the complexity of the problems requiring the operation that will be presented to the student or whether the student will generate those problems.

   In reading, locating information may be the goal. The teacher determines the vocabulary loading and idea density that each student is able to handle successfully and the degree of imbedding or surfacing of the information that is necessary to make its location challenging but visible to the learner.

   Long-range goals need not be academic. The same task analysis procedures apply to affective psychomotor or action pattern goals.

2. *Learner behavior decisions.* A second category of decisions the teacher makes is focused on what the student will *do* to learn. Will the student read, listen, observe, discuss, experiment, record? This decision also may be delegated to the learner, but total responsibility for the student's learning can never be delegated. In making a decision about learning behavior, the teacher must consider two factors:

   (a) Is what the student is to learn "appropriate" to what is to be learned? This question supplies the reason that the decision about learning behavior must be made after making the decision about content. The behavior of reading may contribute information for discussion, but one cannot achieve skill in discussions by utilizing only the process of reading. The student needs to engage in discussion. In learning how to discriminate between fact and opinion, the learner may observe, listen, read, and so on, in order to tell the difference, but he or she must also practice making discriminations. It is only *after* the student demonstrates accomplishment of the learning (the student discusses or discriminates successfully) that the teacher knows the next more difficult learning task is achievable and that the student may proceed to it.

(b) Is what the student is doing "working" for the student? It is obvious that "looking" would not "work" for a blind student nor would "listening" "work" for the deaf. Not so obvious, but equally handicapping, is the use of only *diagrams* for a student who finds them difficult to comprehend or only *words* for a student who needs to see relationships through a visual representation. Usually, it is not necessary for a teacher to diagnose a student's perferred learning behavior, but the teacher must ascertain whether the learning behavior or "input system" being utilized is working for that student. If it isn't working another learning behavior needs to be added to or substituted for the less successful one. Inherent in this decision is the responsibility for helping students develop a repertoire of learning behaviors rather than "majoring" in a preferred one.

The combination of appropriate behavior and the specific content being learned constitutes the instructional objective for that student. That objective may be in the affective domain (the learner will choose poetry as a leisure time activity); the psychomotor domain, (the learner will sight read and play a musical selection); or the cognitive domain (the learner will design an experiment that will substantiate or impeach the hypothesis). Learning objectives may be set by students, by teachers, or by both. The teacher's responsibility is to see that decisions that promote successful student achievement are made and implemented.

3. *Teaching behaviors. After* the first two decisions have been made (content to be learned and behavior of the learner to achieve that learning) and the instructional objective has been ascertained, the teacher can make the decisions that utilize principles of learning to affect students' motivation or intent to learn, the rate and degree of that learning, and the retention and transfer of that learning to new situations that require problem solving, decision making, and creativity. It is in the use of these psychological principles that the greatest artistry in teaching occurs. Designing needed practice so that it is exciting rather than boring, making material so interesting

that the student becomes intrinsically motivated to continue learning, using reinforcers that enhance a student's self-concept, relating new academic learning to a student's own life so that learning becomes meaningful and useful—all are hallmarks of educational artistry.

We must continue to remind ourselves that teaching is a decision-making process. Teaching decisions are a synthesis of what is known about human learning in general, what is known *or* inferred *or* intuited about a particular student or group, and what is known about the ambience, constraints, or requirements of the current situation, as well as future possibilities and probabilities.

Teaching becomes a profession only when information from funded knowledge, experiential knowledge, knowledge of student, and knowledge of present and future life press are synthesized in pedagogical decision making. Along with, but not in lieu of, this conscious decision making, there is plenty of need for the use of intuition, that highly functional but inarticulate knowledge, and for extra sensory perception, if available. It has been said that all teachers should have an "advanced degree in wizardry." That, too, is indicated, because at times "wizardry" seems to offer the only solution to complex problems in education.

Excellence and artistry in teaching can be ascertained by a sophisticated observer. Excellence and artistry can be *achieved,* however, only in the way all artistic and effective performance behaviors are achieved and validated: by practice with observation of performance, which yields feedback to effect improvement. While other behaviors may be indicators of excellence in performance—what one says, knows, and writes about performance plus results from that performance—only observation can attest to the consonance of that performance with funded knowledge and current perceptions of student and situation. Only observation can yield suggestions for ways to increase both effectiveness and artistry.

In his 1979 ASCD Conference address, Elliot Eisner labeled this yield from observation of performance "connoisseurship in education" and likened it to the connoisseur in music and art who interprets and evaluates performance in terms of commonly agreed upon meanings that describe the excellence of the performance or its needs for improvement.

Connoisseurship in education has been singularly absent. Not for want of intent or desire, but for lack of two essentials. First, there has been no common vocabulary by which teaching performance could be described in agreed upon terms. That vocabulary now exists. Second, funded knowledge in human learning had not been couched in terms intelligible to practitioners and, therefore, was not translated into performance behaviors in the classroom.

Suppose the skills of football players were described only in terms of physics, chemistry, anatomy, and kinesiology. No matter how accurate, those words would be of little help to the player and coach. Only when that information has been translated into passing, blocking, tackling, running, or kicking, can football be described, interpreted, evaluated, and improved. That same translation is essential to improving performance in teaching.

Translation of research-based theory into practice has now been accomplished, so we can describe and substantiate much of what is effective in teaching.

A number of "templates" can be used to describe, interpret, and evaluate either formatively, to improve the process of teaching, or summatively, to categorize the quality of teaching. One template in common use is an examination and interpretation of teacher decisions and behaviors in terms of the three previously described categories.

Analysis of Decisions in Teaching

1. *Content.* Are the teacher's decisions about the degree of difficulty and the complexity of content to be learned (cognitive, affective, or psychomotor) appropriate for the intended learners? If the learner has made the content decision, is it achieveable in the foreseeable future, or is that learner's level of aspiration too low or too high? Regardless of who made it, a content decision that is "over the learner's head," because its attainment is highly improbable, or "under the learner's feet," because that learning requires very little effort or has already been attained, constitutes a pedagogical error for which the teacher is responsible. For example, is it appropriate that a particular learner participate in a discussion, or should he or she be learning to guide or summarize the discussion, or be learning to listen without interfering with the discussion?

2. *Learner behavior.* Is what the learner is doing in order to learn appropriate not only to the learning to be achieved but also to that learner? Does observable behavior validate that learning has occurred? For example, if discussion skills are the objective, are ways of successfully acquiring those skills available to the learner in a mode he or she can assimilate? Is there behavioral validation that simpler skills have been acquired before more complex skills are introduced? Does the learner eventually demonstrate productive participation in a discussion?

3. *Teacher behavior decisions.* What evidence indicates the teacher is using principles of learning to accelerate achievement? Or, is the teacher unaware of or abusing those principles by overuse or omission? For example, is the teacher linking new learning to students' past knowledge and experience to make new learning meaningful and its acquisition enhanced by transfer? Is the teacher testing the

meaningfulness of new learning by encouraging students to generate examples from their own lives? Is the teacher regularly reinforcing productive new behavior when it emerges, but changing to an intermittent schedule of reinforcement for productive behavior that is not new? Or is the teacher committing pedagogical errors by persevering with potential reinforcers that are not needed, hammering in meaning when there is evidence it already is present, massing practice for fast learning, but forgetting to distribute that practice for long-term retention?

The template of the three categories of decisions in teaching provides a common and defensible frame of reference by which teaching decisions and actions can be described, interpreted, discussed, evaluated, and improved.

Design of Effective Lessons

A second template is lesson design or "a basic white sauce of teaching." This format for *designing* (not necessarily *conducting*) the lesson was deliberately given the name "basic white sauce" because seldom does a creative cook use a plain white sauce. *Techniques* used in making the basic sauce, however, are employed in more elaborate culinary masterpieces. So it is with teaching. Because making a basic lesson design explicit was "welcome news" to so many educators, it has unfortunately become a rigid measuring stick of "correctness" in teaching. That was never its intent.

Many observers find the template of the seven elements in lesson design to be helpful in interpreting the effectiveness or ineffectiveness of direct teaching and in identifying what is needed should lessons be ineffective. These elements have been developed elsewhere so only a brief listing will be included here.

1. *Anticipatory set.* Has the teacher developed in the students a mental set that causes them to focus on what will be learned? An anticipatory set may also give some practice in helping students achieve the learning and yield diagnostic data for the teacher. *Example:* "Look at the paragraph on the board. What do you think might be the most important part to remember?"

2. *Objective and purpose.* Not only do students *learn* more effectively when they know what they're supposed to be learning and why that learning is important to them, but teachers *teach* more effectively when they have that same information. Consequently, in words that are meaningful to the students, the teacher often states what will be learned and how it will be useful. *Example:* "Frequently people have difficulty in remembering things that are important to them. Sometimes you feel you have studied hard and yet you don't

remember some of the important parts. Today, we're going to learn ways to identify what's important, and then we'll practice ways we can use to remember important things."

3. *Input.* Students must acquire new information about the knowledge, process, or skill they are to achieve. Regardless of whether that information comes from discovery, discussion, reading, listening, observing, or being told, the teacher must have task-analyzed the final objective to identify knowledge and skills that need to be acquired. Only then can the input phase of the lesson be designed so that a successful outcome becomes predictable.

4. *Modeling.* "Seeing" what is meant is an important adjunct to learning. Usually, it is facilitating for the learners to directly perceive the process or product they are expected to acquire or produce. So that creativity will not be stifled or generalizability impeded, several examples should be a routine part of most (not all) lessons. Demonstrations, live or filmed, of process and products are facilitating rather than restricting to student initiative and creativity.

5. *Checking for understanding.* Before students are expected to do something, it is wise to ascertain that they understand what it is they're supposed to do and that they have the minimum skills required to do so. Sometimes this checking occurs verbally before actual student action. Sometimes it occurs simultaneously with the next element.

6. *Guided practice.* Students practice their new knowledge or skill *under direct teacher supervision.* New learning is like wet cement; it is easily damaged. An error at the beginning of learning can easily "set" so that it is harder to eradicate than had it been apprehended immediately.

7. *Independent practice.* Independent practice is assigned only after the teacher is reasonably sure that students will not make serious errors. After an initial lesson, students frequently are not ready to practice independently, and the teacher has committed a pedagogical error if unsupervised practice is expected.

One of the most typical errors in supervision is the assumption that "all good things must be in every lesson." Each element must be *thought* about by the teacher and its exclusion be a matter of professional decision making rather than default. Only the teacher, however, is in a position to make the final decision. As long as that decision is thoughtful and theory based, when theory is available, and "wizard based," when theory is not, then that teacher is operating as a professional.

Should a teacher, on the basis of emerging data *decide* to skip guided practice, later to find students practicing errors, the inaccurate practice can be stopped until supervised practice can be scheduled. That teacher knows what's wrong and how to correct it. A teacher who is oblivious to the function of guided practice will interpret errors as due to students' "not listening" rather than realize the problem is pedagogical. Questions asked during an instructional conference can separate one teacher from the other.

The TA III

A third template for describing and interpreting performance in teaching is the TA III (Teaching Appraisal for Instructional Improvement Instrument). This instrument was developed for an outside evaluation to document changes in teachers' decisions and behaviors and to validate the positive influence of those changes on student learning gains in terms of academic achievement, positive self-concept, reduced problems of discipline and vandalism as well as increased teacher satisfaction. This project took place in an inner-city school where previously both teachers and students had been unsuccessful and discouraged. Observed teacher growth, as documented by the TA III, correlated highly with significant student achievement gains. Subsequently, the TA III has been used with different students to measure different goals.

In using this instrument, the following questions are answered and documented from observation:

1. *Are teacher and learner effort and energy directed to a learning?* Are teacher and learner effort and energy contributing to attainment of a perceivable learning objective, or are their behaviors random, resulting from free associations or ad hoc inclinations? This question does not imply that teaching should be rigid or unresponsive to emerging data. Rather, teaching should be rigorous and maximize learning gains from time and energy expended by teacher and student. It is teaching wisdom to change objectives when such a change is indicated by student boredom, audiovisual failure, misjudgments in appropriateness of level of difficulty of learning task, or emergence of a more appropriate objective; all of which occur in the real world of teaching. It is pedagogical folly to follow, in the name of creativity, each possibility that emerges or to engage in a series of free associations that lead nowhere except perhaps to confusion.

   For example, when map reading skills are the learning objective and a student volunteers, "I'm going to Disneyland on my birthday next Saturday," the teacher has several options, none of which is always correct. The teacher may use the response to add meaning and facilitate attainment of the objective by saying, "If John lives here on our map and Disneyland is here, what direction will he be traveling next Saturday? What direction will he be traveling when he returns home?" Another teaching option might be to ignore John's response or acknowledge it with just a smile or "Oh." A third option might be to change objectives and move to a discussion of the critical attributes of an amusement park, developing categories of activities that are in most parks. A fourth option might be to respond with "Help me to understand how that relates to reading a map."

No particular one of these possibilities is always correct. If the state test on map reading is to be administered the following day, the teacher will probably continue with the original map reading objective. If this is the first time John has ever volunteered a remark, the teacher may abandon the map reading objective and encourage further comments from John by a discussion of amusement parks, thereby building a bridge to a report of the trip on the following Monday. If John's remark is simply the result of not attending to the map lesson, the teacher will attempt to refocus him but not dignify his extraneous contribution. The teacher's knowledge of the learning that is necessary to read maps, knowledge of John, and sensitivity to current and future situations must be synthesized to determine an appropriate teaching action for this particular situation. Teaching is decision making!

2. *Is the learning objective at the correct level of difficulty for these students?* This is the second question of the TA III. To answer it, the teacher must have diagnosed the students, either formally (using some reliable instrument), informally (by observation, sampling, or signaled responses), or inferentially (basing present interpretations on similar past performances). The observer of teaching does not need to look at diagnostic data, IQ's, or yesterday's lesson plans to determine whether the level of difficulty is appropriate for these students. It will be apparent that, as the lesson progresses, students are moving from apathy to enthusiasm, from less certainty to more certainty, from halting to more fluent responses, from errors to more accurate performance; all of which will attest to the correct level of difficulty defined as that place where old learning leaves off and new learning can begin.

3. *Is the teacher monitoring students' learning and adjusting teacher and learner behaviors as a result of information revealed?* An inexperienced teacher may dutifully plan a lesson, then teach those plans regardless of indications that suggest adjustments need to be made. The effective teacher is constantly validating or modifying teaching and learning behaviors on the basis of cues that are surfacing or being elicited during the lesson.

For example, in teaching a three-step process, a teacher may let the students see the "big picture," then teach the first step, check to see that it has been learned, and reteach or remediate when indicated before moving on to the second step. By the time the third step has been concluded, the teacher has a good idea of who knows and who doesn't and either builds remediation into the present lesson or make plans for future help for those who need it.

There is no one best way to check learning achievement. Taking papers home to correct may give accurate information, but that information is available for teaching tomorrow, not today when it is needed. To make sure needed information is constantly emerging, the teacher may use signaled responses, choral responses, samples responses, partnership responses, or *brief* written responses, which the teacher circulates to inspect. All of these techniques have the potential to give information *while* teaching, the time when information about achievement is most needed.

4. *Is the teacher using principles of learning effectively?* This question is the same one asked in the template that focused on the three categories of teaching decisions. To answer, the observer must be familiar with those principles of learning, recognize them in action, and determine, on the basis of objective evidence, whether they are being used appropriately, being ignored, or being abused.

For example, if a teacher comments on the excellent quality of a student's thinking and the student increases his productive participation in a discussion, reinforcement principles are being used effectively. If, instead, that student becomes self-conscious and silly and makes remarks that derail the discussion, the teacher will not call attention to him again but will attempt through other means to refocus his participation so it is more productive in the group. If the teacher continues to make comments drawing attention to that student, it is evidence that the teacher is ignoring the results from an unsuccessful attempt to use reinforcement and mindlessly following the false absolute that "praise is good," rather than using student response and current situation to modify a teaching decision.

5. *How will the observer help the teacher continue to grow?* Continuing growth is one hallmark of a professional. The use of science and art in teaching also applies to the teaching of teachers. Just as analysis of a student's performance reveals what the student knows and is ready to learn, observation and analysis of teaching performance attest to knowledge and art already translated into teaching performance and what can next be learned to increase the excellence of professional decisions and action patterns. Analysis of teaching is most effectively accomplished with the use of a script tape—anecdotal notes of what transpired during the teaching performance. Temporal relationships are revealed in those notes, which in turn suggest possible cause-effect connections between teaching decisions and behaviors and student learning.

Through the use of script tapes, which capture what "happened" in the lesson, the six categories of information listed below can be made available to teachers. In addition, options that hold promise for extension of professional skills can be identified for teachers' future investigation and selection. These have been developed in detail elsewhere (Six Types of Instructional Conferences), so they will be listed only briefly here.

1. *Identifying and labeling productive behaviors.* Teachers grow when they receive specific feedback as to student behaviors that were productive, the teacher decisions and behaviors that probably evoked those students behaviors, plus the label for that cause-effect relationship and the research-based reasons for the observer's assumptions.

   Example: The students were listening intently to your explanation. A probable reason for this was that you let them choose their area of interest and then stated that students who could demonstrate they understood the assignment would be able to work on their own. This gave them a reason for listening and a reward if they did. You make excellent use of the principles of *interest* and *level of concern* to increase student *motivation* or intent to listen and learn.

   Knowing what they did well and why fosters professional growth among teachers because so much of their knowledge has been experiential or intuitive and, therefore, inarticulate. They may have known that something "worked" but didn't know why, so that "something" could not be accurately generalized to new situations. Competence in knowing what we're doing, why it works, and doing it on purpose is reassuring to all of us.

2. *Developing productive alternative behaviors.* A second kind of feedback that accelerates the development of teaching excellence is the professional stretching that results from identifying alternatives to decisions and actions that were successful in the previous lesson but that could be less successful in a different situation. Developing in advance a cluster of alternative possibilities, for a future time when they might be needed, produces fewer surprises and more successes.

   Example: "Your students were listening intently. Your cartoons on the chalkboard certainly captured their interest. Sometimes when the teacher is doing something that is amusing, some students can get silly and start making 'remarks.' What might you do if that happened in your group so that one student didn't spoil it for everyone?"

   An instructional conference is not a spectator sport. The observer who is conducting the conference should be thinking and working harder than the teacher because the observer is now assuming primary responsibility for that teacher's learning even when the teacher is a willing collaborator and an active participant (something that is not always the case). Consequently, the observer must be ready to suggest several possible alternatives, not *the* right one, while also encouraging the teacher to develop alternatives. The teacher then needs to predict which one or two alternatives would best fit students, situation, and the teacher's style.

Example: "One possibility might be to reinforce those students who were not acting silly by saying 'Some of you are showing that you're mature enough to have fun in learning without getting silly.' Another possibility might be to prompt those students who are out of order, 'I hope you can handle yourself without needing help.' A third possibility might be to raise everyone's level of concern, 'Now, while I am erasing the board, review the main points so you're ready to answer a question when I call on you.' A fourth possibility might be, 'Pretend you're the teacher and be ready to ask the group a question to test how well they have been listening.' "

The observer encourages the teacher to develop additional alternatives and, then, in light of students and situations, estimate the most productive teaching behavior in a similar future situation. Developing alternatives and selection from that repertoire of alternatives constitutes the science *and* art of teaching.

3. *Analyzing one's own teaching.* One of the most powerful techniques for producing professional growth is introspection into one's own teaching. A third possible objective of an instructional conference is to encourage the teacher to identify what was learned from teaching a lesson that might be useful in subsequent teaching or of assistance to someone else who is going to teach a similar lesson. The teacher may identify something that did not go as anticipated or desired and, with the observer, can analyze possible causes and then suggest alternative actions. Again, those alternatives may be developed by the teacher, but the primary responsibility for analyzing possible causality and suggesting remediation rests with the observer who was there for the purpose of promoting professional growth. The observer may be tempted to suggest what he or she used to do or would prefer to do. The objective of supervision is not to clone oneself but to stimulate growth in another. Teaching behavior that fits the observer's style may not fit the teacher's.

4. *Identifying areas that need improvement.* In the past, the most common message in teacher conferences was identification by the observer of what didn't go well; a message that may or may not be conducive to teacher growth. Occasionally, identification of unsuccessful teaching decisions and behaviors may be necessary. Frequently, the three previous types of messages, all of which are positive, can eliminate the need for identification of pedagogical errors and can even encourage the teacher to initiate a request for additional possibilities for improvement. When unsuccessful teaching decisions and actions are identified, the observer must be sure to use objective data, "The students were distracted. This could have occurred because

you were introducing fractions by dividing cupcakes. The students were so concerned with 'do we get to eat them after the lesson?' that they had a hard time focusing on what was being taught. If you decide to use food to stimulate high interest, you might use soda or graham crackers or apples or vegetables and divide them into sections. Students will enjoy eating them afterwards but won't be in such a frenzy of anticipation." In addition to the observer's suggestions, teachers are always encouraged to design their own alternatives.

Remember, the observer identifies only those problems to which there are potential solutions, or acknowledges that a problem exists though solutions, at this time, seem nonexistent.

Example: "I know the students were disinterested in learning the difference between restrictive and nonrestrictive clauses, but for the life of me I can't think of a way to make it important to them even if you use sentences about those students. I'll work on it and see if some productive ideas emerge."

5. *Identifying the next steps to promote the continuing growth of excellent teachers.* Most neglected have been our "X" cellent teachers who, because of their superior performance, have been left to learn on their own. We would not think of treating our gifted students in this manner. We would continue to stretch, stimulate, and open new avenues of interest and investigation for them. We need to do the same for our gifted teachers. Remember, even champions need coaches in order to continue to excel. An "X" conference should represent collaborative effort between teacher and observer so the final results are a synthesis of the best thinking and planning both have to offer. Exploring a new teaching technique or curriculum goal, doing professional writing that requires clarification or articulation of effective teaching behaviors, developing new ideas, working in different content or with different ages, making videotapes or doing demonstration lessons—all of these stimulate professional growth, particularly if teacher and observer become partners in the new venture so each has stimulation and feedback from the other. This type of professional interaction is so growth evoking that it becomes addictive. Once a professional has experienced it, nothing less is satisfying.

6. *Evaluative conferences.* All of the above conference interactions are formative in their function. The objective is to effect change in the direction of continually increasing professional excellence. As a summation of many such interactions, the evaluative or "E" conference is regarded by both teacher and observer as a fair assignment of a teacher to the category of "excellent," "satisfactory," "needs improvement," or whatever characterizations have been adopted by

the district. Categorizations are based on and supported by evidence secured from many samples of teaching performance rather than from one deterministic observation, prejudice, or irrelevant and static "shoulds" and "should nots," which formerly plagued evaluation. Teachers will see as fair and just those evaluations that can be supported by evidence from many instructional conferences.

This brings us to the criticality of the observer's skill. This role may be assumed by the principal, superintendent, supervisor, or by another teacher. However, most principals have responsibility for evaluation; therefore, they need inservice opportunities to acquire skills in observation, analysis, and instructional conferencing.

The Role of the Principal

The importance of the role of the principal in creating an effective school has always been assumed, but only recently has the criticality of that person's skills been affirmed and documented. To fulfill that responsibility, contemporary principals need a newly articulated set of skills: those of analyzing the process of teaching and reinforcing and/or remediating and/or stretching from both a curricular and a pedagogical theory base.

No principal can be a curriculum specialist in every area of content but can observe, assist with, and evaluate the effective translation of any content into students' understanding and successful use. The principal can also determine, in most cases, students' perception of the value of what is being learned: whether it is to please the teacher, to pass the test, or to be useful and enriching in the present and future.

The principal *must* be a pedagogical specialist in order to stimulate, observe, and validate constantly escalating effectiveness in instruction—the business of the school. The principal has a unique professional obligation and opportunity in that he or she is an administrator whose primary function concerns the education of each student, but who must work through the skills of teachers. Consequently, enhancement of those teaching skills becomes a principal's primary concern. To nurture, develop, and escalate instructional excellence is the single most important function of the principal: a function for which most principals have had little or no systematic training and for which there seems never to be enough time.

When one considers how many of a principal's problems would be alleviated, if not removed, by satisfied, successfully learning students, it is surprising that the principal has not been more systematically and successfully prepared for this function. Probably the reason is that, until recently, the science of the art of teaching had not been articulated in language useful to the practitioner. Now we can describe in words and translate into action those supervisory skills that promote increased instructional effectiveness.

In assisting each principal to acquire the necessary skills, we need to follow those same universal principles of effective instruction that apply to students and to teacher preservice and inservice education rather than the more typical admonitions to principals that they should become educational leaders.

Most principals were effective teachers, but their skills may have been intuitive and therefore inarticulate. While highly functional and not to be underrated, inarticulate knowledge and skills have two problems: (1) Intuition is sterile and therefore dies with its posessor because it cannot predictably be reborn through transmission to others, and (2) Intuition is not "on call." Many a teacher has hoped that what to do would "come in a burst of insight," and it hasn't. Articulated knowledge while not providing omniscience has neither of these problems. A person can "reach into a memory bank" and retrieve knowledge. Principals need to learn how to articulate, explain, and demonstrate the cause-effect relationships that exist between teaching and learning.

Consequently, the first learning objective for the principal who is to become an educational leader is a knowledge-based one. The principal must be able to *state:* (1) a learning objective in performance terms, (2) diagnostic procedures that will reveal what a student knows and indicates the next learning steps, (3) ways of translating input into various learning modalities and learner styles, (4) ways of eliciting student performance that is not only perceivable but validates that a learning has been achieved, (5) principles of learning and ways they can be used to facilitate that achievement, and (6) evaluative techniques that do not drain a teacher's time and energy but validate or impeach student's achievement.

After bringing much formerly intuitive knowledge to a conscious level and adding articulated, research-based knowledge, the principal needs to develop the skill to transmit or discuss both kinds of knowledge with another professional.

The next learning tasks of the principal are performance ones.

1. *Performance that reflects knowledge.* First, the principal must internalize pedagogical knowledge so it becomes characteristic of performance in the act of "principaling." This not inconsiderable feat is usually best accomplished by practicing *deliberate* incorporation of effective teaching skills while working with a small group of students. Nothing is more enabling and humbling than experiencing, firsthand, how easy it is to state what should be done and how difficult it is to do it. No other activity will so effectively build the skills and empathy necessary to work productively with teachers as well as develop credibility from having "tried it" with students. In addition, this "field testing" will produce the rigor and competence necessary to being helpful in a supervisory relationship. The princi-

pal may have once been a great teacher, but will find skills have rusted and memory of how difficult teaching is will have faded. An added bonus from practice with students will be the exhilaration of finding how much better one can teach when deliberate science supports intuition. No small dividend will be the credibility developed with teachers when the principal is willing to reveal and examine his or her strengths and weaknesses in teaching with the purpose of minimizing or eliminating those weaknesses. Videotaping a teaching episode, looking at it privately, erasing it if necessary, and finally having an observer analyze the lesson with the principal is the ultimate growth-evoking activity.

2. *Staff meetings that reflect application of knowledge about teaching.* A second way that the principal needs to translate newly articulated old skills and newly acquired research-based skills into performance behavior is by designing, conducting, and evaluating staff meetings. It has been stated, sometimes accurately, that the poorest teaching in the world occurs in a staff meeting. Through meetings, the principal can provide a way for teachers to directly experience the results of scientific *and* artistic planning and instruction.

3. *Script taping teaching.* A third learning task for the principal who aspires to instructional leadership is the application of knowledge of cause-effect relationships between teaching and learning to the analysis of short episodes (2-10 minutes) of teaching. The objective at this point is *not* to help a teacher, but to assist the principal to acquire the skills of capturing with anecdotal notes the temporal sequence of teacher and learner behaviors as they emerge. This provides the principal with a "script tape" of what happened. The script tape becomes a primary data source for analysis of instruction and future principal-teacher interaction. From the script tape, an audiovisual record of the lesson can be recreated.

It should be noted that most people (student teachers, teachers, supervisors, principals, superintendents, and professors) can learn to do a very accurate script tape in about two hours. Because it is counter to what they are used to doing, which is making judgments rather than capturing data, most people are convinced by their beginning efforts that it is an impossible task and wish for shorthand skills, a tape recorder, or a video recorder, none of which is necessary or in many cases desirable.

Script tapes have the following advantages:

- They require only a pen and pad, materials available in any school and materials that the observer can easily transport and use whenever needed.
- The observer can quickly "swing" focus from one part of the group to another (something not possible for a camera). This enables an observer to scan and record many parts of the room

almost simultaneously. The script tape can show what was happening in each area.

- From the script tape, the observer can recreate the sequence of the lesson, determine the objective of the lesson, identify salient teacher and student behaviors that were enabling, useless, or even interfering to achievement and, from those data, design the objective for a subsequent growth-evoking instructional conference to be held with the teacher.
- During the conference, the script tape can be used to "play back" the sequence of the lesson, teacher and student actions, comments, or whatever is needed to recall the lesson to the teacher and to validate what occurred.

A script tape can be skimmed and edited by the observer so that only relevant parts will be addressed in the conference. Should the teacher wish to focus on another part of the lesson, a record of that part is available.

At times, lessons may be videotaped. Videotape has the advantage of enabling the teacher to "see and hear" what happened, something that is not always possible in the "heat" of a lesson. Videotapes, when viewed, have the disadvantage of taking all the time the lesson took to teach, plus the time needed to analyze and talk about it. They also have the disadvantage that they are not edited, which means "seesawing" through to find the special part to be discussed. Videotapes also make highly visible some things you'd rather forget. In addition, there is the time, energy, and space required to set up the recorder. Even when a lesson is videotaped, it is useful to do a script tape; the latter is a resource for the parts of the lesson not captured by the videotape. Still, videotapes should occasionally be used to "see ourselves as others see us," something the script tape can't accomplish as vividly.

Audiotapes have advantages and disadvantages similar to videotapes. Both audiotapes and videotapes are useful tools in examining the process of teaching, but are not essential to that examination.

4. *Analysis of teaching.* A fourth activity essential to the role of the principal as an educational leader is the analysis of teaching in terms of both curriculum and pedagogy. This analysis must reflect the principal's knowledge about human learning as applied to a teaching episode, thereby, identifying possible cause-effect relationships. An inviting "booby trap" exists in the false absolutes that certain behaviors in and of themselves are "good" (questioning, discussing, discovering) and others are "bad" (lecturing, telling, using negative reinforcers, or punishment). All classroom behaviors must be interpreted in terms of their purpose and the immediate and long-term results from their use. Behaviors are not "good" or "bad"

in themselves. Getting rid of this bias is one of the most difficult tasks for the typical principal.

5. *Task analysis of teaching effectiveness.* A fifth ability essential to educational leadership is the application of skills in task analysis to the task of continuing growth for a teacher. What is the teacher next ready to learn? What are the components of that learning? Each component must be addressed and acquired before the more complex teaching behavior can be expected.

6. *Monitoring teaching performance.* A sixth procedure inherent in successful leadership is the principal's monitoring of teaching performance and adjusting supervisory guidance on the basis of that monitoring; the same skill expected of teachers in the classroom. Monitoring can occur in classroom observations, in instructional conferences, in staff meetings, and in ongoing principal-teacher interactions.

   A serious omission in supervision is the attention that should be given to guided practice. Teachers learn about important aspects of effective teaching and are then expected to engage in independent practice within their own classrooms without the necessary guided practice and feedback from an observer.

7. *Developing conferencing skills.* Finally, the principal must be able to demonstrate conferencing skills that exemplify effective pedagogy, regardless of whether the interaction is with a teacher, student, parent, central office or community worker.

   Criteria for an effective conference are the same as those for an effective lesson. Any conference can be analyzed and made more effective by using the same templates that are used to interpret a lesson. One hallmark of principal growth in instructional leadership is that he or she encourages others to observe instructional conferences and give feedback designed to improve the principal's performance. Whether this is done "live," by video or audiotape, depends on the availability of people and hardware. It is an anxiety-provoking but a growth-evoking procedure.

8. *Working with discipline.* Skills of using principles of learning in human interactions can be singularly absent when working with discipline cases, even though such work must follow the same principles used in teaching. The misbehaving student must not only learn and practice more acceptable behavior but learn to choose that behavior in preference to previous unacceptable behavior. The teacher must learn how to more predictably elicit the acceptable behavior and learn how to deal productively with the unacceptable behavior should it occur. Parents must learn how to modify their parenting to achieve the jointly agreed upon new behaviors and learn how to collaborate with the school in those expectations. All of

this is *new learning* or the problem would not exist. The responsibility for evoking this learning achievement by everybody concerned rests primarily with the principal.

Working in collaboration with a teacher on a discipline problem frequently provides the basis for trust and belief in the competence of another professional. That collaboration can pave the way for the more anxiety-evoking process of the principal's observation and analysis of teaching. Building rapport and trust is an essential element in productive supervision, so the skill to accomplish this should be demonstrated by the principal in all interactions.

Formative evaluation information from frequent principal-teacher conferences following brief observations (5-20 minutes) plus systematic, *useful* theory-based inservice sessions for which the principal is responsible (even though he or she may not conduct but *does* attend), provide the data for a summative evaluation conference at the end of the year. Group inservice for efficiency of input plus classroom observation and feedback for accountability for output are both essential to a fair and accurate end of the year evaluation. Teachers see this basis for evaluation as fair and just, but they resent evaluation based on one formal observation plus indirect or hearsay evidence. (Unfortunately many evaluations are still based on the fact that parents or custodians approve of the teacher or he or she helps the principal in the supply room.)

Inservice plans, like teaching, should be an educational prescription based on diagnostic procedures. Teachers' desires should certainly be taken into account, but so should their needs. The way those needs can be ascertained fully is through observation of teaching performance in classrooms. The same is true of any performance behavior whether it concerns artists, salesmen, athletes, or principals. A person's ability may be judged by a product, but that product can be improved only by analysis by self and others of the performance that produced the product. Continual improvement of instructional skills is probably the single most important performance responsibility of both teacher and principal.

All of this instructional leadership appears to be a tremendous professional load for the principal. It is! But it is a responsibility that nobody else can assume for the following reasons:

1. The principal is continuously "on site," unlike supervisors, consultants, or central office staff who are only occasionally at each school. Even though someone else may do inservice or work with teachers in classrooms, unless that person is consistently available when needed, a request for help as well as the validation of subsequent effective performance by the teacher must be met by the principal.

2. The principal controls the "reward" system of the school. Correctly or incorrectly, the principal is perceived as the dispenser of "good" assignments, supplies, yard duty, committee responsibilities, stu-

dents, classes, and, most importantly, "the boss's approval." Principal's "warm fuzzies" or "cold pricklies" constitute a powerful reinforcement system that operates within every school. If a principal, with integrity, chooses to use the system to improve instruction, the results are dramatic.

3. The principal evaluates teachers. In the final outcome, a teacher's evaluation is directly related to the "impressions" of the principal. It is important to the mental health of both teacher and principal that those impressions have a documented basis of reality in the cause-effect relationships of human learning with evidence from many observations of teaching performance.

As principals' and teachers' roles and responsibilities are described, one is reminded of the "Renaissance man." How can a human acquire all these skills and still maintain some semblance of a normal life outside of school? It isn't easy, but it can be done. The answer resides in adequate preservice education of both principals and teachers plus continuing inservice, renewal, and revitalization to bring lagging skills back to criterion, and to infuse newly emerging skills with excellence derived from current research findings translated into artistry in daily performance behavior.

The Role of Preservice and Inservice Education

To achieve the "now possible" in effective schooling, we need to re-examine, revitalize, or reform the preservice and inservice education of teachers, principals, and supervisors. The foundation for this renewal should be research-based knowledge of relationships in teaching and learning. Implementation of this knowledge should begin in the teaching decisions and behaviors of the professors of teacher education and continue in the leadership and supervision behaviors of teachers, principals, supervisors, and inservice leaders.

Observational learning—learning from the behaviors of significant others—is a powerful source of future behavior. One has only to put a student in charge of a class to see a mirror of one's own teaching behavior. Unfortunately, many teachers have been subjected to "do what I say, not what I do" models and have, as a result, learned, through observation, teaching behaviors that were not so productive. (The never-use-a-preposition-to-end-a-sentence-with syndrome.) Consequently, reform in teacher education should begin with preservice education providing effective models of what is being "taught." Professors of education as well as superintendents, principals, and supervisors are no exception to deliberate, theory-based teaching.

Education professionals need to move from the extremes of either intuitive or "recipe-based" behavior to deliberate professional decision making based on research plus experiental wisdom. There still remains plenty of room for intuition. Clearly, we desire educators who are inspired, empathetic, and sensitive to the needs of students and dedicated to the value of education. Those traits are more likely to emerge and be sustained, however, if educators see that students learn successfully as a result of effective teaching.

There exists a body of knowledge and skills that should become the foundation of all teacher education programs: the "anatomy and physiology of teaching." In the same way that a medical student learns what is known about anatomy, physiology, and pharmacology and then applies that knowledge to promote health, the future teacher needs to learn what is currently known about cause-effect relationships in human learning to promote student achievement. In addition to, but not in lieu of, this knowledge foundation there are varying methodologies and philosophies that constitute a series of beliefs and prescriptions that represent the ideosyncratic orientation of the practitioner.

To use another parallel medical example, humans need protein to grow and remain energetic and healthy. That generalization remains fundamental to a successful nutrution program. To implement that program according to one's beliefs, it is possible to use soybeans, chili beans, octopus, fish, chicken or steak, prepared and served in one's preferred style.

Teachers need to infuse their instruction with the "protein, vitamins, and minerals" that accelerate human learning but to "serve it up" with their own teaching styles in a form that is "palatable and digestible" by the learners being served.

Most critical to successful preservice and inservice is the bridging of the chasm that exists between theory and practice. Granted, researchers exist to widen the gap between what is practiced and the frontier of new knowledge, but there exists also the responsibility for someone to "midwife" new ideas so they are born in the constant revitalization and renewal of practice.

Needed in education are "bilingual" professionals who know and speak the language of both theory and practice and who can translate the knowledge of research into the techniques of practice. I believe this bilingualism has been the critical "missing link" that has prevented already overburdened theoreticians and clinicians from respecting, stimulating, influencing and, correcting each other through the use of a common vocabulary. This yearbook was conceived, developed and "born" to become a milestone in such interactive communication.

The preparation of the future teacher should begin with a theory base that is directly experienced as it is modeled by instructors as well as vicariously experienced as it is viewed on selected films and videotapes, so the invariancies of teaching and learning are perceived, identified, and understood. With films and videotapes, what is viewed can be determined in advance and reviewed if necessary; something not possible in live instruction. Critical to the viewing process is the simultaneous verbal categorization and labeling of teacher or student behaviors, the results of those behaviors, and the theory that would support or impeach the teaching decisions manifested.

Example: "Notice that the teacher dignified the student's incorrect response of 'Lincoln' to the question, 'Who was our first elected president?' by stating 'Tom, you remembered that Lincoln was one of our most important presidents. Lincoln was our sixteenth president. Our national capitol is named after our first president.' The teacher dignified Tom's error, helped him know where that information belonged, and then prompted a correct answer. Notice, Tom continued to volunteer answers. Had he been humiliated by being told 'no' and by the teacher going to another student for the correct answer, Tom might not have participated so eagerly in the rest of the lesson."

Next, future teachers need the opportunity to design some "mini" teaching to try translating theory into *guided* practice with a small group of "nonexceptional" students. Feedback and labeling by a sophisticated supervisor provide guidance essential at this phase. We know that the beginning of any learning sequence is the "prime time" for learning. The beginning of teaching real students is no exception. Consequently, beginning teaching efforts must be carefully monitored, so translation of theory into practice can be reinforced or remediated.

Finally, as student teachers, future teachers are placed in classrooms with supervising teachers who are highly trained in the analysis of instruction, who model the best in teaching, who label the student teacher's productive and nonproductive practice, and remediate the latter, always linking interpretations of teaching and learning behaviors into research through the use of a common vocabulary, yet simultaneously stimulating intuition and artistry. I believe that such teacher preparation should be followed by a year of "residency" in a regular classroom where systematic and productive feedback on teaching performance would frequently be available from master teachers, supervisors, and principals to make that significant first year a productive, growth-evoking, and successful one.

While supervision, feedback, and infusion of new ideas into teaching performance may lessen as a teacher gains more experience, such feedback is the sine qua non of a continually growing profession. Consequently, systematic and significant inservice must be planned; budgeted for in terms of time, money, and support; then implemented in classrooms with accountability for its infusion into the program being systematically monitored. Quite an order, but one that is essential to a growing profession.

Making What We Teach Worth Teaching

Pedagogy, the science and the art of teaching, is one "leg" on which effective teaching is supported. The other "leg" is curriculum. To teach exquisitely that which is not worth the effort or to teach poorly that which is essential to a productive, satisfied, contributing member of a global society are equal educational sins.

The goals of education need to be thought through and agreed upon by the lay public and education professionals. These are the philosophically based ends that our artistic and scientific means help us achieve. Much needs to be done to revitalize curriculum. Even more needs to be done to bring pedagogy up to what we now know so that "all students learning" becomes a reality.

To achieve effective and artistic pedagogy, which successfully implements a curriculum worth the effort, will take massive re-examination of both. This can begin "tomorrow." Necessary knowledge and research are available. We desperately need the implementation of that research-based knowledge in preservice education of teachers, supervisors, and principals, followed by continuous inservice as a part of the professional contract. Only when both professional preparation and continuing renewal reflect emerging knowledge, and accountability for artistic implementation based on that knowledge becomes the license for educational practice, will teaching become a profession.

Utilizing Educational Research: The Hunterian Approach

SUSAN B. LEAHY

Madeline Hunter, along with others, has turned her attention in recent years to the identification of specific teaching behaviors that foster student learning. Her research findings indicate, among other things, that the teacher is one of the most critical factors related to successful achievement and learning.

Teaching and learning, she says, are intimately interwoven and spring from what the teacher does, not what the teacher "is." Disputing the myth that good teachers are "born," not made, Hunter asserts that effective and predictable teaching is a transmittable professional skill. Simple strategies based on research findings related to effective teaching are now at the fingertips of the educator.

An example of a theory-based teaching practice for checking understanding would be, "Now that I've started using number cards in math and the class flashes their answers at me, I can tell immediately who is with us and who isn't. It's made a big difference for me to know in an instant how well the kids are doing. Sometimes I can speed up, sometimes I have to slow down. But, the best part is that it makes me feel in control of the learning."

Research findings recently translated from theory into practice offer teachers' proven methods upon which to base decision making concerning the selection and presentation of material to students. The scientific view of teaching behavior makes it possible for every teacher to consciously recognize, evaluate, and improve basic teaching skills. According to Hunter, teaching is a process of professional decision making, which should be task oriented and self-analyzed, and incorporate human learning principles. The science of teaching, she states, is generalizable to all goals in all content areas.

Certain teaching behaviors are now recognized as contributing to student learning regardless of the subject matter. Active teaching coupled with high teacher visibility, for example, has been found to provide motivation for students and for the teacher a way to check for understanding. As one high school history teacher states:

> I've started moving around the room when I teach. I walk up and down the aisles, around the back of the room, everywhere. What I've noticed is that the students turn their heads toward me, follow me with their eyes, and seem to stay interested longer in what we're doing. I

Susan B. Leahy is Elementary Teacher, Kishwaukee School, Rockford, Illinois.

guess I was always visible before, but now I'm so much more active and mobile that it really keeps the class on their toes. I can check up on them individually, too, in a way I never could before perched on a chair or at my desk in front of the room.

Research findings reveal new ways for teachers and students to behave. Research may even provide answers to long-asked questions about how to deal with the differences in children. It just may be that teaching decisions appropriately made can minimize constraints present in the students or the students' environment. What a teacher may construe as a disobedient child may really just be a child no one will listen to at home.

Joanne blurts out all the time—answers to questions, personal comments, questions she has about assignments. The more I told her not to; that she was disturbing the class, that it wasn't fair for her to monopolize discussions; the worse she seemed to act. Well, I learned to ignore instead of focusing even more attention on her behavior. I learned to call on someone else and at the same time to reinforce Joanne's new behavior when she raised her hand or waited for her turn to speak. Joanne still slips, but I'm so consciously tuned in to ignore that behavior that we both feel better about it. I'm no longer frustrated with her behavior and she's slowly learning new ways to act in school.

Learning new ways is the offering held forth by educational researchers. The studies of cause-effect relationships associated with effective teaching and learning have also in some cases simply reinforced the intuitive knowledge of teachers. But, what is most important is that both research and knowledge are *available* to guide the decisions and resultant action of the teacher in all three areas of decision making outlined by Hunter: (1) the learning objective, (2) the learning behavior, and (3) the teacher behavior. It is against this backdrop that the artistry and creativity in selecting teaching options occurs:

As I watched myself teaching an English lesson on videotape, I became embarrassed. Everytime a student gave a correct answer, I said "excellent." I bet I said "excellent" ten times in ten minutes. I could see that "excellent" came to mean nothing to the class because I was overworking it. So, I made a list of phrases I could use instead. Then, I listed my new reinforcers on a 3-by-5 card that I carried around the room with me. Everytime I used a new phrase, I put a star after it on my card. It occurred to me that I was positively reinforcing myself at the same time as I was adding to my repertoire of reinforcement theory teaching behaviors.

A repertoire of teaching behaviors mired in choices, constraints, and conscious analysis, the merging of intuitive and scientific sources of professional knowledge, and recent psychological research findings that apply to all of life's dealings with others—these are the basic elements in teaching and learning—the successful, interdependent, and complex interaction between humans and knowledge—has entered a new era of understanding. Educators stand on the threshold of an explosion of professional knowledge, which when supplemented by insight and intuition will lead to improved and effective teaching practice and increased learning for the student. By combining the best of both the scientific and intuitive worlds, educators spurred on by the work of researchers like Madeline Hunter can lead students to their highest potentials of learning and living.

A Reaction to Hunter's Knowing, Teaching, and Supervising

ARTHUR L. COSTA

Those acquainted with Eisner and Vallance's *Conflicting Conceptions of the Curriculum,* [1] will recognize the philosophical nuances of Hunter's tour de force. Such terms as "launch pad," "task analysis," "input," "systematic," and "template" provide initial clues to form hypotheses, which are then corroborated as one reads about increasing speed and efficiency of learning and categorizing the acts of teaching, learning, and supervising into precisely three decisions, seven steps, and six types. Hunter's chapter is expressed in the language of *technology.* Much like engineering is defined as an applied science utilizing knowledge of physics, chemistry, and mathematics, so, too, is teaching defined as an applied science utilizing knowledge of psychology, neurology, anthropology, and sociology.

Consistent with this philosophy, Hunter explicitly addresses *direct* teaching for which outcomes are preconceivable, analyzable, and measurable, and for which the psychological principles she identifies are well suited. Awareness of the different purposes, and the pedagogical comparisons between direct and indirect teaching methods helps to maintain proper admiration for her contribution. [2] Other significant instructional strategists who operate under different psychological and philosophical conceptions might conceive the acts of teaching, learning, and supervising quite differently: Taba, Lozanov, Adler, Glasser, Bruner, and Montessori, to name a few. [3] Indeed, some of the world's more inspired teachers—Jesus, who spoke in parables; Socrates, the insatiable questioner; or Buddha, the master of "wait-time"—probably never performed a task analysis!

---

[1]For a complete description of five conflicting conceptions of the curriculum, see Eisner and Vallance (1976).

[2]Reference is made here to the contrast of indirect and direct teaching methods by Penelope Peterson (1979).

[3]For a greater expansion and comparison of various teaching strategies and their proponents, see Joyce and Weil (1981).

Arthur L. Costa is Professor of Education, California State University, Sacramento.

The Unscientific Interpretation of the Science of Teaching

While this chapter focuses on the art and science of teaching, there is little to illuminate the art and much to consider about the engineering. It is more the definition of science than the definition of teaching with which I am concerned. The inadequacy of the former causes confusion in the latter. Perhaps an alternate view of the nature of science may help draw different analogies to teaching.

Teaching as a Mode of Inquiry

In this chapter the science of teaching is characterized as an application of the *products* of scientific research. While scientists do, of course, use knowledge and theories acquired elsewhere, they apply this knowledge in a problem-solving *process*. The cyclical scientific method of inquiry involves focusing on a problem or discrepancy, formulating theories to explain this discrepancy, and testing those theories by gathering data through experimentation and verification. So, too, should the science of teaching be characterized as a process that employs scientific methods in the solution of instructional problems.[4]

A Passion for Certainty/A Need for Doubt

Scientists search for truth yet view all conclusions with humble tentativeness and healthy skepticism. Most of us can remember memorizing scientific "truths" (such as Saturn having nine moons), only to have this knowledge subsequently replaced with more accurate conclusions supported by data gathered through more refined research methods and technology. Hunter's statement, "Translation of research-based theory into practice *has now been accomplished,* so we can describe and substantiate much of what is effective in teaching," conveys an attitude of conclusiveness that most scientists abhor. Furthermore, if teaching is indeed part art, then, like the *Mona Lisa's* smile, it will be inscrutable forever.

At a time when educators are being pressured to account for quality by specifying and measuring teaching competencies, it is tempting to adopt a list of specific behaviors as certainties. But as Einstein aphorized, "As far as the laws of mathematics refer to reality, they are not certain; as far as they are certain, they do not refer to reality."[5]

---

[4]Several authors have described teaching as a mode of inquiry. See Coladarci (1959) and Shavelson (1976).

[5]In reacting to Hunter's chapter, I relied heavily on Capra's *The Tao of Physics* (1975). In his work, Capra brings together the thinking and contributions of many scientists and philosophers. My quotes are taken from his book. This one is on page 27.

Reductionism: An Obsolescent Goal of the Scientific Enterprise

The concept of science portrayed throughout this chapter is one of reducing teaching, learning, curriculum, and supervision to their lowest common denominators. Through task analysis of teaching and learning, we can supposedly identify the "basic building blocks" or "smallest particles" that compose these acts. This concept of science was popularized by the ancient Greeks over 2,000 years ago when Democritus pictured matter as consisting of several basic building blocks. This view was furthered by the systematic and organized mind of Aristotle, expressed mathematically by Galileo, divided and classified by Descartes, and attained its zenith with Newtonian Physics.[6]

Over the last 50 years the scientific enterprise has undergone a paradigm shift. One of the most important events in the history of scientific methodology was J. J. Thompson's discovery of the electron, which he described as a "splinter of the atom." Up until that time the atom had been considered the ultimate material unit of the universe. Over the ensuing years other particles and antiparticles have further lessened the scientist's enthusiasm for thinking of the universe as composed of static substances. Modern physicists admit that physical objects have an atomic structure, but the atom, too, has a structure that cannot be described as wholly material. Matter, it turns out, is highly packed energy, "communicating" with other energy processes such as light, motion, and heat.

Einstein thrust us into viewing the world as relative and probabilistic. As a result, modern quantum scientists no longer search for the ultimate particle. Instead, the emphasis is on structure, process, and interaction between a number of elementary particles and processes that may well be infinite. Modern scientific method is based on the search for unity among events, conditions, and phenomena rather than analysis, isolation, reduction, and quantification. While these techniques are used as the means of science, they are not the ends of science.[7] A more consistent, *quantum* view of the science of teaching and learning would reveal a complicated web: an infinite number of interactions between learning probabilities, teaching processes, and environmental conditions.

The Dichotomy of Scientific vs. Intuitive Methods

The rational part of research would be useless if it were not complemented by the intuition that gives scientists new insights and makes

---

[6]Capra (1975), pp. 40-71, and 124.
[7]Restak (1979), p. 236.

them creative. In the same manner that a scientist, who wants to repeat an experiment in modern subatomic physics, must undergo many years of training, so, too, a deep mystical experience requires many years of training so that the intuition can be reliably "on call." The "repeatability of the experiment" is as basic to scientific training as it is to mystical training.[8]

Intuitive insights come to the scientist suddenly and characteristically *not* while working out equations but rather while relaxing in a hot tub, strolling in the park, or during early morning wakefulness. In these periods of relaxation the intuitive mind seems to take over and produce the sudden clarifying insight that gives so much joy to scientific research. But when do teachers use intuition?

Instructional decision making is cited as being performed before, during, and after the teaching act. During the planning and reflective phases—before and after classroom teaching—much information can be brought to bear because the teacher has the time and lack of pressure to call it from memory. Planning and reflecting may be done in a formal setting: thinking, writing, and devoting attention to it; or informally, such as while driving to work or jogging. These unpressured phases are in sharp contrast to the frenzied, in-classroom, interactive phase when teachers must respond quickly to the immediate demands of the situation. Decisions made during teaching may be either impulsive, spontaneous, planned, or a mixture of each. There may be little time to recall data about student's readiness for learning, to consider alternative teaching strategies, or to explore the theoretical consequences of each teaching act. Thus, during the press of teaching, teachers probably rely more heavily on intuition than during the more rational planning and reflective periods. Yet teachers seldom (if ever) receive training in how to use their intuitive powers during teaching, when they may be needed most. Instead, Hunter depreciates intuitive methods as "sterile" and unreliable. Teachers are admonished to mistrust their intuition and to rely solely on rationality.

The Multi-Science Basis of Teaching

Teaching is described as an applied science that utilizes the findings of psychology, neurology, sociology, and anthropology. (I would add philosophy.) Hunter lists many factors derived from *psychological research*. (Sources of these data are unscientifically absent.) Lacking is any comparable list of neurological, sociological, and anthropological factors to guide us.

---

[8]Capra (1975), pp. 18-23.

For example, recent research from the neurosciences has shed light on what happens in the brain and nervous system (contrary to B. F. Skinner) to explain why people think and act as they do.[9] Brain functioning and growth studies are expanding our ideas about instructional methods and critical times when learning new content can be maximized.[10]

Anthropological factors increase our understanding of divergent attitudes toward learning and guide our decisions about resolving value conflicts among teachers and students in multicultural classrooms. Sociological research provides clues as to how children form their self-concept in relation to power and authority and therefore guide the teacher's choice of methods in resolving discipline problems. Because the classroom and the school are pluralistic mini-societies, psychological factors alone are inadequate.

A Word About Words

Heavy emphasis is placed on the building of a common vocabulary and the translation of scientific knowledge into words. Yet the physicist Werner Heisenburg stated, "Every word or concept, clear as it may seem to be, has only a limited range of applicability."[11] While a common vocabulary is useful, the reality of teaching and learning can never be adequately described in words because it lies beyond the realms of the senses and of the intellect from where our words are derived. Words can never convey reality; they are only approximations of reality. Most of the decisions teachers make are based on recent and long-term experiences. Michael Polanyi describes this knowledge as tacit, not explicit.[12]

The Art and Science of Supervision

It is refreshing to note an observer of teaching is not merely a spectator, but a participant. This is very consistent with modern science. Heisenburg says, "Natural science does not simply describe and explain nature; it is part of the interplay between nature and ourselves. What we observe is not nature itself, but nature exposed to our method of questioning." In atomic physics, then, scientists cannot play the role of detached, objective

---

[9]Many implications for teaching and learning from the neurosciences can be drawn from Restak (1979): 418-427.

[10]A very succinct synthesis of Herman Epstein's research, Piagetian theory, and hemisphericity with implications for teaching practice and curriculum development is presented in Johnson (1982).

[11]Heisenberg (1958), p. 125.

[12]For a distinction between tacit and explicit knowledge, see Polanyi (1967).

observers. Rather, they become involved in the world they observe to the extent that they influence the properties of the observed objects.[13]

Throughout Hunter's discussion of the supervisor's role, however, I detect a duality between the observer and the observed. She states: "The primary responsibility for analyzing possible casuality and suggesting remediation rests with the observer," and "The observer identifies only those problems to which there are potential solutions or acknowledges that a problem exists . . ."

Consistency between quantum science and the supervisor's role in helping teachers become better decision makers requires the supervisor *not* to remain detached, but rather to seek harmony with the teaching-learning act. Thus, the observer, the teacher, the students, and the learning are intricately intertwined in a network of values, perceptions, and sensations. Together they share impressions and feelings, as they explore the paradoxes of teaching and the vicissitudes of learning. Thus they *both* become more autonomous decision makers.

The Aesthetic Bases of Teaching

Just as analogies have been drawn between the structure of science and the act of teaching, so, too, can we correlate aesthetics with teaching. Harry Broudy has identified four aspects of the aesthetic response: the formal, the technical, the sensuous, and the expressive.

The *formal* is a response to form: merely a recognition of the name or category of the object or rendition—a fugue, a tragedy, cubist or cabernet.

The *technical* refers to participation in the "techniques" used in the production of the aesthetic piece: "playing" the song, "acting" the part, "sculpting" the form. When we *live* the part we experience it and thereby know more of the aesthetic response.

The *sensuous* refers to knowing through the senses: feeling textures, savoring fragrances, seeing movement and color. It is through awareness of the perceptual processes that we "take in" and heighten our aesthetic knowledge. To "know" the wine we must taste it: to "know" the dance we must move it.

The *expressive* response is a summary of the others in which we assess and interpret the meaning of the aesthetic experience and incorporate that meaning into the self. It is the act of incorporation that makes the aesthetic response significant and unforgettable.

Thus, we can also derive aesthetic factors to use as "templates" to assess the quality of instruction: Does teaching provide for direct experi-

---

[13]Heisenberg (1958), p. 81.

ence in the learning? To what degree are the senses being stimulated? What opportunities are there for expression, interpretation, and incorporation of the learning into each learner's "self"?

Aesthetics is not concerned with what learners memorize nor even with how much they *remember*. Rather, aesthetic teaching is concerned with making learning *memorable*. [14]

Towards the Tao of Teaching

Alfred North Whitehead characterized teaching as a deeply religious experience. Ole Sand defined it as an art based in science. Paul Brandewein deemed it a mercy. Leon Lessinger described it as a performing art. I suggest it is neither of these and it is all of these.

Teaching, like all other forms of human interface with environmental phenomena, is a dynamic interaction between both exterior and interior forces—the exterior world of the classroom and the interior meaning of the teacher. Teaching is an inseparable science/art alliance, which is unified only when the ultimate reality without is identical to the reality within. It is that *search* for unity that transcends either the art or the science.

The inaccessibility of data is similar both in science and in learning. We cannot directly "see" subatomic particles, nor can we "see" the inner-workings of the mind and emotions of the child. Both are inferrential; both are subject to human interpretation. Teaching, therefore, is a synthesis, not a separation—a synthesis of the human mind's rational *and* intuitive capabilities. Neither is comprehended in the other, nor can either be reduced to the other. Both of them are necessary; supplementing one another for a fuller understanding of the realities of teaching and of learning.

We need to transform our conception of teaching to encompass this dynamic interplay between mystical intuition and scientific analysis. So far this has not been achieved in our profession. At present, our attitude toward teaching is too *yang*—too absolute, rational, and aggressive. What is needed is more *yin*—intuition, sensuousness and subtlty—to bring back a delicate balance. Children might then learn those other basics: the wholeness and unity of existence—the art of living in harmonious balance with nature and with each other.

---

[14]Harry Broudy's definition of aesthetic response was reported by Arthur Foshay at the Professors of Curriculum annual meeting in Detroit, Michigan, March 2-3, 1979.

References

Capra, Fritjof. *The Tao of Physics*. New York: Bantam Books, 1975.

Coladarci, Arthur P. "The Teacher as Hypothesis Maker." *California Journal of Instructional Improvement* 2 (March 1959): 3-6.

Eisner, Elliot, and Vallance, Elizabeth. *Conflicting Conceptions of the Curriculum*. Berkeley: McCutchan, 1976.

Foshay, Arthur. "Toward a Humane Curriculum." In *Education in Flux: Implications for Curriculum Development*. Edited by J. J. Jelenek. Tempe, Ariz.: The Professors of Curriculum, 1979, pp. 97-113.

Heisenberg, Walter. *Physics and Philosophy*. New York: Harper Torchbooks, 1958.

Johnson, Virginia. "Myelin and Maturation: A Fresh Look at Piaget." *The Science Teacher* (March 1982): 41-49.

Joyce, Bruce, and Weil, Marsha. *Models of Teaching*. Englewood Cliffs, N.J.: Prentice Hall, 1981.

Peterson, Penelope. "Direct Instruction Reconsidered." In *Research on Teaching*. Edited by P. Peterson and H. J. Walberg. Berkeley: McCutchan, 1979.

Polanyi, Michael. *The Tacit Dimension*. Garden City: Doubleday/Anchor, 1967.

Restak, Richard M. *The Brain: The Last Frontier*. New York: Warner Books, 1979.

Shavelson, Richard. "Teacher Decision Making." In *The Psychology of Teaching Methods*. Edited by N. Gage. Chicago: University of Chicago Press, 1976.

An NIE View of the Problem

MANUEL J. JUSTIZ

O ne of the greatest teachers of all time, Socrates, didn't need any research data to tell him how to be an effective teacher. But then again, Socrates didn't have to deal with computers in the classroom. Or with declining test scores. Or a smorgasbord curriculum.

Obviously, education has undergone many changes since Socrates' time. Today, it is a frustrating, confusing, intractable system to a great many educators, parents, and observers. For some time now, the American public has been expressing misgivings about the effectiveness of our schools. Fortunately, we are in a position, thanks in part to the accomplishments of educational research and development, to take positive action.

We are at a point where developments in educational research make it possible for us to achieve more significant school improvements than at any time in the past. The substantial and growing base of research knowledge now available to educators wasn't available just a few short years ago. In fact, only five years ago, researcher Gene Hall, now acting director of the NIE-funded R&D Center for Teacher Education in Austin, Texas, wrote, "In very few areas of teacher education are there solid, empirical findings or coherent concepts and theories to guide future research efforts. There is a definite need for description, analysis, exploration, mapping and theory building."

We have not met all those needs yet. In fact, research of this sort is still in its early years. And yet, in the past 15 years, educational researchers and other social scientists, underwritten to a great extent by federal research funds, have built a rich store of knowledge for improving schools. In light of this, I think it is fair to say now that educational research has been accepted by the country's scholarly and research communities as a legitimate and significant enterprise. The question of whether education research is itself a science is not relevant. It is clearly at the conjunction of several academic disciplines and applied fields.

Manuel J. Justiz is Director, National Institute of Education, Washington, D.C.

Educational research in recent years has attracted top scholars from both the education communities and the academic disciplines, has advanced the state of the art of the field, and has produced sound studies with convincing findings on subjects that matter. Such positive advances indicate research will play a big role in the future of education.

Consequently, it is in this research field that the federal government can make a substantial and direct contribution to education. By conducting research and development through the National Institute of Education (NIE), the research agency of the Department of Education, the government can provide the education system a means for improving without intruding at the state and local levels.

It is NIE's responsibility to provide leadership in identifying and analyzing significant problems in American education, in supporting research to solve these problems, and in translating that research into practical applications.

"Translating the research"—therein lies a problem. All too often research results are stored on a shelf, left to gather dust. We know that research results *can* be used to improve education if we get them off the shelf and out into the education community. Take the effective schools research, for example. Schools in New York City, St. Louis, and Chicago have successfully used NIE's body of effective schools research as the basis for school improvement programs. Many other school districts around the country are trying out the tenets of this same research. Some are having little success; others report encouraging improvement. But most importantly, we have captured a certain essence of school effectiveness—one with great intuitive appeal as well as forceful simplicity—that we have been able to communicate to educators across the country. They, in turn, have been able to begin trying local school improvement efforts.

We have seen the same thing happen with reading research. Teachers in Harlem report the reading comprehension of their students jumped dramatically after New York City devised a program based on NIE-supported reading research. When the project began, only 26 percent of the students could read at their grade level; today that figure is 52 percent.

Frank Macchiarola, chancellor of the New York City Public Schools, told a House Education and Labor Subcommittee on Select Education that, for the first time in 11 years, New York City students' reading scores this year exceeded the national average. He attributed this in part to the benefit of federal research and development. And in Hawaii, an early childhood education program used NIE research on reading comprehension to develop reading skills in low-achieving students where prior programs had failed. The project brought the students up to national norms in reading and is being adopted by the school system statewide.

We can go a step further and use research findings to improve practice in other elements of the education system—publishers, testing firms, and the like. For example, James Squire, senior vice president of the Ginn and Co. publishing firm in Lexington, Massachusetts, says that recent reading research "will force editors and authors to think through their basic assumptions in reading programs and look at how they are taking into account the experience and knowledge of pupils."

These examples show what can be accomplished when the results of research are made available. It also indicates how important it is that researchers make sure the results of their projects are not only useful, but are readily available to educators.

All too often, education research projects are labeled too esoteric and of interest to a limited few. Researchers must shed this tarnished image. One way to do this is to work closely with schools and those individuals closely associated with education. It's time that researchers realize that teachers have been "researchers" all along. They can provide a wealth of information to our work. Reflection, problem solving, craft knowledge, and personal innovation are the trademarks of the excellent teacher—of which this country has many. Often what we researchers believe we have "discovered" are simply these teachers' long-standing practices. It is high time we involve teachers more actively in our research.

NIE got off to a good start this past year at a seminar the Institute sponsored at the annual meeting of the American Association of Colleges for Teacher Education. The seminar brought together teams of faculty and administrators from ten teacher training institutions as part of an extended effort to change their teacher education programs. These teams spent two days assessing their programs, determining what they wanted to change, and devising draft action plans to take back and share at their own institutions. For the remainder of the year, they implemented these changes, carefully documenting the process. This year, the team members will share their experiences with their convention colleagues. Because this research was undertaken by individuals directly affected, other faculty and administrative personnel from teacher colleges will be better able—and perhaps more willing—to relate to the results.

Effective teacher research is another example of how important teacher involvement is. Here, teachers and researchers worked together to define and carry out research to help us learn more about effective teaching. Like effective schools research, results of effective teaching research have been put into practice across the country. The positive results that have ensued are just one indicator that where teachers are involved in research, startingly, revealing and useful work results. These two steps—striving to keep research down to earth and actively involving teachers in this research—are two giant steps forward the research community has taken.

But there remains a third step—that of finding better ways of spreading the word about the results of education research. Simply to have a base of knowledge is not sufficient. And neither are the past ways of dissemination which we have used. One way to get the word out, so to speak, is to change the relationship researchers have with the rest of the education community. The word that we at NIE are beginning to use to describe this changed role is "partnership."

"Partnership" is but a term to suggest the beginning of what psychologist Sheldon White calls "an overarching enterprise that begins and ends in educational practice." Partnerships are the arrangements that must be formed between research and practice communities, between administrators and policymakers, and between federal, state, and local governments. These are the first beginnings to removing the obstacles to coherence in education and to making the results of R&D truly effective in improving the quality of education.

NIE already has begun forming these partnerships. The Institute's lab and center competition is a prime example. NIE asked teachers, administrators, legislators, parents, and researchers for help in setting its research agenda for the future. In another NIE partnership, several labs and centers, together with the American Association of School Administrators and the National Association of State Boards of Education, have launched a campaign to promote effective schools.

Many communities already have begun to adopt this partnership strategy. Columbus, Ohio, has forged an exciting coalition for education planning and governance among its school, industry, university, and community leaders. Under the inspiration of Boston University, that city has been negotiating a new alliance that will unite the mayor's office, surrounding school systems, businesses, and higher education in meeting educational, economic, and social demands.

The future holds an immense challenge for both researchers and educators. For researchers, it is to provide reliable, down-to-earth research for the teaching community; for educators, it is to use this research to develop sound, creative responses to the changing demands of our schools. Even Socrates, I'm sure, would approve.

Board of Directors

Executive Council
1983-84

President: Lawrence S. Finkel, Executive Director, Institute for Curriculum Development, Dobbs Ferry, New York

President-Elect: Phil Robinson, Principal, Clarence B. Sabbath School, River Rouge, Michigan

Immediate Past President: O.L. Davis, Jr., Professor of Curriculum and Instruction, University of Texas, Austin, Texas

Arthur L. Costa, Professor of Education, California State University, Sacramento, California

Sidney H. Estes, Assistant Superintendent, Atlanta Public Schools, Atlanta, Georgia

Robert Hanes, Deputy Superintendent of Schools, Charlotte-Mecklenburg Schools, Charlotte, North Carolina

Francis P. Hunkins, Professor of Education, University of Washington, Seattle, Washington

Luther L. Kiser, Assistant Superintendent for Curriculum and Instruction, Ames Community School District, Ames, Iowa

Marcia Knoll, Principal, Public School 220, Queens, Forest Hills, New York

Elizabeth Lane, Principal, Mount Pisgah Elementary School, Memphis, Tennessee

Nelson (Pete) Quinby, Director of Secondary Education, Joel Barlow High School, West Redding, Connecticut

Stuart C. Rankin, Assistant Superintendent, Detroit Public Schools, Detroit, Michigan

Bob L. Sigmon, Director for Elementary Administration, Richmond City Schools, Richmond, Virginia

Board Members Elected at Large

(Listed alphabetically; the year in parentheses indicates the end of the term of office.)

Roger Bennett, University of Wisconsin, Oshkosh, Wisconsin (1987)

Doris Brown, University of Missouri, St. Louis, Missouri (1987)

Gene Raymond Carter, Norfolk Public Schools, Norfolk, Virginia (1985)

Gloria Cox, Board of Education, Central Area, Memphis, Tennessee (1984)

Geneva Gay, Purdue University, West Lafayette, Indiana (1987)
Elaine McNally Jarchow, Iowa State University, Ames, Iowa (1985)
Lois Harrison-Jones, Richmond City Schools, Richmond, Virginia (1986)
Marcia Knoll, Public School 220, Queens, Forest Hills, New York (1984)
Jessie Kobayashi, Berryessa Union School District, San Jose, California (1986)
Elizabeth Lane, Shelby County Schools, Memphis, Tennessee (1986)
Marian Leibowitz, Teaneck Board of Education, Teaneck, New Jersey (1986)
Betty Livengood, Mineral County Schools, Keyser, West Virginia (1985)
Gloria J. McFadden, Western Oregon State College, Monmouth, Oregon (1984)
E. Gaye McGovern, Miami East School District, Casstown, Ohio (1985)
Arthur D. Roberts, University of Connecticut, Storrs, Connecticut (1987)
Ann Converse Shelly, Bethany College, Bethany, West Virginia (1986)
Arthur Steller, Shaker Heights City School District, Shaker Heights, Ohio (1987)
Claire H. Sullivan, Secondary School Services, Clearwater, Florida (1984)

Unit Representatives to the Board of Directors

(Each Unit's President is listed first; others follow in alphabetical order.)

Alabama: Paul Wylie, State Department of Education, Montgomery; Milly Cowles, University of Alabama, Birmingham; Mabel Robinson, University of Alabama, Birmingham

Alaska: Dolores Dinneen, University of Alaska, Anchorage; Donald McDermott, University of Alaska, Anchorage

Arizona: Carolyn Hawkins, Public Schools, Phoenix; Ellie Sbragia, Arizona Center for Law Related Education, Phoenix; Elizabeth Manera, Arizona State University, Tempe

Arkansas: Nancy Lawson, Public Schools, Arkadelphia; Jerry Daniel, Public Schools, Camden

California: Doris Prince, Santa Clara County Schools, San Jose; Walter Klas, Public Schools, Alameda; Nancy Comstock, Public Schools, Bakersfield; Dorothy Garcia, Public Schools, Bloomington; Don Halverson, Public Schools, Redwood City; Carolyn Haugen, Public Schools, Walnut; Bill James, Public Schools, Paso Robles; Loren Sanchez, Public Schools, Upland

Colorado: Cile Chavez, University of Northern Colorado, Greeley; Donna Brennan, Public Schools, Englewood; Gordon Brooks, Public Schools, Littleton

Connecticut: Bernard Goffin, Monroe Board of Education, Monroe; Arthur Roberts, University of Connecticut, Storrs; Edward Borque, Public Schools, Fairfield

Delaware: George Kent, Delaware State College, Dover; Melville Warren, Public Schools, Dover

District of Columbia: Judine Johnson, Public Schools, Washington, DC; Roberta Walker, Public Schools, Washington, DC

Florida: Mary Giella, District School Board of Pasco County, Land O' Lakes; Jean Marani, Department of Education, Tallahassee; Hilda Wiles, Alachua County School Board, Gainesville; Mary Jo Sisson, Okaloosa County School Board, Fort Walton Beach

Georgia: Scott Bradshaw, State Department of Education, Atlanta; Joe Murphy, Augusta College, Augusta; Ann Culpepper, Bibb County Board of Education, Macon

Hawaii: Claire Yoshida, Hawaii State Department of Education, Honolulu; Mary Logasa, Public Schools, Honolulu

Idaho: Gary Doramus, Public Schools, Caldwell; David Carroll, Public Schools, Boise

Illinois: Patricia Conran, Public Schools, West Chicago; Kathryn Ransom, Public Schools, Springfield; Rodney Borstad, Northern Illinois University, DeKalb; Alvin Cohen, Public Schools, Deerfield; John Fletcher, Public Schools, Park Ridge; Richard Hanke, Public Schools, Arlington Heights; Sybil Yastrow, Education Service Region, Waukegan

Indiana: Marjorie Jackson, Public Schools, Indianapolis; Donna Delph, Purdue University, Hammond; Ken Springer, Public Schools, Decatur

Iowa: Tom Budnik, Heartland Area Education Agency, Ankeny; Betty Atwood, Heartland Area Education Agency, Ankeny; Harold Hulleman, Linn-Mar Community School, Marion

Kansas: Tom Hawk, Public Schools, Manhattan; Jim Jarrett, Public Schools, Kansas City; Harold E. Schmidt, Public Schools, Salina

Kentucky: Jack Neel, Western Kentucky University, Bowling Green; Judy Minnehan, Oldham County Schools, LaGrange; Jim Guess, Henderson County Schools, Henderson

Louisiana: Emilie Hinton, Public Schools, New Orleans; Julianna Boudreaux, Public Schools, New Orleans, Kate Scully, Public Schools, New Orleans

Maine: Irving Ouellette, Public Schools, Bath; Ralph Egers, Public Schools, South Portland

Maryland: Joan Palmer, Public Schools, Towson; Thelma Sparks (retired), Public Schools, Annapolis; Ruth Burkins, Public Schools, Harford County

Massachusetts: Robert Munnelly, Public Schools, Reading; Peter Farrelly, Wachusett Regional Schools, Holden; Morton Milesky, Public Schools, Longmeadow; Gary Baker, Public Schools, Acton

Michigan: Charles King, Michigan Education Association, East Lansing; Virginia Sorenson, Western Michigan University, Kalamazoo; Rita Foote, Public Schools, Southfield; Dixie Hibner, Public Schools, Saline; James Perry, Public Schools, Muskegon

Minnesota: Joan Black, Public Schools, Bloomington; Arnold Ness, Public Schools, St. Anthony; Merill Fellger, Public Schools, Buffalo

Mississippi: Juliet Borden, Public Schools, Amory; Bobbie Collum, State Department of Education, Jackson

Missouri: Warren Solomon, State Department of Education, Jefferson City; Patricia Rocklage, Public Schools, St. Louis; Frank Morley, Public Schools, La Due

Montana: Kay McKenna, Public Schools, Helena; Henry Worrest, Montana State University, Bozeman

Nebraska: Dave Van Horn, Public Schools, Lincoln; L. James Walter, University of Nebraska, Lincoln; Dee Hall, Public Schools, Omaha

Nevada: Fred Doctor, Public Schools, Reno; Melvin Kirchner, Public Schools, Reno

New Hampshire: Jean Stefanik, Public Schools, Amherst; Mary Ann Pank, Public Schools, Milford

New Jersey: Sid Sender, Public Schools, Middletown; Judith Zimmerman, Public Schools, Metuchen; Paul Braungart, Public Schools, Moorestown; Ruth Dorney, Public Schools, Randolph; Paul Manko, Public Schools, Mt. Laurel

New Mexico: Bill Childress, Public Schools, Farmington; Delbert Dyche, Public Schools, Las Cruces

New York: Anthony Deiulio, State University College, Fedonia; Dorothy Foley, State Department of Education, Albany; Robert Brellis, Public Schools, Oakdale; Donald Harkness, Public Schools, Manhasset; Gerard Kells, Public Schools, Henrietta; Timothy Melchoir, Public Schools, Valley Stream; Arlene Soifer, Nassau BOCES, Westbury; Nicholas Vitalo, Public Schools, Lynnbrook

North Carolina: Betty Nichols, Public Schools, Statesville; Hilda Olson, Public Schools, Hendersonville; Mary Jane Dillard, Public Schools, Sylva

North Dakota: Richard Warner, Public Schools, Fargo; Glenn Melvey, Public Schools, Fargo

Ohio: Arthur Wohlers, Ohio State University, Columbus; Eugene Glick (retired), Public Schools, Medina; Robert Bennett, Public Schools,

Gahanna; Billy Bittinger, Public Schools, Dayton; Ronald Hibbard, Public Schools, Chagrin Falls

Oklahoma: Jerry Hill, Central State University, Edmond; Nelda Tebow, Public Schools, Oklahoma City; James Roberts, Public Schools, Lawton

Oregon: Tom Lindersmith, Public Schools, Lake Oswego; Jean Ferguson, West Oregon State College, Monmouth; Art Phillips (retired), Public Schools, Ashland

Pennsylvania: Robert F. Nicely, Jr., The Pennsylvania State University, University Park; Jeanne Zimmerman (retired), Public Schools, Lancaster; David Campbell, State Department of Education, Harrisburg; Robert Flynn, Public Schools, Lemoyne; Anthony Labriola, Public Schools, McVeytown

Puerto Rico: Ramon M. Barquin, American Military Academy, Guaynabo; Teresa de Dios, American Military Academy, Guaynabo

Rhode Island: Nora Walker, Public Schools, Cumberland; Guy DiBiaso, Public Schools, Cranston

South Carolina: Edwin White, University of South Carolina, Spartanburg; Edie Jensen, Public Schools, Irmo; Ron West, State Department of Education, Columbia

South Dakota: Virginia Tobin, Public Schools, Aberdeen; Janet Jones, Public Schools, Martin

Tennessee: Margaret Phelps, Tennessee Tech University, Cookeville; Robert Roney, The University of Tennessee, Knoxville; Marshall Perritt, Public Schools, Memphis

Texas: Ann Jensen, Public Schools, Garland; Wayne Berryman, Region VII Education Service Center, Kilgore; Robert Anderson, Pedamorphis, Inc., Lubbock; Bob Coleman, Region X Education Service Center, Waco; Carol Kuykendall, Public Schools, Houston; Dewey Mays, Public Schools, Fort Worth

Utah: W. Scott Whipple, Public Schools, Magna; Corrine Hill, Public Schools, Salt Lake City

Vermont: Larned Ketcham, Public Schools, Charlotte; George Fuller, Public Schools, Orleans

Virgin Islands: Mavis Brady, State Department of Education, St. Thomas

Virginia: Nancy Vance, State Department of Education, Richmond; Delores Greene, Public Schools, Richmond; Marion Hargrove, Public Schools, Bedford; Nancy Jones, Public Schools, Virginia Beach

Washington: Bob Valiant, Public Schools, Kennewick; G. Richard Harris, Public Schools, Tacoma; Monica Schmidt, State Board of Education, Olympia

West Virginia: Joyce Clark Waugh, West Virginia College of Graduate Studies, Institute; Helen Saunders, State Department of Education, Charleston

Wisconsin: Roland Cross, Public Schools, Oregon; John Koehn, Public Schools, Oconomowoc; Arnold Chandler, Department of Public Instruction, Madison

Wyoming: Ed Porthan, Public Schools, Lander; Donna Connor, University of Wyoming, Rawlins

International Units:

Germany: Robert Lykins, Department of Defense Dependents Schools

ASCD Review Council

Chair: Elizabeth Randolph (retired), Charlotte-Mecklenburg Schools, Charlotte, North Carolina

Barbara D. Day, Professor Early Childhood Development, University of North Carolina, Chapel Hill, North Carolina

Gerald Firth, University of Georgia, Curriculum and Supervision, Athens, Georgia

James House, Wayne County Intermediate School District, Detroit, Michigan

Charles Kingston, Thomas Fowler Junior High School, Tigard, Oregon

ASCD
Headquarters Staff

GORDON CAWELTI/*Executive Director*
RONALD S. BRANDT/*Executive Editor*
DIANE BERRETH/*Associate Director*
JEAN HALL/*Interim Associate Director*
JOHN BRALOVE/*Business Manager*

SARAH ARLINGTON, HARRIET BERNSTEIN, JOAN BRANDT, ELAINE C. DULL, ANITA FITZPATRICK, DAVID GIBSON, JO ANN IRICK, DEBORAH A. JOHNSON, TEOLA T. JONES, JACQUELYN LAYTON, INDU B. MADAN, AGATHA DEBORAH MADDOX, BARBARA A. MARENTETTE, CLARA M. MEREDITH, FRANCES MINDEL, NANCY CARTER MODRAK, DOLORES MOORE, CYNTHIA MORAWCZYNSKI, MOJGAN PHAM, GAYLE ROCKWELL, ROBERT SHANNON, CAROLYN SHELL, BARBARA J. THOMPSON, AL WAY, COLETTE A. WILLIAMS